Sacred Habits

The Rise of the Creative Clergy

Intersections
Theology and the Church in a World Come of Age

Series Editor, Rev. Dr. Christopher Rodkey
St. Paul's United Church of Christ, Dallastown, PA

Advisory Board

Introduction to the series

The past century has seen an increased and increasing divide between the guilds of academic theology and the inhabitants and practitioners within the church—especially among American Protestants. So much is this the case that entire seminaries, colleges, and networks of educational institutions exist primarily to shield or suppress the richness of contemporary theology from the church's leadership and its laity. Diminished resources of theological schools and religious publishers have relegated theology and theological reflection to be a luxury for those who splurge in such intellectual desires.

This series from Noesis Press, Intersections: Theology and the Church in a World Come of Age, takes the perspective that theology is not an excess by-product of church practice, but a *necessary* and *foundational* task which fuels and animates the increasingly multifaceted roles of clergy and church leaders in the present. The subtitle of the series is an intentional nod to Dieterich Bonhoeffer, whose call for a church in a "world come of age" is to affirm a forward-thinking and self-critical approach to Christianity, even at the expense of Christendom. Of course, Bonhoeffer's contemporary apologists have attempted to galvanize and redefine this to be a clarion call to affirm the past and resist the future.

Bonhoeffer, too, stood at the intersection of the academy and the church. He brought his learned sophistication into the practice of youth ministry and ecumenical dialogue. When the systems of the church and theological schools failed in their mission by affirming the easy triumphalism of nationalism and racism, he led efforts in the confessing church and underground seminary movements. As an intellectual, Bonhoeffer was willing to challenge central theologies of Luther and radically reconsider the relationship of Christ and the church, even pointing toward the possibility of a post-Christendom Christocentrism.

The works presented in this series seek to embody and inhabit these intersections, engaging and inviting church practitioners to think theologically anew, and enticing theologians to return to the ecclesiology, of the contemporary church and its tasks. These works are not presented with a specific confessional or theological bias, but encourage challenging perspectives and introductory texts to concepts and ideas for clergy and laity to envision the future of the Christian faith, whose participants seek to re-connect to the rich intellectual heritage of the church.

Christopher D. Rodkey, *The World is Crucifixion: Radical Christian Preaching, Year B,* with a foreword by Katharine Sarah Moody and an afterword by Carl Raschke

Jeff Nelson, *Coffeehouse Contemplative: Spiritual Direction for the Everyday,* with a foreword by John C. Dorhauer

Chad R. Abbott, *Sacred Habits: The Rise of the Creative Clergy,* with a foreword by Carol Howard Merritt

Bruce G. Epperly, *The Gospel According to Winnie the Pooh*

Sacred Habits

The Rise of the Creative Clergy

Chad R. Abbott

Foreword by Carol Howard Merritt

Noesis Press
Aurora, Colorado

Library of Congress Cataloging-in-publication data:

Names: Abbott, Chad R., author.
Title: Sacred habits : the rise of the creative clergy / Rev. Chad R. Abbott
  ; foreword by Rev. Carol Howard Merritt.
Description: Aurora, Colorado : Davies Group, Publishers, 2016. |
Series:
  Intersections: theology and the church in a world come of age |
Includes
  bibliographical references and index.
Identifiers: LCCN 2016036665 | ISBN 9781934542392 (alk. paper)
Subjects: LCSH: Pastoral theology. | Creation (Literary, artistic,
  etc.)--Religious aspects--Christianity.
Classification: LCC BV4011.3 .A23 2016 | DDC 253--dc23
LC record available at https://lccn.loc.gov/2016036665

Printed in the United States of America

0123456789

Contents

Foreword

Rev. Carol Howard Merritt

"Do not change anything for the first year," our professor advised when I attended seminary. I dutifully wrote down his instructions in my notebook at that moment and etched them in my brain as I entered into the church as a newly-ordained pastor. The words felt wise and sturdy, like massive columns on an ancient library.

I loved the progressive denominational church because it didn't change. The liturgies were ancient, the hymns had theological depth, and the architecture was soaring. The words, melodies, and stones were not something that we could rig up overnight, and I loved them for their durability. The solid consistency of it attracted me from my evangelical upbringing, which seemed to be chasing the next version of cool. I was never good at keeping up with trends and felt irritated by the exertion. Venerable wisdom shouldn't have to wear skinny jeans. So the warning to not change anything felt like a great comfort.

However, when I started in my first congregation, my perspective evolved. My first church was small and getting smaller. It wasn't their fault. A factory at the edge of town had closed down, leaving a massive concrete shell and unemployed workers who had to move. The demographics of the area just didn't support growth. Adding to the difficulties, the church was in a rural area that couldn't attract a lot of candidates, so they had been hobbling along with part-time preachers for years. They didn't have any educational or administrative structures in place. The building needed a lot of updates. So I had to eschew the counsel, roll up my sleeves, and get to the hard work of change. Thank God, they appreciated the changes and labored right beside me. I think they understood how desperate the situation was, because other (bigger) churches I served weren't so willing to alter.

I began to think that perhaps the words "do not change anything" were meant for a different generation, one in which the church was on the soaring uptick and the pastors needed to keep their hands off so they wouldn't disturb the rapid growth. After a year, the pastor would become accustomed to the congregation's quirky ways and would forget what he or she wanted to change in the first place. But the church-at-large reflected my tiny congregation, and it was changing. It was dwindling and we could not, in good conscience, allow it to continue. As my pastor friend, Doug Hagler reminded me, "No one says 'you're very sick and in decline, so let's not change anything for a year.'"

When we began to walk from seminary into our churches, many of our congregations felt as if they were moving toward a genteel dilapidation, like a grand old building whose inhabitants faded away decades ago. We looked the other way as windows cracked, plaster peeled, and doors sagged, as if embarrassed. We neglected our gardens as tenacious vines crept over flowers. We tended bedsides and forsook communicating beyond our walls. The funerals took up so much time that we hardly realized that we didn't have any baptisms.

For some pastors, the longing to try something (anything!) new, became as acute as labor pains. But the resistance could also be strong, and so pastors would be cut off from their hopes, and on some occasions, they would be sent packing. The chastened ministers became cautionary tales for the rest of us, reminding us, yet again, "Don't change anything."

In those early days, my creative yearnings struggled with those inert forces. I longed for a creative life, and I didn't quite know how to go about it. Then I found great comfort in Paul Tillich's *Courage to Be* (please forgive Tillich for the exclusive language):

> Nonbeing threatens man as a whole and therefore threatens
> his spiritual as well as his ontic self-affirmation. Spiritual

self-affirmation occurs in every moment in which man lives creatively in the various spheres of meaning. Creative, in this context, has the sense not of original creativity as performed by the genius but of living spontaneously, in action and reaction, with contents of one's cultural life. In order to be spiritually creative... one must be able to participate meaningfully in their original creations. Such a participation is creative insofar as it changes that in which one participates, even if in very small ways.[1]

The words hit me like a shot in the arm. They pulsed in my blood as the cure for my spiritual stagnation, and gave me a glimpse into our overall denominational malaise. Nonbeing threatened us, because we were not encouraging congregations to change, but we were asking its leaders to not change. We wanted to cut off their vision, stunt their innovative life, and surrender to that inert enemy.

Creation is an act of God, and when we create, we participate in God's work. So, as we were admonished not to change anything, we stemmed the Spirit's moving. But, Tillich also gives a remedy. We can change things in very small ways. We can turn this ship around, one degree at a time.

Now, our denominations have no choice in the matter, as members die, churches close and pastors retire, a new generation of clergy step into their callings knowing that much of the church will never be the same. Just as the economy has moved from agriculture, to industry, to technology, we understand that the nature of how we worship together also amends. We are imagining new structures of sustainability and practice. We are thinking generationally, at the deep-rooted issues of our cultures. We are starting new worshiping communities. We are wrestling with social justice, hoping for the world as it ought to be.

---

1. Paul Tillich, *Courage to Be* (New Haven: Yale University Press), 46

In the midst of the painful and difficult work of this creation, the authors in this volume come as an inspiration and balm. These creative clergy move us beyond the nitty-gritty to do lists of what needs to be changed. They let us peek under the grand schemes and help us to see the daily habits of visionary pastors. They understand Tillich's admonition to be spiritually creative, to change the ministries in which we participate, even in small ways.

I sit, with my teeth on edge, waiting for the work to come. There is much hand wringing, but there's excitement too. We might be ministering in the midst of some rubble, but we're no longer expected to read off someone else's worn-out script. We are being called into a creative life, listening to our own labor pains, and opening ourselves to the Spirit's movement.

Acknowledgments

Growing up I witnessed my mother patching together quilts of many different colors and sizes. Her quilting was a gift passed on to her from her grandmother and what I discovered in watching her put them together over the years is that it is a craft. One has to measure and cut material in just the right way in order for it to fit together with all the other pieces. Material can come from all kinds of sources, I would discover, but my favorite quilt was the one where the material was all my mother's clothes from when she was a child. Quilts are a labor of love, a measure of precision, creativity, and artistry that one can find in fields like architecture, engineering, the culinary arts, and dare I say, the ministry. My mother is a creative and she taught me to dream and construct something beautiful with my work. And so, a book like this comes as a labor of love in the tapestry of my life's work in pastoring churches.

I came to dream of a book on the creativity of clergy from reading the Zen Habits blog and listening to podcasts on entrepreneurship. I also came to realize that I know a great deal of clergy for whom I deeply admire all the passion they are pouring into their context of ministry. I have had the good fortune of being in a group of clergy in their 20s and 30s in the United Church of Christ and in this group alone are so many people using creativity to transform the Church. My desire to publish this book came from the realization that the world needs to hear about these amazing creative clergy and the astonishing things they are doing with their work. Thank you, UCC 2030 Clergy Network and may these pages be worthy of all your beautiful diverse voices. In light of all these intersections in my life, I invited over a dozen clergy and scholars to join me in thinking through the transformative habits that change the work of the Church. I am deeply indebted to all those printed in this book who said "yes" to my reaching out to them and for all their incredible wisdom into this sometimes strange work we are called to as pastors. Thank you, authors, for all of your writing and exceptional challenging ways of thinking.

I am indebted to many in my training who have helped me to formulate my theology, my pastoral and leadership approaches, and given me guidance over the years. I am thankful especially for Brian Hartley, Rick McPeak, Ruth Huston, and Craig Boyd, who provided me with a strong foundation at Greenville College. I was sharpened even further by Mark Lewis Taylor, Luis Rivera Pagan, Robert Dykstra, and Brian Blount at Princeton Theological Seminary. I consider myself blessed by several clergy and academic colleagues throughout the years who have challenged me beyond my own limits, especially, Gregory C. Ellison II, Toby Sanders, Jonathan Walton, Everett Mitchell, Erica Thompson, Tim Kennedy, Chris Hays, Blair Bertrand, Ajit Prasadam, Matthew Nygren, Kevin Armstrong, Mike Mather, Danny Walker, Greg Pimlott, Dearthrice Dewitt, Rachel Metheny, Duane Carlisle, DeAmon Harges, Sharon Baker, Gary Zola, Ryan Taylor Byers, Alicia Taylor Byers, and Tom Eden.

This book would not have been published without the inspiration of all the parishes I have served. I am thankful to Sydney Sadio and the folks of the United Methodist Church at New Brunswick for letting me get my feet wet with you in seminary. I am so glad I was able to serve my first parishes at Andover United Methodist and First United Methodist Church of Newton, NJ. I was so young and you were so forgiving and compassionate. I give thanks for the opportunity to pastor with Sharon Baker at Lockerbie Central where I learned so much about experimentation as a model for the church. I am so glad that I met Mike Mather and that he invited me to be on his staff at Broadway Church in Indianapolis while I was in a time of transition to the United Church of Christ. I learned so much in those short years we were together and Broadway not only saved my ministry, but changed the scope and future of how I looked at the work of a pastor. I am also thankful for my UCC clergy group in Northern Kentucky, a wellspring of wisdom and support. Finally, I am so blessed to serve with the fine folks at St. Paul's United Church of Christ in Alexandria, Kentucky. You all have taught me what it means to begin again and how to fall in love with God's Church.

In the formative stages of this book, I was approached by Christopher Rodkey about submitting a proposal for the Intersection Series with The Davies Group, Publishers. Thank you, Chris, for encouraging me to do so. And, thank you, James Davies for helping this get to print. In the process of writing and editing this book, I am thankful to Eliza Buchakjian-Tweedy, Rachel Hackenberg, Joshua Patty, Bromleigh McCleneghan, and especially Christopher Rodkey for helping me with some of the editing and giving me sound advice on several chapters. And, thank you, Carol Howard Merritt and Gregory C. Ellison II for your terrific bookends to this volume.

As much as I love the people mentioned above, I could not write any book without my family. Thank you, Shannon Norman Abbott, for your unending support of my writing and for being the best partner I could have asked for. I am so proud of my kids, Isabel and Solomon, as they are growing up to follow their dreams. I am glad you will get to see your daddy in print. I am so fortunate that I get to share this moment of writing with my parents, Marty and Marilyn Abbott, whose support is something I cherish a great deal.

In the end, this is a book about clergy, their habits, and the creativity with which they engage the work of the Church. May the voices in these pages offer wisdom and challenge to a Church that so desperately needs a new way of being.

Contributor Biographies

Rev. Chad R. Abbott is a pastor having served churches in both the United Methodist and United Church of Christ traditions. Abbott received his B.A. in religion and philosophy from Greenville College and his M.Div from Princeton Theological Seminary. His area of focus and research has been in the field of spirituality and spiritual practices, especially as it relates to the work of interfaith dialogue. Abbott is a contributing author to the book *The Justice Project* and is the co-editor for the book *Breaking Silence: Pastoral Approaches for Creating an Ethos of Peace*. Abbott currently serves St. Paul's United Church of Christ in Alexandria, Kentucky, where he lives with his wife, Shannon, two kids Isabel and Solomon, and wire haired terrier, Zoe.

Rev. Teresa Blythe has worked with hundreds of people in spiritual direction since receiving her Diploma in the Art of Spiritual Direction from San Francisco Theological Seminary in 2000. She is the founder of the Phoenix Center for Spiritual Direction and has served as Director of the Hesychia School of Spiritual Direction at the Redemptorist Renewal Center in Tucson, Arizona since 2005. Blythe is an ordained United Church of Christ (UCC) minister who lives and works in midtown Phoenix, AZ and is the author of *50 Ways to Pray*. She works with clients in person, by phone and skype. Contact her for more information at teresa@teresablythe.net.

Rev. Ryan T. Byers is an avid lover of green tea brewed three times a day, fairly traded dark chocolate & espresso, and delicious craft beer. Married to Alicia, they have two young sons. Adopted at four weeks old, Ryan's birth name was Juan Ortega, but he was raised by two great Euro-Americans who instilled in him a taste for Tex-Mex. He is a pastor of a United Church of Christ congregation in Fort Thomas, Kentucky.

Rev. Elizabeth Dilley serves as Minister for Ministers in Local Churches on the Ministerial Excellence, Support and Authorization ministry team in the national setting of the United Church of Christ. She and her spouse make their home in Cleveland, Ohio, where they parent Bacon Baby (now Bacon Kid) and two dogs.

Dr. Gregory C. Ellison II is the Associate Professor of Pastoral Care and Counseling at Candler School of Theology at Emory University. Ellison has written several articles and speaks extensively on issues related to adolescence, hope, marginalization, and muteness and invisibility in African American young men. He is the author of *Cut Dead But Still Alive: Caring for African American Young Men* and the co-founder of Fearless Dialogues, a grassroots community empowerment initiative to improve the lives of African American young men. His current research focuses on caring for marginalized populations, pastoral care as social activism, and twentieth- and twenty-first-century mysticism. Ellison has two books in progress with Westminster John Knox Press, *Fearless Dialogues: The Civil Rights Movement of the 21st Century* and *Anchored in the Current: The Eternal Wisdom of Howard Thurman in a Changing World.*

Rev. Dr. Bruce G. Epperly is Pastor and Teacher at South Congregational Church in Centerville (Cape Cod), Massachusetts. Ordained in the Christian Church (Disciples of Christ) and United Church of Christ, he is the author or co-author of over thirty-five books, including *Tending to the Holy: The Practice of the Presence of God in Ministry*; *A Center in the Cyclone: 21st Century Clergy Self-care*; and *Process Theology: Embracing Adventure with God.* He serves on the D.Min. faculty at Wesley Theological Seminary and has taught at Claremont School of Theology, Lancaster Theological Seminary, and Georgetown University.

Rev. Dr. Jeffrey M. Gallagher is the Senior Minister of the United Congregational Church of Tolland, United Church of Christ, in Tolland, Connecticut and author of the book *Wilderness Blessings: How Down Syndrome Reconstructed Our Life and Faith.* Gallagher holds a Bachelor and Masters degree in English Literature from Salem State College, a Master of Divinity degree from Andover Newton Theological School, and a Doctor of Ministry degree from Bangor Theological Seminary. He enjoys writing, running, playing and coaching soccer, New England sports, and currently makes his home in Connecticut with his wife and two sons.

Rev. Rachel G. Hackenberg is an author and United Church of Christ minister, whose books include the popular Lenten devotional

Writing to God and the revitalizing *Sacred Pause: A Creative Retreat for the Word-weary Christian*, which RevGalBlogPals said "will change your life. Not might. Will." Hackenberg is also a soccer mom and an unapologetic Starbucks fan; she and her family reside in Cleveland.

Rev. Dr. Kristina Lizardy-Hajbi is an Ordained Minister in the United Church of Christ and currently directs the denomination's Center for Analytics, Research and Data. She has served in various vocational roles and settings including parish ministry, hospital chaplaincy, non-profit youth ministry, and higher education teaching and administration. Kristina and her spouse Ali reside in Aurora, Colorado.

Rev. Dr. Andrew Hart was born in Philadelphia, Pennsylvania and grew up in Wayne, Pennsylvania. He went to college at Wake Forest University in Winston Salem, North Carolina. Feeling the call from God, he went to Princeton Seminary. He served churches in South Carolina, Long Island, and recently in Chambersburg, Pennsylvania. He also is a chaplain for the Civil Air Patrol as well as an elected board member of Presbyterians Caring for Chaplains and Military Personnel. He is married to Laura Hart, another PC(USA) Minster, and has four children.

Rev. Emily C. Heath is the Senior Pastor of The Congregational Church in Exeter, New Hampshire. Heath is a member of the United Church of Christ's board of directors, a writer for the *Still Speaking Daily Devotionals, Huffington Post Religion*, and more. Heath's book, *Glorify: Reclaiming the Heart of Progressive Christianity,* is published by Pilgrim Press.

Rev. Dr, Andrew T. Kort is ordained in the Presbyterian Church (USA). He currently serves as the Senior Pastor at the First Presbyterian Church in Bloomington, Indiana. Along with his wife, the Rev. Mihee Kim-Kort, he is the co-author of *Yoked: Stories of a Clergy Couple in Marriage, Family, and Ministry.*

Rev. Dr. Sarah Griffith Lund is passionate about loving her family, God, and being part of faith communities. She is an ordained minister and has served as pastor to churches in Brooklyn, New York, Minneapolis, Minnesota, and New Smyrna Beach, Florida. She holds degrees from Trinity University, Princeton Theological Seminary, Rutgers University, and McCormick Theological Seminary. She is on the leadership team for Bethany Ecumenical Fellows, a mentoring program for young clergy, and serves as the Vice Chair for the United Church of Christ Mental Health Network. Rev. Dr. Lund received the Dell Award for Mental Health Education at the 30th General Synod of the UCC. She currently serves as a Vice President for Advancement at Christian Theological Seminary in Indianapolis, Indiana. Sarah is the author of *Blessed are the Crazy: Breaking the Silence about Mental Illness, Family and Church*. She blogs at HuffPost and at www.sarahgriffithlund.com.

Rev. Michael Mather is the pastor of Broadway United Methodist Church in Indianapolis, Indiana. He is also the author of *Sharing Stories, Shaping Community*.

Rev. Dr. Rick McPeak is an Associate Professor of Religion and Philosophy at Greenville College and an experienced pastor in the Free Methodist Church. McPeak held the position of Youth Pastor at the Greenville Free Methodist Church for seven years in Greenville, Illinois. He was the Senior Pastor at Lakeview Free Methodist Church in Seattle, Washington. He is currently an Administrative Pastor of St. Paul's Free Methodist Fellowship in Greenville, Illinois. In addition, he is an artist and first displayed his work in 1999. Entitled "Eastern Pilgrimage," his show featured an installation of thirteen works of mixed media collages made of contemporary icons and pages of biblical text. He continues to teach and design art, continually pulling together the intersection between religion and art.

Rev. Carol Howard Merritt has served Presbyterian (USA) churches in the swamps of Cajun Louisiana, a bayside village in Rhode Island, and an urban neighborhood of Washington, DC. Her committee and board work with the church includes serving as Moderator of the Special General Assembly Committee on the Nature of the Church in the 21st Century. This breadth and depth of practical experience informs her consultations with denominational governing bodies, publishing houses, seminaries, and local churches. The award-winning author of *Tribal Church: Ministering to the Missing Generation* and *Reframing Hope: Vital Ministry in a New Generation*, Carol is a frequent contributor to books, websites, magazines, and journals. She is a regular columnist at the *Christian Century* where her blog, "Tribal Church," is hosted. Carol is a founder and host of UNCO, an open-space "unconference" that attracts church leaders across denominations and generations. She co-hosts the thought-provoking podcast, God Complex Radio, with Rev. Derrick Weston.

Rev. Leah Robberts-Mosser lives in Urbana, Illinois, with the other Rev. Robberts-Mosser, her husband David. Together, they have two daughters, Chloe and Violet. Leah is Pastor/Head of Staff of Community United Church of Christ, a progressive, justice with peace, LGBTQIA open and affirming congregation, located in the heart of the University of Illinois. In the midst of being a mother, partner, and pastor, she cooks, practices yoga, watches "The Walking Dead," and is currently writing a serial killer novel. Before entering the ministry, Leah was a professional face painter.

Rev. Dr. Kay Mutert is a Master Teacher with Veriditas, the worldwide labyrinth organization founded by Rev. Dr. Lauren Artress. In that faculty capacity Kay offers pilgrimages, retreats, labyrinth workshops and facilitator trainings for the organization, both nationally and internationally, and is a member of the Veriditas Council. Her work focuses on creative expression and renewal of spirit. She is a United Methodist minister, musician and author, a breast cancer survivor and the parent of an adult son lost to lymphoma. Her vision is that we walk together on the path.

Rev. Dr. Christopher D. Rodkey is Pastor of St. Paul's United Church of Christ in Dallastown, Pennsylvania, and teaches at Lexington Theological Seminary. He is a graduate of the University of Chicago (M.Div.), Meadville Lombard Theological School (D.Min.), and Drew University (Ph.D.). His books include *The Synaptic Gospel*, *Too Good to Be True*, and *The World is Crucifixion*, and is the series editor of Intersections, published by Noesis Press.

Rev. Dr. Robert Saler is Research Professor of Lutheran Studies and Executive Director of the Center for Pastoral Excellence at Christian Theological Seminary in Indianapolis, where he also directs the Lilly Endowment Clergy Renewal Programs. He is the author of *Between Magisterium and Marketplace: A Constructive Account of Theology and the Church* (Minneapolis: Fortress, 2014).

Rev. Callie J. Smith is Associate Director of the Lilly Endowment Clergy Renewal Programs at Christian Theological Seminary in

Indianapolis. She is an ordained minister in the Christian Church (Disciples of Christ) and was co-founder of Studio Ninety-Six—a community of theologians, worship designers, and artists in the Indianapolis area.

Rev. Zayna Hart Thompson is an ordained pastor in the United Church of Christ and is currently serving two congregations in the beautiful Driftless Region of Southwest Wisconsin. Her greatest loves include theater, coffee, hiking, and airports. She shares a home with her ever-supportive partner Matt and a beloved ten year old collie, Brett.

Rev. Michelle L. Torigian is the pastor of St. Paul United Church of Christ, Old Blue Rock Road in Cincinnati, Ohio. Torigian worked in fundraising and marketing for non-profits as her previous career. She graduated from Eden Theological Seminary in 2010. Torigian is the author of a number of articles on the Huffington Post Religion page including "Between Childless and Childfree," a reflection for Mother's Day. She also blogs for RevGalBlogPals feature "The Pastoral Is Political" and the United Church of Christ's New Sacred. Recently, Torigian's essay "Always the Pastor, Never the Bride" was published in the book *There's a Woman in the Pulpit* (Skylight Paths Publishing, 2015). She regularly posts her musings on current events, justice issues, pop culture, and theology at www.michelletorigian.com.

Rev. Courtney Stange-Tregear is a student of the Great Books, advocate for maternal rights, United Church of Christ pastor, wife and mother. She works for social justice and partners with community leaders and organizations to improve the quality of life for all her neighbors. Courtney's interest in health and wellness includes running, yoga, and anything else related to mind, body, and spiritual wholeness.

Rev. Caela Simmons Wood is a United Church of Christ pastor currently serving First Congregational UCC in Manhattan, Kansas. Caela previously served First United Church in Bloomington, Indiana and is a graduate of Christian Theological Seminary in Indianapolis and Perkins School of Theology in Dallas. She is passionate about understanding and confronting systemic injustices, especially relating to race, sexuality and gender, economic inequality, and the environment. Wood enjoys cycling, hiking, cooking, and reading everything she can get her hands on. Caela and her husband David are parents to two young sons.

Introduction

The Rise of the Creative Clergy: Habits, Clergy and the Future of the Church

Rev. Chad R. Abbott

I can remember the intake interview like it was yesterday. Clearly, I was there to save the church. They had spent the last five years with an otherwise retired pastor working part time and the church figured that now was the time to make a move towards transformation. They and my then Bishop turned to me. I was young, which meant everyone assumed I could bring in young families. They told me, "We have $150,000 in the bank, which we calculate will get us three years under your financial package. We are going to give this all we have for three years and if we aren't successful then we will just close the church." They assumed that decades of decline could be turned around in three short years. We were all nearly doomed from the start.

This story is not atypical in the American context of the mainline church. Our churches have spent the decades since the 1960s in steady decline. Very few have any answers as to how to transform our congregational cultures, and turn around such decline. A great deal of ink has been poured out in the last several years, outlining the historical and sociological reasons for the shift in the church. Many more books have targeted ways in which mainline and even evangelical churches can reach more and more of the shift in religiously unaffiliated or "nones," as they have come to be known. But, in the end, the data is abundantly clear: *the American church is in crisis.* In fact, religion scholar and regular commentator on American religion, Diana Butler Bass, writes: "the line of segregation is between those who go to church and those who do not. And, judging by the number of cars parked in driveways on Sunday morning in most American cities and suburbs, it is not hard to figure out which group is growing."[1]

As one who is leading a church in this twenty-first century context, I, like many of my clergy colleagues, am painfully aware of these startling realities about our future. Declining membership, increasing numbers of non-affiliated religious people, and more pastoral burn-out than ever before all threaten the vitality of the holy space that we love so much and on which we have staked our lives. However, one staggering hope catches my eye: *I continue to see a deeply held spiritual hunger in our ethos.* Many are not interested in the institutional church, but have come to see themselves as "spiritual, but not religious." Still, this is not a book about reaching out to those "nones" or the "spiritual, but not religious," nor about church growth in local congregations. We have plenty of books on both. This book focuses upon dreaming of an emerging future for the church, one that embraces creativity and experimentation in the pastorate in the midst of such a context. This book foresees the developing of an entrepreneurial spirit among clergy who serve in contexts that have illustrious histories and produced grand educational institutions. This book sets hope upon clergy who form habits in their work, calling upon an innovative and creative spirit that frees them not only to encounter the Sacred themselves, but also to open doors to new ministries, in a time when the Church so desperately needs transformed leadership. This is a book about new wineskins (Matthew 9:17) and the possibility that we can examine the work of the pastorate through the eyes of creativity, risk, experimentation, and a theology of hope.

A Culture of Creativity

Near the turn of the twenty-first century, urban theorists began asking questions about what makes certain communities or neighborhoods thrive economically. Many of the theorists at the time assumed that economic vitality lay in the reproduction of existing large and successful conglomerates and companies in as many and varied settings as possible. Much of this way of thinking also assumed that working individuals aimed to spend their entire careers being loyal to one particular employer or location. However, urban theorist, Richard Florida encountered data that suggested that there was an entirely new movement and class of people transforming the economy, the community, and the way people live their everyday lives. This movement of people demonstrated less interest in remaining loyal to particular companies and communities for life, and were much more interested in setting their own work schedule, living among others who thought like them, and being committed to utilizing creativity in both work and life. This movement of creative people began to change the definition of a community or economy. Florida came to call this the "rise of the creative class."

While this rise of a new and innovative class mostly viewed the world in economic terms, Florida also saw here a cultural shift beginning to shape and transform the way people live everyday life. Florida remarks, "In this new world, it is no longer the organizations we work for, churches, neighborhoods or even family ties that define us. Instead, we do this ourselves, defining our identities along the varied dimensions of our creativity."[2] As of 2002, nearly 38 million people made up what Florida called the creative class, working in areas of education, the arts, technology, architecture, and entertainment. The basic utility of this group is to "create new ideas, new technology, and/or new creative content," under a common ethos that "values creativity, individuality, difference, and merit."[3] Most importantly, according to Florida, the work of creativity is multi-dimensional. This means that such a creative culture is not simply interested in individuals creating new products to be sold on an assembly line. The work of creativity and its associated economy goes much deeper than this. Further: "It is a mistake to think, as many do, that creativity can be reduced to the creation of new blockbuster inventions, new products, and new firms. In today's economy creativity is pervasive and ongoing: We constantly revise and enhance every product, process and activity imaginable, and fit them together in new ways."[4] In other words, creativity is a comprehensive way of being that encompasses not just specific products that produce economy, but is rather a way of examining the entire process and systems of production in the first place.

What Florida most readily discovered in his research was that this class of people utilized the work of creativity in every area and aspect of their lives and that their creativity began transforming the way in which communities were living. Creativity began transforming both individuals and institutions because a culture of creative means infiltrated both thinking and habit formation. For example, a company's best practices and habits were regularly reviewed and reinvented. Florida suggests, "Creativity involves distinct kinds of thinking and habits that must be cultivated both in the individual and in the surrounding society. Thus, the creative ethos pervades everything from our workplace culture to our values and communities, reshaping the way we see ourselves as economic and social actors--our very identities."[5] Florida argues that the future of economic success hinges on the power of creativity in our communities. He concludes, "Powering the great ongoing changes of our time is the rise of human creativity as the defining feature of economic life."[6]

What exactly do thriving economies and creativity have to do with the future of the church? Some might suggest nothing at all. But the act and culture of creativity have a great deal to teach those of us who are experiencing a cultural shift in the life of the church. Crucial to Florida's argument about the creative class is this notion that the utilization of creativity transforms both habits and culture. My argument in this book is that clergy and faith communities possess the capacity for the transformation of habits and culture through creativity. We are creatures of habit. The work of spiritual growth, both individually and communally, is founded upon the notion that a discipline is formed ritualistically and regularly enough to fuel the story and life of a person towards God and the Sacred.

Beyond this, habits also assume a sense of creativity, of discerning and refining what speaks to a particular individual or community. We theologically make sense of this if we draw upon the notion that since God created us, as it is written in the opening verses of the Genesis narratives, we are co-creators with God. We are told in Genesis, "So God created humankind in his image, in the image of God he created them; male and female he created them." (Genesis 1:27) Thus, if God is a creator and we are created in God's image, then we too are designed to utilize the gift of creativity that lives within us. I believe that nurturing and living out this innate creativity lies at the heart of any positive transformation of the church and its future. Just as creativity has been utilized in urban centers to transform economy and cultural life, so too, can creativity be transformational in the church and play a role in what theologian John Phillip Newell calls the "Rebirthing of God." One of the places that creativity plays itself out in this transformation is in the lives of clergy and the habits they form in their work, which is the core purpose of this book.

Clergy and Creative Habits

While I do not think that clergy who use creativity in their work and habits represent the only contributing factor to the transformation of the church, such issues are at the very least a crucial part of the discussion. Theologian John Philip Newell, in his *The Rebirthing of God* forcefully argues clergy to have the space to respond to the collapse of Christendom:

There are three main responses or reactions to this collapse. The first is to deny that it is happening. The second is to frantically try to shore up the foundations of the old thing. The third, which I invite us into, is to ask what is trying to be born that requires a radical reorientation of our vision. What is the new thing that is trying to emerge from deep within us and from deep within the collective soul of Christianity?[7]

In her book, *Christianity After Religion,* Diana Butler Bass reminds us of the revival language of the Old and New Lights. During the First Great Awakening in the United States, the creativity of the emerging clergy was highly resisted by those who wanted to preserve the old ways, creeds, and traditions. These "New Lights" were interested in the transformation of society, culture, religious practice and how it is that we hear from God. Bass strongly argues that this language of Old and New Light is relevant to the crisis of the church as we today look towards solutions for the future. She argues, "Today's New Light awakening starts with a vision of humanity created in the divine image and moves toward the hope of universal connection and wholeness through God's spirit. New Light spirituality emphasizes creation, restoration, and shalom."[8] This New Light, according to Bass, is a building on the use of creativity to make sense of where we have been, where we are, and where we are going as communities of faith. The most formative notion of her idea of New Light is that it is grounded in an authentic experiential faith fueled by creativity. She writes, "For New Lights, the primary agency of experiential faith is the individual-in-community, following a freely chosen spiritual path, based on principles of empathy and compassion, and judged by internal authenticity."[9] The agency of New Light and the rebirthing of God is partially found in the use of creativity, not just in the church writ large, but in the leadership of its clergy.

In my estimation, many examples exist demonstrating how we might build off of creativity and the forming of habits among clergy. However, two examples in particular shine as of particular notice: Mahatma Gandhi's use of experimentation, and Jesus' use of parables. Gandhi was interested only in one thing: *truth*. Gandhi expressed interest not just in truth, as such, but in the *kinds of truths* that would lead him into direct relationship with God. In his autobiography he writes, "What I want to achieve, what I have been striving and pining to achieve these thirty years, is self-realization, to see God face to face, to attain moksha."[10] In striving towards self-realization and experiencing God, Gandhi's methodology was that of experimentation. He experimented with everything from vegetarianism to, psychology and thoughts of his mind, by way of dress, fasting, and the social and moral value of non-violence as a theory and practice. In the end, he said of his experiments, "I claim for them nothing more than does a scientist who, though he conducts his experiments with the utmost accuracy, forethought and minuteness, never claims any finality about his conclusions, but keeps an open mind regarding them."[11] The habits that Gandhi formed were based in creativity because he desired with every fiber of his being to be faithful to what was true of himself and of God. This approach is profoundly important for clergy whose primary work is to be present to the self, God, and the people of God.

Jesus is also another prime example of someone who understood the power of creativity and habit in his context. The power of the work of Jesus and his cousin John the Baptist lay in the geographical location of their ministry, that is, away from the structure of the Temple cult. In Jesus' day, it was understood that God's presence on earth was centered within the Jerusalem Temple. The people of Jesus' day, including his own family, traveled yearly to Jerusalem to make offerings at the Temple and to receive forgiveness of sins by the priests and religious leaders. John the Baptist was considered a rabble rouser in part because he called people out of this Temple focus, and suggested that the presence of God could be experienced by coming out to the desert to be baptized and repent of their sins.

This movement, as we all know, eventually got John beheaded, in part because John focused his efforts only at the Jordan river.

Jesus himself came to be baptized at the Jordan and he followed in John's footsteps in arguing that the presence and way of God could be experienced outside of the temple. In fact, Jesus even suggested that the Kingdom of God was within human beings, that we were the temples where God dwells. Jesus, then, formed the habit of walking from town to town, engaging with people in relationship and helping them to foster a connection with God, wherever they were in life, physically or spiritually. But Jesus had a very specific way of teaching that was partial to storytelling and parables. He taught by creatively placing himself in the geographic and emotional location of his audience, and then utilizing their daily images to weave the stories and parables that would challenge them in following his radical way of love. He told stories of vineyards, seed sowing, grand banquets for children who had lost their way, land owners and the wages of their workers, and an injured person found on the side of the road taken care of by a foreigner but ignored by his own people.

Additionally, so much of the Jesus story that we have in the gospel narratives is told through the lens of the Exodus: the story of the Israelites coming out of Egypt. Jesus went through the waters of baptism just like the Israelites went through the Red Sea. Jesus went out into the wilderness for forty days and nights just as the Israelites were in the desert for forty years. He gave his interpretation of the law by sharing the Sermon on the Mount, just as the Israelites received the Law with Moses on Mt. Sinai. In many ways, Jesus had become the re-created Moses, living out the very story of Israel. Jesus was, himself, a living parable. His creativity sparked a movement of followers, who would eventually carry on his work after his death and resurrection. Many years prior to the life and work of Mahatma Gandhi, Jesus understood and lived out these experiments and creativity among the people in the land in and around Roman-occupied Judea. These examples provide a clear foundation for understanding habits as the backbone of discipleship. Therefore, clergy are not unique in our ability to form habits through the power of creativity, but if a new way and future is to be made as the church then we must be willing to live into their example.

A New Old Way

The ways of rebirth in the church and among the people of God is both a new and yet a very old way. The future of Christian faith and the work of local churches will not be able to survive the current crisis so long as we continue by *only* reclaiming the old ways, the Old Light. Great power is found in creeds, in the reading of scripture, in liturgy, and in old habits. However, the movement of present and future culture will not always rest on such things. We must get back to John Philip Newell's question of "What is the new thing that will emerge from deep within us?" Allowing New Light to emerge from within us to revive the church requires several things: deep listening, letting go, compassionate relationships, and an open mind to new and creative ideas that emerge within both individuals and communities. There is nothing particularly new about these things, but they can lead us to the new. This makes the future of the church a New Old Way.

Deep Listening means spending time with individuals and communities and leaving behind any preconceived notions of what is and should be happening in our lives and churches. God can only emerge and birth a new way if we are willing to clear our minds, our hearts, and listen for what the Spirit is saying to us. Deep listening requires an intent focus on being attentive and mindful to the present moment and to what is right in front of us. We have missed so many opportunities in the church by not listening or trying to reclaim something old that does not speak to modern people. We must listen deeply to one another, to our inner life, and to the God who calls us.

Letting Go is a willingness to surrender all things so that what is right and true can emerge. One of the dangers of always clinging to patterns of thinking or behaving is that there is a false sense of security in them. In fact, the idea of security represents an illusion, unless we are speaking of the strength and assurance of God. What if we let go of our need for security? What if we opened ourselves up to experimentation and the possibility that God and the truth of our lives and communities can emerge as the world unfolds? We must let go to make room for that which is emerging within us and all around us.

Compassionate Relationships, as Diana Butler Bass reminds us, build on empathy. The power of empathy allows us to see each other as One and not as separate. If we are interconnected in our relationships, then what happens to my neighbor also happens to me. When our relationships build on compassion and empathy then we are far less likely to cause harm or injustice towards one another. We can hear and see one another as children of God created in God's image, which differs from seeing one another as enemy, as other, or as unworthy of being included in the people of God. We must embrace compassionate relationships if the church desires to live into the very calling of Jesus who asked that we be One just as he and God are One (John 17:21).

Creativity is the power to awaken the voice within us that speaks of a God making all things new within us and in all of creation. Creativity offers the power to speak and breathe new life into parts of the world that have been in spaces of deep decay and withering death. In the church, creativity represents opportunities for us to open ourselves to what God is speaking and saying yes to, and allowing the Spirit to move in ways unexpected and unforeseen in our lives and communities. We must be creative if we hope to offer ourselves as any kind of midwife in the birthing of a new way in the church and in the lives of those who attend our churches.

In the work and lives of clergy, there is a crucial path for new life in the church as we form creative habits that embody deep listening, letting go, compassionate relationships, and creativity. In our creative sacred habits we find a new old way of being that can open our lives to God and what God has in store for our future.

Jazz and The Rise of the Creative Clergy

My favorite music is jazz. I could sit in a jazz lounge for hours listening to a pianist flow up and down the keys, the bass uttering its deep and low voice, the trumpet or saxophone offering their sharp dialogue with clarity and vision. As a lover of music, jazz more than any other art form speaks the language of my personal journey. I believe this to be so because I deeply value the power of human connection and conversation. I believe that when conversation is taking place that transformation, change, justice, and hope are entirely within our grasp. Whether it is politics, community, theology, spirituality, or psychology, the sharing of our stories is what can help us to reach a shared future. The power of jazz music ultimately can be found in assembling a collection of voices sharing in a meaningful conversation about our lives together. The language is music, the stories are about human connection. The great trumpet player, Wynton Marsalis, described that, "The real power of jazz and the innovation of jazz is that a group of people can come together and create art, improvised art, and can negotiate their agendas with each other and that negotiation is the art," concluding that this "is our art, the four of us can now have a dialogue, we can have a conversation, we can speak to each other in the language of music."[12]

This book offers a collection of such voices in negotiation, a gathered dialogue among people whose practices and vision help shape the future of the church. The voices in this book coalesce into a work of spiritual and intellectual jazz, where the expression of a habit or pastoral practice as a place of creativity functions as improvisation. Our practices and habits function as experiments in what it means to be clergy, to live in community with other people of faith, and how the future of the church, in part, depends upon our willingness as clergy to use creativity in our work. Building off of each other's voices in this book, our spiritual jazz offers a broader conversation about the future of theology, the church, and spirituality.

The voices in this book come from varying theological traditions, racial or ethnic heritages, genders, sexualities, lived socio-cultural spaces and social locations. These various social locations offer us the chorus of voices that will play the music of this book and, just like jazz, our conversation together has real consequences in real communities, congregations, and theological institutions. What binds us together is that each author has chosen to share a particular habit or pastoral practice that is changing the way we live and understand church. In this text, we have chosen four areas of focus upon which to express the rise of the creative clergy: 1) *habits of the parish*, 2) *habits of community*, 3) *habits of spiritual discipline*, and 4) *habits of self care*. Before delving into these practices, I would like to define the categories which I have chosen as a means of introducing my readers to the concepts, topics, and authors.

Habits of the Parish The work pastors do within our immediate congregations is crucial. Each author will give voice to different aspects of this work, but this section in particular is focused on pastoral work in the church. Leah Robberts-Mosser opens up the book centering our work in four principles for understanding how creativity functions as a pastoral act. Andrew Kort then sets the tone for this section by focusing on how using a common "rule" can aid in the structural work of congregations. Christopher Rodkey reminds us of the importance of theological study as a pastor and a similar regular study of scripture will be taken up by Emily Heath. Michelle Torigian will situate our work in developing creative worship services specifically to be mindful of the context and lived experiences of those in our parishes. Finally, Ryan Byers will share in the work of creativity among young adults and millennials that is now defining the work of our parishes very differently.

Habits of Community Certainly community can be defined in a variety of ways, but the critical way of defining it for this section would be habits that are formed for the purpose of work outside of the walls of our churches. Mike Mather will engage us in the creative work of community engagement, which is a model built on asset based community development. Caela Simmons Wood situates the work of pastors within the habit of developing points of connection and community for the sake of simply building community, both in and outside of the church. Andy Hart will call us to a practice of creating sacred space with those experiencing trauma, in particular our veterans who are in our communities struggling with PTSD. Zayna Hart Thompson will speak to the habit of community office hours and the impact this has in creating sacred space for pastoral work outside of the church. Elizabeth Dilley will point us to the practice of creative work done in the community of social networking and technology. To round out this section, Bruce Epperly will bring synergy into the ministry of clergy by reminding us of the need for pastoral excellence groups in creating health and balance.

Habits of Spiritual Disciplines A book on clergy habits certainly would not seem complete without a section on creative spiritual disciplines. Rick McPeak speaks to the habit of prayer as a place of artistic and creative discovery. Jeff Gallagher awakens us to the habit of exercise as a specific incarnational mode of theological and spiritual discipline that transforms church culture. Sarah Lund will call us to the habit of silence and how it provides moments of clarity and discernment for our work as pastors. Finally, Kay Mutert reaches our spiritual lives into the spiral of memory and longing with the ancient path of labyrinth walking.

Habits of Self-Care The final section will address important practices that clergy use to take care of themselves and that nurture healthy habits for longevity and excellence. Rob Saler and Callie

Smith will speak to the habit of sabbaticals and how the invitation to step away can transform both pastors and congregations. Kristina Lizardy Hajbi awakens us to the work of mindfulness as it relates to clergy mental wellness. Teresa Blythe reminds clergy that the ancient art of spiritual direction can keep pastors healthy and centered in our work in congregations. Courtney Stange-Tregear offers us a new vision of a home practice of family ritual that steeps us in good boundaries of self care. Finally, Rachel Hackenberg disrupts our understanding of Sabbath-keeping as a practice of the pastorate and re-centers us in God and Other.

My readers should not assume that this discourse attempts to directly address the ecclesiological and missiological questions regarding the rebirthing and transformation of the twenty-first century church as it responds to, and tries to live under, the weight of decades of dramatic decline. I simply believe that through creativity and the formation of habits, a new way can emerge among clergy, which can play a role in the transformation of the church. Like a good piece of jazz, I defer any expertise on creativity and sacred habits to the voices in this book who are living them and transforming their communities of faith as a result. In each chapter, the authors will draw on their own experience in forming a habit, constructing a theological and sociological interpretation of that habit, and the reflecting implications of transformation in the context of the church and beyond. In the end, this collection of essays will demonstrate the power of habits and creativity to transform the lives of clergy and to offer "New Light" and new models of rebirth in the work of our faith communities.

Following on Richard Florida's assumption that the rise of the creative class is crucial for the transformation of economy and community in urban centers, I argue that the creativity of clergy will function as one of the key factors in the transformation of the Christian faith. The creativity utilized in urban communities is a creativity that motivates and permeates all arenas of city life and changes the entire way communities are choosing to live. If clergy can experiment with creativity to build habits and culture within congregations, then what can emerge from the rubble of the declining church is a vision of beauty, compassion, transformation, and hope that changes the way communities of faith choose to live.

Do I believe that our current decline in the church is destined to end a painful death? No, I do not. I believe a new old way is forming, a new class of clergy is emerging, and that if we will listen deeply, let go, invest in compassionate relationships, and risk our faith creatively, we will see that a new church is being born. A new kind of clergy is leading the way. Welcome to the rise of the creative clergy.

Notes

1. Diana Butler Bass, *Christianity After Religion: The End of Church and the Birth of a New Spiritual Awakening* (New York: HarperOne, 2012), 18.

2. Richard Florida. *The Rise of the Creative Class: And How It's Transforming Work, Leisure, Community, & Everyday Life* (New York: Basic, 2002), 7.

3. Ibid., 8.

4. Ibid., 5.

5. Ibid., 22.

6. Ibid., 21.

7. John Philip Newell. *The Rebirthing of God: Christianity's Struggle for New Beginnings* (Woodstock: Skylight Paths, 2014), xi.

8. Bass, 229.

9. Ibid., 229.

10. Mahatma Gandhi, *Gandhi An Autobiography: The Story of My Experiments with Truth* (Boston: Beacon, 1993), xxvi.

11. Ibid., xxvii.

12. Ken Burns, dir., *Jazz*. ep. 1 (Hollywood: Florentine, 2000).

Part 1
Habits of the parish

Chapter 1

The Pastor as Creative: Four Principles for Centering Pastoral Life in Creativity

Rev. Leah Robberts-Mosser

Coloring books were contraband in my house as a kid. "They stunt creativity," my artist and art educator parents mused. Coloring books signified the antithesis of everything they valued. Why learn to color inside the lines when you can draw your own? The coloring book became metaphor for our way of life: Why learn to stay inside prescribed lines when you can learn to draw your own on the page, and beyond, on into life?

So began my apprenticeship into the creative class.

In her transformational book *Drawing on the Right Side of the Brain*, Dr. Betty Edwards wrote, "Drawing is not really very difficult. Seeing is the problem, or to be more specific, shifting to a particular way of seeing."[1] Edwards spends the rest of her book teaching people how to see in a particular way, then to interpret what they see. What does that have to do with being a pastor in the twenty-first century? It's what creativity is: it's all about how we see and interpret the world. When we practice creativity, we employ our attention to really, truly, see the world around us; then, utilizing our attention, imagination, skill, and spirituality, we produce original ideas and innovative works, building on what's come before us to create new paths, while discovering solutions to problems both big and small. Whether painting, sculpting, or pastoring, the same holds true: creativity is the ability to see and interpret the world in expansive ways. See why my parents who made their bread and butter being creative banned coloring books? It's hard to see in expansive ways when there are lines already on the page.

"Sure, easy for you to say," my color-by-number friends quip, "How does that work? What are the mechanics? How does being creative happen on a daily basis?" The answer is in our bones. Each of us is born a creative. Every child plays make believe. Every child spins stories. Every child draws. Every child creates and concocts and conceives grandeur daily. Creativity is the work of childhood. Then, somewhere along the road to adulthood…wham! Creativity is cast aside and imaginative endeavors are traded in for the practicality of adulthood. Practicality is creativity's kryptonite—not one of us is immune to it. What's the antidote? How might we practice our creativity as adults as freely as we did when we were kids, so it is a transformational, revelatory, rejuvenating habit of adulthood? This is a key question. Even those of us raised on creativity as a way of life must tend to our creativity with regular nurture, upkeep, and maintenance. Guarding against that which renders it worthless, we must practice our creativity much like we practice our faith.

Perhaps this metaphor is wholly, and holy, unnecessary here. Might we practice our creativity as a practice of our faith, as essential and necessary, like the air we breathe? My answer is, yes. In this new millennium, we can and we must. Creativity is faithful. It is a faithful response to the life with which we are gifted. For if we believe God to be Creator, then practicing creativity is to participate in divine acts. It is blessed work. It is life-giving action. It is prayer.

We find ourselves in a unique position in this age when little of what we know about the how-to of doing Church continues to apply. As acknowledged in the introduction of this book, the twenty-first century Church is facing a crisis that demands of its clergy a willingness to take old forms of faith, which have always defined it, and transform them, allowing them to speak in new, life-giving ways for our time. Those of us who are clergy are both private practitioners of an ancient faith and public leaders who guide others in the way of that sacred path. How might we as clergy give voice to new paths and new forms of expression, while discovering solutions to problems big and small? When the norm is change, what better tool to use in the practice of public, pastoral leadership than the discipline of creativity itself? Creativity, then, is an essential practice for those who want to be faithful as clergy in the twenty-first century.

As a life-long practitioner of creativity and as a pastor, I will tell you the truth: this creativity-as-spiritual-practice thing morphs as I move through life. How it manifests itself changes. What renewed me as a married young adult failed to fulfill me as a grad student. How I practiced creativity daily as a young associate pastor with no children, just a three-and-a-half-legged dog and plenty of free time, simply doesn't sync with my life as Pastor/Head of Staff with two kids and a husband, with a love of family life and more laundry than you can imagine. What remains the same, as I move through life, though, are four principles that I seek to inhabit. These four principles set the tone for the rest of this book by centering creativity, this way of seeing and interpreting the world, at the forefront of our work as clergy.

These four principles are: 1) taking a creator's view of the world, 2) hushing the inner critic, 3) feeding the creative soul, and 4) trusting the process. Perhaps you will find, as you endeavor to take up creativity as a spiritual practice and practical tool, as a clergyperson and a practitioner of the Christian faith, that these markers will serve you as profoundly as they have served me. If so, no doubt, they'll serve the Church profoundly, too.

Principle One: Taking a creator's view of the world

One of the inaugural activities of my father's "Introduction to Art" class was an assignment called "50 Things to Do with a Brick Other than Build Something." The instructions were simple: make a list of 50 things you can do with a brick without listing "build" as one of them. I started making this list when I was a kid. You try it. What can you do with a brick?

Make a paperweight out of it.

Get a second one, heat them…make paninis!

Use it as a book end.

Rub your heels on it—instant exfoliation!

Place it on the gas pedal in lieu of using cruise control. (Don't really do this, but perhaps think of this idea when we get to the next principle.)

That's five. We could go on and on but you get the picture. The practice of creativity requires thinking about and seeing the world in expansive ways rather than prescribed ones. That means noticing the particularity of things while not being confined to those particularities. Creativity requires being able to readily think outside the lines.

Georgia O'Keefe, the American painter of southwestern landscapes and flowers as big as a Mack truck, said, "Nobody sees a flower—really—it is so small it takes time—we haven't time—and to see takes time, like to have a friend takes time."[2] Perhaps her practice of taking a creator's worldview best sums up this practice. She looked at flowers; she had to in order to paint them in detail. But she saw them from a perspective never taken before. O'Keefe managed to look intently at the details of a tiny thing, pistol, petal, stamen, stalk, and see them in another way, a way that was not bound by convention. It's as if every time O'Keefe went to the canvas, she played "50 Things to do with a Flower other than make a Flower Arrangement." What can you do with a flower, Georgia?

Blow it up bigger than life allowing you to see the tiniest parts.

Drench the canvas with hues and pigment, flooding the viewer with color and, consequently, emotion.

Paint in such a way that the viewer thinks they are looking at some colorful vulva, when they're actually looking at a painting of an iris.

That's three. What else can you do with a flower, Georgia? Georgia O'Keefe could do plenty. Again, we could go on and on, but you see. You understand how to see differently.

In keeping this principle of the practice of creativity, I spend a lot of time looking at the world, looking and wondering. I use the macro lens and take the panoramic view. Both the details and the broad expanse prove important. I stop to watch ants move along the sidewalk and follow their train; I think about converting an inch to a mile and the size of an ant to that of a human being and wonder what kind of ground those industrious little things are covering. I stop to watch the wind blow across the corn field; I am taken by the way the tassels move in waves, like the ocean spread before me in green and gold. I wonder if other people see this splendor and get lost in the majesty of corn fields. I stop to look at trees in winter, their leaves gone; I am stunned by the branches against the flat gray sky. The branches look like bones. I wonder if that's what we look like when we get exposed.

When we learn how to see with a creator's view, we can readily see possibilities that didn't exist before. What would happen if we played "50 Things to do with Worship other than Worshippy Things?" How could worship be infused with new energy and transformed by creativity if only we could see it in a different way? What could you do if you played this game? You try.

Taking a creator's view, and therefore, The Creator's view of the world means learning to see both what's in front of our eyes and what's in the mind's eye. If we can learn to see the world not just as it is, but how God longs for it to be, then we truly learn to see.

Principle Two: Hushing the inner critic

In the movie "Inside Out" we watch the inner workings of a young girl's mind. Five emotions, fear, anger, sadness, disgust, and joy, manage Riley's inner life, assessing each situation she encounters and taking control accordingly. Critics—the people who scoff and say, "You can't do that. Pfft! Why would you do such a thing?"—are controlled by disgust, the feeling of profound disapproval. In the practice of creativity, most of us get waylaid by our inner critic before we ever face any actual critics lurking out there in the world. When we begin to practice creativity, our own feelings of disgust start up, and unless we've learned to hand the controls over to another emotion, we allow disgust to guide us, steering us in another direction.

Inner critics are crippling to creatives. Most people who deal in creativity as their bread and butter employ practices to silence the inner critic. Don't let successful creatives fool you: everyone has an inner critic and everyone has to find the technique that works for them in hushing it up. Years ago, I attended a workshop about utilizing mandalas in our private meditation practices. Mandalas are sacred circles used and utilized by faithful people from religious traditions the world over. The workshop leader taught us this practice based on Jeri Gerding's book *Drawing to God: Art as Prayer, Prayer as Art.* Gerding outlines a nine step process for drawing and praying with mandalas.[3] Her instructions describe the process of centering oneself, choosing the colors, and beginning to doodle within that sacred circle. Step Three instructs, "Begin to fill in the circle with color and form."[4] At this point in the workshop, the leader broke free from the printed instructions and expounded on this point. "You may hear that little voice inside your head say, 'What are you doing? You can't draw.'" Everyone in the room chuckled at the workshop leader's personification of the inner critic we had all heard time and again in our heads. The leader went on, "When you hear this little voice, remind it that it's not its turn to speak. It should be quiet and sit down." The room erupted in applause. Yes! Finally, someone speaks up and shuts down the inner critic. Bam! Be gone, inner critic, with your crippling critiques and shame-filled assessments: it's not your turn.

This recognition of that skeptical part of myself proved revelatory. Expecting that I would someday be able to silence my inner critic once and for all is unrealistic at best. Frankly, it is impossible. We will always have doubts. Unequivocally censoring our inner doubter makes us prone to naiveté; learning to hush our inner critic in the practice of creativity dispenses its wisdom judiciously (like when you shouldn't actually place brick to pedal in lieu of cruise control), allowing us to dream, imagine, and endeavor beyond convention. The inner critic values productivity and practicality, but artists will tell you that form does not always follow function. For innovation, imagination, and originality to take hold, the creative must be willing to pull the inner critic aside and say, "Hush. It's not your turn to talk," then enforce the boundary.

When Jesus prayed, "Forgive us our trespasses as we forgive those who trespass against us," perhaps he was talking about more than our outward relationships. Perhaps he was also talking about our inner relationships as well. This principle is as necessary in the practice of creativity as it is in pastoring. So, learn to set the boundary, hold to it, and forgive yourself when your inner critic crosses the line. It's only in this gentle flow that we are able to navigate the creativity landscape courageously.

Principle three: Feeding the creative soul

An "artist date" is what Julia Cameron calls the practice of feeding the heart, soul, and imagination in her sacred text for the creative class called *The Artist's Way: A Spiritual Path to Higher Creativity*. Cameron says, "An artist date is a block of time, perhaps two hours weekly, especially set aside and committed to nurturing your creative consciousness...an excursion, a play date that you preplan and defend against all interlopers."[5] I learned the concept of The Artist Date as a young adult and have carried it with me ever since, allowing its employ to shift accordingly. In certain seasons of life, I've let this principle of the practice of creativity go and the results were dreadful. I thought I could live without it. After all, only so many hours exist in each day.

Even so, you must find a way for this principle of soul-feeding to fit in your life. A two-hour chunk may not fit into your week. It is not the logistical container of the two-hour artist date that will feed your soul; it is what you put in there that matters, so spread it out over the week in tiny bits if you must. Do it however it works for you. The point is this: you must feed your creative soul. You must practice this principle, as my wise friend from Seminary, Edwin, would often say, because, "If you don't feed your soul, you'll feast off the people you're trying to serve."

Currently as a pastor, I feed my creative soul in these ways. I read poetry nearly every day: I need the weaving together of words in beautiful and unexpected ways; I also need to learn from people who employ an economy of words—as a preacher, being able to speak in transformative sound bites is paramount. I look at images and art work every week while planning worship: I think in pictures and am able to consider a sacred story differently once I've seen how artists have interpreted it—what detail did they see and expound upon on canvas? I watch movies, TV, and read fiction: I need the skill of storytellers to strike my fancy and the imaginary worlds they create to coopt my mind for a while. I consider modern day parables to matter, especially when we, as people of faith, find their connection to the parables of Jesus, the campfire stories of the Original Testament, the history lessons, and the letters contained in the Bible. I travel: I need to go other places, see other things, eat other food, and feel other weather than I do on a daily basis; I do love my cornfields but if I'm in them too long, my vision is stunted.

Lastly, I've stopped shopping: like any child of the '80s and '90s, going to the mall served as standard practice in my younger life. But I found that if I spent my creative energy in consumption—I waste it. Instead, now, I go to my studio space and play. Now, if you just read that last sentence and thought, "Well, I don't have a studio in my house, how am I supposed to do that?" Pull your inner critic aside, gently remind it that it's not its turn to talk, then hear this: Emily Dickinson only had "a table, 18 inches square, with a drawer deep enough to take in her ink bottle, paper and pen. It was placed in a corner by the window facing west."[6] We can all find 18 inches in our life to dedicate to our creativity, can't we?

The Gospels tell us that Jesus went away often. He went away by himself and with the disciples. He went away to pray and ponder, to wander and to wonder. This was what fed his ministry. What practices feed yours?

Principle four: Trusting the process

Last winter, my husband took me to a David Wilcox concert. The singer-songwriter opened his concert by telling a story about how he writes a song. He laughed as he described the inaugural act of this process: he goes up to his song-writing space where he fidgets and fiddles around until the song arrives. It's not productive, but productivity isn't what's crucial here—this is just how the process works. Often when we do other things and stop thinking so intently about the issue at hand, with our conscious mind occupied on some other task, our subconscious is free to do the work—when we get out of the way, the idea bubbles up. That light bulb moment will not happen by staring at the computer screen or chaining ourselves to the chair until we finish the work. Trusting the process means respecting the fertile spaces between where creativity takes root and new ideas are born.

I went through a phase early on in ministry, after being mentored by a few talented pastors with engineer brains, where I thought "trust the creative process" to be a forsaken notion. In the name of scheduling my week in the most efficient and productive manner possible, I duped myself into thinking that worship for the coming Sunday needed to be planned completely and totally, every hymn chosen, every prayer written, in total by work day's end on Monday. Most weeks I met my goal, then found myself rewriting liturgy and choosing new hymns on Thursday after I'd walked around with those sacred texts for a few days. When I reminded myself that the fidgeting and fiddling around are necessary to the creative process, not wasted time, I gave myself permission to ease up on the deadline, realizing this life-giving truth: it will come when it will come. That's what "trusting the process" is all about, allowing the new thing to be born within us instead of forcing its premature arrival.

These days, after lectionary study on Monday mornings, I do other things when I return to the office. Then, I spend the afternoon looking at art images related to this week's texts, thinking about what the soundtrack for our faith ought to sound like for this Sunday, and writing poems that get transformed into liturgy. Usually, I leave the office with a question or a conundrum about the text for the week. And, then, I go to yoga. In the sacred sanctuary of that rectangle of my mat, in the breathing in and out of the spiritus, in the moments when the teacher says, "Do you feel a stretching? Notice this and breathe into it," the answer to the question or the key to the conundrum often arrives in my head. The yoga teacher may be talking about the stretch screaming in my thigh in pigeon pose, but my subconscious is thinking about that conundrum with which I left the office and is stretching to wrap itself around it. Mid-week, when I get stuck in sermon writing, I set my computer aside and go take a shower. I ought to keep a paper and pen in the bathroom, because more often than not, as the water pours over my head, like in baptism, what was once dead rises to new life. It is as if the sermon writes itself in the water. When I'm mulling over an article I am writing and cannot seem to see what is next, I will regularly relocate my laptop to the kitchen counter and bake. With my mind focused on the leaven, a leavening happens within me.

What is it the disciples said after that meal along the Emmaus road? In the breaking of the bread, their eyes were made open. "Were not our hearts burning within us while he was opening the scriptures to us?" (Luke 24:32) Yes. But they could only see when they were ready to see it, and we're never ready to see if we don't trust the process.

Let's Get Started

Is the Church ready to see in new ways and trust the process? Do our clergy have an awareness of and openness to the ways in which creativity can offer new life in our congregations? I hope so.

Long before my friend, the Rev. Angela Menke-Ballou, and I were pastors, we were just Angie and Leah: church camp buddies who, after college graduation, moved together to Orlando, Florida, to try adulthood on for size. Angie, with her industrial engineering degree, worked as a labor maintenance analyst, while I, with my art degree, worked as a professional face painter. We both toiled away in the theme park industry, Angie donning smart pant suits and heels every day to go crunch numbers, while I often returned from work be-speckled in glitter. We were quite the pair. Our employee ID cards granted us access to the parks and so, many an evening, after work we'd meet, ride a few rides, grab dinner, and watch the fireworks show. As young people, Angie and I both discerned calls to ministry and spent those years in Florida trying to work out the details of our calls. We spent hours under the Florida sun discussing our deeply held hopes for the future, wrestling with who God is (and is not) in relation to the world, and wondering what the world might be like if the Church would live fully into the Way of Jesus. Imagine you're waiting in line to ride Space Mountain and the young women next to you are passionately discussing a wild strategy for practically solving world hunger—this was a normal evening for us.

The magic of Disney captivated us. Watching the artistry of animation is one thing. Walking around the Disney theme parks is quite another. The magic never got old. "Tinker Bell actually flies over The Magic Kingdom! She FLIES!" Angie would squeal. "The leaves on the Tree of Life are on hinges—they move with the wind!" I would exclaim. While floating through the Winnie the Pooh ride, we suddenly realized the whole ride smelled of honey. "Honey!" we declared. "Who thinks of doing that? Who makes that happen?"

Who thinks of crafting such astonishing attractions that bring a smile to your face and raise goosebumps on your arm?

Creative people. That's who.

And what might the world be like if we applied the same degree of creativity to bringing about the Kin-dom of God as we do to creating such amusement? How differently would our churches look if our clergy and laity alike applied creativity to our collective work?

Would not such creativity change the world?

Coloring books are no longer considered contraband—my girls own a couple, as do I. After all, coloring books are the newest meditation tool. So, don't finish up this chapter thinking you have to purge them from your house. There are many ways to learn how to recover the creativity of your childhood and let it grow. These are my tips. The chapters that follow will live into these four principles. The clergy who write them demonstrate how they use creativity to transform their churches and communities. Perhaps employing these four principles and listening to these voices will help you take on a new way of seeing—one that bursts with an abundance of energy and courageous ideas.

God's laid out the paper. You've got the crayons. The Holy Spirit is whispering, "Wanna color?" Just say "yes" and get started.

Notes

1. Betty Edwards, *Drawing on the Right Side of the Brain: A Course in Enhancing Creativity and Artistic Confidence* (Los Angeles: Tarcher, 1979), 4.

2. Georgia O'Keefe, *Georgia O'Keefe,* reissue ed. (London: Penguin, 1977).

3. Jeri Gerding, *Drawing to God: Art as Prayer, Prayer as Art* (Notre Dame, Indiana: Sorin, 2001), 47–48.

4. Ibid., 47.

5. Julia Cameron, *The Artist's Way: A Spiritual Path to Higher Creativity* (New York: Tarcher/Putnam, 1992), 18.

6. "Office Space: Emily Dickinson," *Amherst Magazine*, on line, accessed 4. May 2016.

Chapter 2

Spiritual Structure: A Rule for Church Leaders

Rev. Dr. Andrew T. Kort

I enrolled in a doctoral class titled "Theology of Church and Ministry." My final project was to design a "rule" for my personal spiritual use. However, following the rule and sticking to it were far more challenging than I had originally thought. In some areas I flourished while in other areas I floundered and became frustrated. Nevertheless, the rule helped me come to grips with a hard truth: I was struggling in my own spiritual life. And I am an ordained minister.

In my dozen plus years of ordained ministry in the Presbyterian Church (USA), I have often felt frustration along with a spiritual dryness. The transition from worshiper in the pew to preacher in the pulpit does not necessarily lend itself to an abundance of spiritual practices or being able to, as Thomas a Kempis might suggest, imitate Christ. At least that has been my experience. I know I am not alone in this, but in my case this is due to several factors. They include a calendar overflowing with commitments, meetings, and the general work of a parish minister. I fully understand this is not unique. I also have a tremendous amount of work and commitments at home that very easily consume much of my time, energy, and resources. This is due in very large part to the reality that my wife and I are parents to five-year-old twins and a three-year-old. They are hyper and nonstop. My wife also works for a Presbyterian campus ministry at Indiana University and is an active writer, meaning we have to juggle schedules as we cover for one another at home. All of this means that when I get home from work at the church, I have to quickly step into my role as husband and father; a role that often continues late into the evenings. Like many other clergy I know, I have felt my own life of faith is often neglected to my own detriment.

Therefore, I had been seeking a more balanced way to structure, or order, my life both at work and at home to allow me to grow and increase my spiritual life. In other words, I had been searching for a way to increase, or at the very least solidify, my "holy living." A rule seemed the perfect opportunity to help me in this struggle.

As I engaged in my rule for the class project, I had another thought: as a minister, if I needed help in this regard, what about the leaders of the church? Could a rule not only help their own spiritual lives, but could it also shape the work and ministry of a governing board at a local congregation?

A Brief History and Background to the Rule

In the Presbyterian Church (USA), the Session is the governing board of the church. They approve the budget. They care for the building. They oversee administration and the staff. They make sure worship happens and the sacraments are administered. But more than simply caring for bricks and mortar, or deciding what color paint to use on the classroom walls, the Session is also charged with being spiritual leaders of the congregation. The problem is most meetings of the session tend to focus on budget line items, personnel issues, debates surrounding music, dilapidated buildings with an endless list of repairs needing attention, insurance concerns, policies, and then more consternation about the budget. Beyond a perfunctory opening and closing prayer, most meetings are indistinguishable from a corporate board meeting. Perhaps a rule for them might be useful too. So, I did the unthinkable; I made a change. I instituted a rule for the Session.

It is important to discuss what I mean, and do not mean, by a rule. To begin with, what I do not mean by rule is the hierarchical structure with power dynamics, as in a king who rules over the land.

I do not mean rule in terms of laws or commands that one must follow. As stated in "A Pastoral Rule" by the Office of Theology and Worship of the PC(USA), "When we hear the word rule, we worry about legalism or about who exercises power over others."[1] Instead, I am drawn to another understanding of the term "rule." That is to understand a rule as a way that one measures, like a "ruler" or measuring stick is used in taking measurements. In this case, a rule is the way that one measures the spiritual temperature of people.

The concept of a rule meant to help guide and lead people in their spiritual life and journey can be traced all the way back to ancients like St. Benedict, among others. For this rule I have drawn elements from St. Benedict and St. Gregory the Great, but also from the work of John Calvin and Dietrich Bonhoeffer. The Latin word for "rule" is regula, which means "a way of ordering your life." I will turn now to how and why these four can help order our Christian life together.[2]

St. Benedict and Obedience

St. Benedict, 480–547, was born in Italy under the Roman Empire. Life at that time was unstable, insecure, and there was a lot of civil unrest. Much in life was confusing, and it was hard to know what the future would hold. Benedict's family was wealthy, perhaps allowing for more potential security, as wealth tends to do. However, Benedict had an inner spiritual experience that led him away from security and on a search for God. While undergoing many trials and temptations, he attempted to flee these temptations in order to gain inner peace. Benedict understood that his natural way needed to be "trained," and it was important to learn to control his emotions and passions. For him, like for many of us, this came through struggle. He began seeking others who could help encourage and sustain him, such as his sister Scholastica, who became a deep spiritual friend of Benedict's and even started a female convent. Wanting to help others lead a better life, he started a monastery in Monte Cassino, Italy.

Benedict understood that the way to be close to God is not to become a hermit, but to live together, work together, struggle together, and learn to grow in life in Christ together. He taught others to live in community and grow closer to God in practical ways. Roles were established, as were ways to structure and order daily life. For Benedict, the crux of it all was obedience. Obedience can be tricky and is a somewhat loaded term. We do not like people telling us what to do. We like to decide for ourselves and embrace our independence. Yet Benedict saw obedience as a faithful response to God and the only way to God.

Benedict taught that obedience was gained in a threefold way. It begins with listening, specifically listening to God through the scriptures. We know it is very hard for people to listen. Even today listening is hard and we are too easily distracted, by our phones for example. Benedict had the monks spend most of the day in silence, listening and not talking. But all was not completely silent. The second way toward obedience was through recitation. Psalms, prayers, and scriptures were recited, internalized, and memorized so they became "a part of" the monks. In contemporary circles, this would be similar to "memory verses" children learn in Sunday school. Finally, for Benedict, the way to obedience was by being obedient. Recalling Christ praying, "Not my will, but yours," Benedict thought a monk had to have his will broken in order to truly be obedient. In most cases, they were to be obedient to the Abbot, who was viewed like a commander informed by God. In this rhythm of listening, reciting, and obeying Benedict thought one would be led closer to God. While his rule is many things, obedience is at the heart of the matter for Benedict.

St. Gregory the Great and Holy Living

We know much about Benedict's life because of his biographer, St. Gregory the Great. Gregory knew that St. Benedict had a great inner peace, and he wanted that too. Gregory believed Benedict had attained this inner peace by living in the presence of God. Therefore, Gregory committed to living a holy life. Born in 540 CE in Rome, he was born into a wealthy and privileged family. But like others, including Benedict, Gregory abandoned his wealth.

Gregory's life was one full of tension. In 573 he was appointed mayor of Rome by the Emperor. One year later he gave it all up and entered a monastery. In 579 he left the monastery to serve as a papal representative in Constantinople. After seven years he returned to Rome and to the monastic community. In 590 he was elected Pope. The life of St. Gregory the Great was one of continual tension between his two sides: to be a monk and to be a high church official. He eventually wrote his pastoral rule, which I believe helps those of us with similar tensions to find balance and perspective.

Gregory understood the spiritual burdens of the pastor are heavy. While many are called to enter the ministry, he also knew there are some people who go into the ministry for the wrong reasons (seeking vanity, authority, or accolades). He notes that some people are attracted to the ministry who are not spiritual and are blind to the way of holiness. One must therefore be called by God to this way of life. So, he wanted to know "what is the condition of your soul?" A good question.

Holy living was critical for Gregory. Understanding that monks, like other people, have self-awareness and are still growing in the life of holiness, he wanted the monks to spend time in prayer, reading scripture, and thinking about God. With their self-awareness, he wanted them to become aware of their gifts and how these gifts are needed by the church so that others can lead a holy life. This leading others to live a more holy life, according to Gregory, was the goal of the pastor. To do that, the pastor must help people become aware of sin and those obstacles that prevent you from living a holy life and then help people be revived to a more holy way of life.

Gregory also helps us understand what practices and disciplines can sustain pastors so that they can do the work of ministry: daily meditation on scripture, because scripture is a lamp unto our feet and a light unto our path, is an important discipline; and, self-examination through which people can come to an awareness of our own selves, which leads us to recognize our dependence on God. These are but two practices Gregory puts forth to help pastors and spiritual leaders live holier lives but also so they can encourage others to live a holy life too. If St. Benedict's rule can be summarized by obedience, the rule of St. Gregory the Great can be summarized by holy living.

John Calvin and Right Doctrine

Students of John Calvin know the importance he placed on doctrine. He thought that clergy should be educated and doctrinally sound. Seeking to help people know the truth about the Triune God, Calvin wanted to help shape an environment in which people could also know doctrine, understand the scriptures, and even understand the Mass. Of course, this was in opposition to the Roman Catholic tradition of the time. Yet Calvin believed that a lack of doctrinal understanding led to low morality and corruption.

Calvin's theology, at least according to The Institutes, begins with the knowledge of God, and the knowledge of self. He believed that God created us so that we could know God and that there ought to be a natural knowledge of God. We can look at creation around us and contemplate God. We can look at each other and see a glimpse of the divine because we are created in the image of God. But, instead we look at nature as something to be exploited and we look at each other and see differences. Calvin argued this is because of sin. As God's revelation, Holy Scripture can bring God back into focus. Calvin famously described scripture as spectacles that could sharpen our vision of God, of ourselves, and of the world. For Calvin, this happens by the power of the Holy Spirit and it brings what God has done, and what God is doing, into focus. The scriptures give us promises, good news, consolation, and always point to Christ.

Calvin knew that along with the message, the messenger was also important. Who would bring the people the good news? Calvin knew that we need ministers, preachers, and those who can interpret the scriptures. One simply could not pick up the Bible to fully understand it. As any clergyperson can attest, this delivering the message of the good news of Jesus Christ happens in many ways. Perhaps most often, it happens with the preaching of the Word and the administration of the sacraments. Therefore, the pastor must be theologically and doctrinally astute. While Calvin, unlike St. Benedict and St. Gregory the Great, did not necessarily have a rule, he did have a structured set of guidelines and a process to increase one's life of faith. To do this, Calvin, and others, participated in what is called "the Company of Pastors."

The Company of Pastors was comprised of pastors in Geneva and the surrounding rural areas. Calvin moderated this gathering for twenty years. Looking at some of the activities of the Company of Pastors, we can see they met weekly for Bible studies. During this time, they would begin in worship and then move to a communal study of the scripture. Most often they would study the scripture that was just preached in their worship. The pastors were expected to come prepared to study and discuss. The study was led by one of the pastors on a rotating basis. The leader would give an exegetical lecture. The other pastors would respond, discuss, debate, and give feedback all in order to find the truth or the right doctrine in a passage of scripture. While Calvin and the Company of Pastors did many things, the main concern was for right doctrine and unity in doctrine.

Dietrich Bonhoeffer and Mutual Service in our Life Together

Finally, turning to a more contemporary theologian, Dietrich Bonhoeffer offers us a rhythm for the day. Using his popular work, *Life Together*, we can understand Bonhoeffer's contribution to leading us in a more holy way. Most of us are familiar with Bonhoeffer, his life, writings, and participation in the failed assassination attempt on Adolf Hitler. Therefore, too much background is likely not needed. Instead, briefly I will focus on some of his work at the seminary in Finkenwalde.

As he set up the seminary, Bonhoeffer saw a need to shape pastors. He wanted to give them practices and disciplines that would help them in their life and ministry. The students studied. There were exams to prepare for ordination. And of course, they spent much of their lives together during this time. To help the community, Bonhoeffer established a routine for the days that would lead and guide the community in its holy living. The rhythm of the day included: begin in silence, morning prayer, breakfast, half an hour meditation on scripture, theological studies, half an hour of singing together, lunch, theological studies, dinner, playtime, and evening prayer.

Bonhoeffer believed that the true nature of Christian community is one that must be rooted and grounded in Christ. It is not an interest group or a social club, but a community standing together under the cross of Christ. He believed this rhythm of the day would help keep Christ at the center of the community.

Bonhoeffer believed that the marks of the community called church centered on the Word and the sacraments, but also a disciplined and ordered life together. This disciplined life together includes serving others. At the seminary, Bonhoeffer emphasized the importance of listening to others and holding our own tongues. He stressed learning how to place others, and their needs, before ourselves. In one section, "Ministry of Helpfulness," he encourages the students to assist others with simple everyday matters. One could summarize much of the daily life together as mutual service; that is, serving others and letting them serve you too. In this way, members of the community are being sanctified, and growing in Christ.

The Rule

With these four great spiritual and theological thinkers as my guide, I designed a rule incorporating various elements of each one. As you can see, the rule consists of four distinct categories. They are: Obedience to the Word, based upon St. Benedict; Holy Living, based upon St. Gregory the Great; Right Doctrine, based on Calvin and the Company of Pastors; and Mutual Service, based on Bonhoeffer's Life Together. The rule is as follows.

Obedience to the Word: Being guided by God's Holy Word and worship

At least once a month use a Worship Response Sheet. A Worship Response Sheet allows for responses to the following questions about various elements of worship:

What did you hear God saying to you in the Scripture reading/s?
What did you hear God saying to you in the Sermon?
What was your favorite hymn today and why?
Was there a prayer that was especially meaningful or challenging for you today?
How might you apply what God has said to you today to your life this week?

Holy Living: Being in prayer for one another

One Elder per month will be asked to arrive at worship five minutes early and pray for the worship leaders each Sunday: the pastors, the liturgist, the choir, the music director, the organist, and all of the other worshipers.

Right Doctrine: Growing in our understanding of God

Together as a Session, read through a confession from the PC(USA)'s Book of Confessions. We will spend 15–20 minutes at the start of each meeting discussing and sharing what we have read. Like Calvin and the Company of Pastors, we will do this in a group setting.

Mutual Service: Breaking bread and sharing a meal

Divide the elders into four groups. Once a quarter each group will make dinner to serve at the session meeting.

Experimenting with Church Leadership

I introduced this rule to the Session in January, 2014. This seemed to be a logical starting place since it gave us a whole year to experience this rule together, but also because as new elders rotated onto the board it gave them the opportunity to begin their time of service in this way.

Upon introduction and initial implementation of the rule, I quickly learned that it would take a few months before everyone fully caught on to what we were doing. As previously noted, prior to the rule, we would simply begin our meeting with a brief prayer and then get straight to the agenda. This was something new and different, so it took time to not only explain what I meant by "a rule," but also time to allow some of the nuances of the different categories to sink in. For instance, under "Holy Living" the elders were instructed to arrive to worship early and pray for those leading worship that day. Questions abounded as to what this meant or how to do it. "What do we pray for? How long do we pray for each worship leader? What if I am not in church that morning, do I still pray?" So we spent time talking through these very good questions and coming up with workable answers. If the elder was not going to be in worship on the morning she was to pray for worship leaders, she could still certainly pray for them from wherever she happened to be. This actually happened with some frequency, so we had to learn some flexibility too.

As we began our rule together, I gave them freedom to do as much or as little of the rule as they discerned and decided to do. I would remind them and encourage them, but would not hover over them or reprimand them. However, I would check in with each of them during session meetings to see how it went, or how the practice of the rule is going. In other words, I was taking the spiritual temperature of the people.

At the meetings we talked about what was good and what was hard. They were honest in their responses. Others listened with great attention, and it was beautiful to witness these spiritual leaders take an interest not only in their own lives, but also in the spiritual lives of their colleagues around the session table. Together we learned that each category brought its own successes and its own shortcomings. I suppose this is true anytime a group of people do something together for a year.

"Obedience to the Word" was one that was especially and equally fruitful and challenging. When the elders engaged in this exercise, they commented on how connected they felt to the worship service and how they could now more fully see how the flow and theme of the service tied together. They talked about really engaging and thinking through the prayers and the theology of the hymns. Several of them commented about how they understood what God was saying in the scripture readings and they were able to compare and contrast that to what was said in the sermon. Or they described how the sermon helped them understand the scripture passage now that they were listening in new ways. I certainly benefited from their feedback. One elder even jokingly suggested this made him stay awake during the service. But there were challenges with this as well. For instance, not only was it an adjustment to remember to do this on a Sunday morning, it was also hard for them to remember the questions posed in the rule or to write their responses down.

In our "Holy Living" portion, the elders reported a sense of peace, comfort, and connection with God as they sat in the sanctuary and prayed for the worship service to come. For the elders this was a dramatic change to the ordinary Sunday morning routine that usually included cups of coffee and chit-chat conversations before scurrying into the sanctuary as the prelude begins on the organ or piano. For others, especially those who attended adult education classes prior to worship, it was challenging to be able to actually get into the sanctuary early to pray as the classes often run right up to the start of worship. Some of the elders, especially chairs of committees like Property, described the experience of being interrupted in their prayer by someone wanting to share an issue with the building in need of attention. One elder even said this got so bad he had to go into the chapel to pray instead of the sanctuary. This provided a great opportunity to talk about boundaries and the importance of letting people know you are not always available. Others were able to sit and pray without interruption or, as described earlier, would do so elsewhere. Interestingly, several elders have described continuing to pray for worship and worship leaders every Sunday, even when it was not their assigned month to do so.

To guide us in our "Right Doctrine" portion of the rule, we used the "Brief Statement of Faith" found in the Presbyterian Church (USA)'s Book of Confessions. I divided the confession into twelve sections, one per monthly meeting. I would email the entire confession and the highlighted section to the elders along with the agenda prior to each meeting. During our time together I would ask questions about the confession or help lead a conversation. We discussed how the confessions help us understand scripture and guide and shape our theology. We were challenged and inspired. Even those who did not read the assignment (which rarely happened) were still able to participate in the conversation. As a pastor, it was a tremendous joy to hear the spiritual leaders of the church openly share and talk about their faith, their questions, their struggles, and their understanding of what God is doing in the world. Several of the elders described knowing about or hearing about the Book of Confessions, but the level of familiarity was not the same as with the other part of our constitution, the Book of Order. This introduction to a book of theological and doctrinal documents and statements has been a tremendous benefit to our communal theological understanding. The main drawback to this is that we had to limit our time to twenty minutes of conversation.

The final portion of the rule, "Mutual Service," ended up being the most popular and enjoyable part of our shared experience. After dividing the elders into four groups, each group was responsible for providing a meal at the start of a meeting. This happened once per quarter, but could easily be adjusted to happen every meeting. As we began we thought about the many ways in scripture that Christ was revealed around food and drink. We talked about table fellowship and what it meant to break bread together, with strangers and with friends. The elders delighted in bringing food to share. And it was always delicious! Since our meetings begin at 6:00 PM, we found that the meal nourished us in many ways. With full stomachs we were able to focus and not worry about having to get home for dinner. One elder remarked that this shared meal helped to relax the environment and made for very civil and respectful conversation throughout the remainder of the meeting. Along the way we learned that it was a challenge to talk and work through the rest of the rule or agenda while we ate. The elders preferred to eat, socialize, and simply be together. So we adjusted and now the meals are shared at 5:30 and the work of the agenda begins at 6:00. To my great pleasure and satisfaction, no one complains about coming early to a session meeting!

The rule generally takes about 20–30 minutes at the start of our session meetings. I promised the elders we would adjourn in two hours. We have found the rule has not kept us past 8:00 or infringed on any business at hand. Ultimately, I believe the rule has helped our session to intentionally live into ancient spiritual disciplines in an easy, accessible, and modern way. We have found the rule helps shape and guide the remainder of the meeting and informs the work and the decisions we face. Not only has this rule benefited our own spiritual lives, I believe it has made us better leaders as together we serve the children of God.

We live in a world that seems to be more increasingly built upon chaos and distraction. This is true for clergy who serve parishes and for those whose work lives are outside of the church, but who come to volunteer and demonstrate leadership in our churches. Between the frenetic pace of our lives, the twenty-four hour news cycle, and social media, there is always something demanding our attention. But, these things are not the rule of our lives as people of faith. We lean on something much deeper, much richer, much more whole than anything these distractions can provide. In our churches, however, we have found ourselves distracted from a structure, an order, a rule and way of life that can point us to that deeper wholeness. One way we can change the conversation from chaos and distraction to wholeness and order in the church is by establishing a practice, a habit if you will. We chose to establish a rule by which to not just govern, but to live our entire lives by and it has been transformative for all of us.

Leaning on some of the spiritual greats of the past, our leadership has grown closer in our work and life together. We give thanks for the spiritual disciplines of obedience, holy living, understanding right doctrine, and mutual service as we continue to grow and mature in our faith today.

Notes

1. "A Pastoral Rule," (Louisville, KY: Office of Theology and Worship, Presbyterian Church, USA), 3.

2. Notes on St. Benedict, St Gregory the Great, Calvin and the Company of Pastors, and Dietrich Bonhoeffer come in part thanks to the lectures of John Burgess at Pittsburgh Theological Seminary, June 17–21, 2013.

Chapter 3

Theological Reflection as Pastoral Practice

Rev. Dr. Christopher Rodkey

St. Augustine of Hippo may rightly be called the prototypical visionary of what would later be known as a liberal arts education. He converted to Christianity and became a Bishop in a church that had learned to erase its past and obfuscate its own origins out of a fear of external challenges. Prior to Augustine, priests were not to study mathematics lest the priestly candidates become lured to the cult of the Pythagoreans. Greek philosophy and literature were frowned upon because of their so-called "pagan," which is to say non-Christian, origins. Serious study of other religions was shunned because they were false and the similarities between Zoroastrian eschatology and Mithraism were considered dangerous; and studying Judaism within its own contexts would place Judaism within a very different light than what Christian supercessionist thinking demanded.

Augustine, himself arriving to Christianity from Manichean-ism—and whose conversion is attributed to the pious prayer of his mother, St. Monica of Hippo—had a different perspective. Following Augustine, priests were now expected to learn the intellectual foundations of the Christian faith, which meant taking seriously the knowledge previously forbidden by diocesan training. The role of the priest as teacher demanded clear intellectual focus: in a move gestured from Plato, rhetorical speaking became prioritized as a skill of the priest, and doing so required a broad education in philosophy and rhetoric.

To these ends, Augustine wrote in *De Doctrina Christiana*:

In a word, the function of eloquence in teaching is not to make people like what was once offensive, or to make them do what they were loth to do, but to make clear what was hidden from them. If this is done in a disagreeable way, the benefits reach only a few enthusiasts, who are eager to know the things they need to learn no matter how dull and unattractive the teaching may be. Once they have attained it, they feed on the truth itself with great delight; it is the nature of good minds to love truth in the form of words, not the words themselves. What use is a golden key, if it cannot unlock what we want to be unlocked, and what is wrong with a wooden one, if it can, since our sole aim is to open closed doors? Learning has a lot in common with eating: to cater for the dislikes of the majority even the nutrients essential to life must be made appetizing.[1]

The office of teaching is not to do what Socrates was famously accused—to "make the worse appear the better cause,"[2] that is, to confuse and insult its audience for the sake of being iconoclastic—but rather persuasively educating the plain truth of the Christian faith, to "make clear what was obscure," in eloquent and straightforward manner. The priest must find the right balance between speaking the truth, making it pretty, but not making it too unattainable, that is, "flavored to meet the tastes of the majority": not be so esoteric that only the insiders of a secret faith know the true meanings of words.

Today clergy find themselves as products of liberal arts educations that did not necessarily teach the liberal arts, and graduates of theological schools and programs that did not really teach theology. The majority of those who teach in seminary ministerial formation programs themselves did not spend much time in the pastorate; in fact, had they spent significant time working in a church and not enough time publishing books and articles, they would have been disqualified from being hired to teach in the first place. Theological education has always been accused of being insufficient to meet the demands of contemporary congregations, scapegoated by clergy and congregations alike. The response has been to teach less and less intellectual foundation for pastoral work and to emphasize the practical, praxis without substantial theory. I am not being hyperbolic when I report that an average recipient of a Protestant Master of Divinity degree today has not read more than a handful of major theologians in her course of study and could likely not recount the history of theology, let alone the influences of philosophy, literature, and other religions upon the Christian faith.

Beyond this, we may make a safe assumption that lay ministry academies are studying even less theology and less hermeneutics than seminaries—and in many denominations, unaccredited academies are the future of ministerial training.

Returning to St. Augustine's historical contexts, his proposal for a more liberal education of the church's priests should also be understood within Augustine's identity as a public theologian. Augustine was an intellectual whose commitments were to the church and the community; his ministry and intellectual gravitas tremendously influenced, and continue to influence, Christianity in every way today. But those great influences grew out of his philosophical interests and drives, combined with a deep Christian faith, and it was precisely Augustine's intellectual pursuits which changed and shaped the church and its theology.

Augustine's desire for priests to be trained differently meant that the priest, as the representative of the diocese in every town and village, would be the one whose training, education, and faith would be well disposed, in the broadest sense, to a Platonic ideal of "wisdom." In many cases, this priest would be one of the few, if not the only one, literate individuals within the parish. As one trained in rhetoric, philosophy, literature, and the arts, the priest would have been, in theory, sufficiently trained to engage the non-Christians— for Augustine, the "pagans"—and defend the faith in reasonable and creative ways from theological innovators—who were for Augustine, "heretics." Pagans were better than heretics in Augustine's view, since pagan philosophies and religions have some truth in them, but heretics deny the truth of the orthodox Christian church. The priestly office, then, demanded the intellectual ability to discern the truths outside of the church, to provoke those adherents to search for a higher level of truth within the church, and to concurrently articulate and defend the proper teachings of the faith to those within the walls of the church.

As a clergyperson, occasionally I reflect upon all of the different tasks I have performed in the prior week or two. To even list those tasks in an entirety would sound pretentious; and our congregants often have no idea just how diverse our skill sets must be—and how carefully we need to be attuned to our weaknesses. From premarital counseling to social justice work, from preaching to interpreting state laws, from music to nonprofit business management, clergy are put to the test at any time. What ties all of it together? For me, my drive is rooted in my faith and in my sense of vocation, but in my drive to answer my call as best as I can, these are also ingredients for unhealthy self-inflation and burnout.

But beyond my own personal and localized experience, what ties it together is a theological worldview that honors and prioritizes these activities, that negotiates drive and purpose, a theological worldview whose audience must not, and cannot be the church alone: the Good News proclaimed boldly outside of the church's walls.

We would not be so pretentious today to draw such clear divisions upon the world beyond the church as Augustine did as heretics and pagans—although these divisions are often demanded by the institutional church. Rather, the church of the future must be—and I am pretentious in claiming this to be obvious—a missionary faith to the secularized and secularizing world in which we live outside of the institution. I do not necessarily see atheism, agnosticism, postmodernism, secularism, or new religious movements to be the enemy of the church. Rather, they are the opportunity for the mission field.

To put this thinking in some context: when I was a student at the University of Chicago Divinity School, our ministry practicum invited Hans-Dieter Betz to give a retirement talk just to the ministry students. Betz, one of the world's great interpreters of the New Testament, came and gave us the background of his academic career; like many theological scholars of his day, he spent his first years working in the parish. He said that he, like other clergy, understood his work—pastoral and scholarly—to be a kind of response to Nietzsche, and that one should not underestimate the efficacy of Nietzsche's influence upon his generation of German intellectuals.

A student present asked how he prioritized his scholarly work while working as a busy pastor. "I just set aside a day of my work every week for study and reflection," he said. And if it didn't happen one week, fine, but it was a regularly scheduled event.

Clearly, not all clergy need to aspire to be one of the top scholars of their generation. But clergy do need to understand the intellectual traditions of the church and the "religious situation," as Paul Tillich called it, in which the church finds herself.

Prioritizing study is an essential part of my week, and by "study" it can be broadly defined as continuing education and any scholarly activity that I pursue. Some of this study includes the required sexual ethics courses that my Conference requires, for example, but more regularly the study involves three primary categories.

First, I pursue study in the field of congregational development, evangelism, and culture. In addition to the typical periodicals (like *The Christian Century*), this includes reading fine journals like *The Chronicle of Higher Education*, excellent newspapers, popular books, and blogs on popular culture. I have developed a good relationship with an independent Christian bookstore whose blog and owner's personal contact keeps me abreast of the current literature. When

I was a campus minister and youth pastor, this time involved watching MTV, reading *Spin* and *Rolling Stone*. The point here is to understand the church in culture, and questioning, like H. Richard Niebuhr, whether, or how the church might move to transform culture.

A second focus of my study time is pursuing my own theological interests. As a part-time professor, one of my pet peeves is when seminarians refuse to identify or have an affinity for any particular school or historical trajectory of Christian theology as an excuse for remaining ignorant of the great traditions of the church and its intellectual gifts; that simply side-stepping theology gives permission to avoid it. And yet still identifying as "Protestant" or with any denomination has more to do with being drafted like a professional sport than participation in an ongoing tradition. It is true that many parishioners and congregations certainly wish we could keep things so unengaged and bland-vanilla, but I hold to the position that these anti-theological views hurt the church and apprehend our gifts as clergy to the mission field.

For myself, I identify with the American radical theology tradition, with interests in neo-Orthodoxy, Christian existentialism, feminist theology, and Continental philosophy. My primary reading in my second focus area is to deepen my awareness of these interests and identifications, and keeping current with the ongoing conversations. Most of these schools of theology are surprisingly small with only a handful of major thinkers. It is my experience that most of these theological communities would especially welcome clergy engaged in the same questions and issues; in fact, clergy involvement for many of these academics gives their own theological inquiry what I call "eek cred," ecclesial, church credibility.

But I also challenge myself every year to deepen my knowledge of another school of theology, major figure, or important text, and in nearly every case these explorations have had fruitful results. Whether it was exploring the philosophy of René Girard; or the major texts and biographies of Jonathan Edwards and Dietrich Bonhoeffer; or a deeper study of Aristotle's term logic, all of these have been directly helpful in preaching, teaching, and leading.

Third, and finally, a focus of my study time is upon the Bible and its interpretation. When I occasionally perform a preaching series or Bible study on a particular book of the Bible, I schedule a minimum of four hours per week of study specific to that subject. This time is hard-scheduled, which is to say, not negotiable, and I usually hold it in my study that has no phone or in a coffee shop where it cannot be interrupted. Over the years I have identified favorite commentary series, and I challenge myself to read new commentaries from theological positions foreign to my own. This has not only made me a better and more effective preacher, but my knowledge and grasp of the Bible has grown exponentially, and I believe that my regular church attenders benefit directly from this time that I spend every week.

How do laypeople benefit from the pastor's study? I believe that the robust churches who will survive the current transformation, this ongoing new reformation, this desecularizing, decolonizing, postmodern crucible—whatever we want to call it—will be developing, teaching, and practicing theology in an explicit way. If one goal of the pastor is to inculcate a sense of the priesthood of all believers in a local parish community, the laity should simply not be passive pupils to the pastor's teachings but rather be trained in practicing a critical theology that engages culture and actively applies hermeneutics to the world itself, inside and beyond the physical walls of the liturgical space.

This overall effort might sound lofty, and sometimes my projects or focus on a text or figure gets extended to an eighteen-month study and is often taken reading on my phone's reading app while waiting for a hospital patient to return from rehab for a pastoral visit or during the inevitable half hour late start of nearly every wedding rehearsal. As Betz taught, this practice needs to be prioritized, and technology has made this easier.

Theological reflection and study are necessary for clergy to be inspirational theologians for the present church and effective evangelists for the future church; they can also keep us balanced in terms of our call and sense of vocation. Not all clergy are called to be academic theologians, but all clergy should be able to communicate and understand academic theology (and similarly, academic theologians need to understand the pastoral and practical theological contexts in which we operate). Not all clergy need to earn higher degrees in theology, but all clergy need to study to push their own theological boundaries and understandings, as well as the boundaries and structures in the geographic locations we are called to serve.

Notes

1. Augustine, *On Christian Teaching*, trans. R.P.H. Green (Oxford: Oxford UP, 1999), Book IV, 72–73 (IV, 11, 26).

2. Socrates says of his own accusation, "he makes the worse into the stronger argument, and he teaches these same things to others" (Plato, "Apology," trans. G.M.A. Grube, in *Plato: Complete Works*, ed. John Cooper [Indianapolis: Hackett, 1997], 19b).

Chapter 4

Reading Scripture as Pastoral Practice

Rev. Emily C. Heath

When I think back on my decision to read the Bible cover-to-cover, I have to admit it came from less-than-noble intentions. I had taken one of those Facebook quizzes that lists the 100 great books that the BBC thinks everyone should read. I went through it, easily ticking off Great Expectations, Harry Potter, and A Prayer for Owen Meany, but one stopped me dead in my tracks.

The Bible

The irony is priceless. I'm a minister, after all. A person who gets into the pulpit nearly every Sunday to preach on a Biblical passage. I can read Koine Greek and Biblical Hebrew. My Presbyterian seminary aspired to teach its students how to exegete pericopes with both the precision of a surgeon and the wonder of a poet. And yet, I didn't know how to honestly answer the question of whether or not I'd read the Bible. And my competitive nature was getting the better of me.

I had read the New Testament cover to cover one Lent. That was done. But the New Testament is only a thin sliver compared to the size of the Hebrew Bible. I knew I had read others of the sixty- six books of the Bible over time too: Jonah, Job, Genesis, Exodus. Add in the courses I took in seminary that required me to be familiar with the Hebrew scriptures, as well as years of being a lectionary preacher, and I was certain I had read most of the Bible. But most is not all.

This revelation disturbed me. I felt, at best, uneducated. At worst, a theological fraud. What sort of clergyperson, I asked myself, has never read the whole book? I reassured myself by saying that it is Jesus Christ himself, not the Bible, who is the preeminent Word of God. The Bible, while the Word, points only to the great Word of God-with-us. However, even my progressive and Reformed theologies could not save me from a sense of unease.

Someday, I told myself, when I have more time…that's when I'll do it right. I'll read it cover-to-cover. Someday didn't come quickly. But it nagged at me enough that it did.

* * *

My wife and I were driving across New York state, on our way home from a visit with her family. We traded off driving halfway, giving me a break. I am the usual driver, and I hadn't brought along anything to read. Bored with obsessively checking Facebook and Twitter, I started to play with the other apps on my phone. I had a rarely-used Bible app that I had installed long ago. I flipped it open and thumbed through the digital pages, with their paragraph-at-a-time recreation of the NRSV. And with hours before us on the road, I decided this was the time to start the read.

The old joke: how does one eat an elephant? One bite at a time.

And so, I took the first bite. Genesis 1:1. "In the beginning when God created the heavens and the earth, the earth was a formless void and darkness covered the face of the deep, while a wind from God swept over the face of the waters. Then God said, "Let there be light," and there was light. And God saw that the light was good…"

I flipped the pages through Genesis that first day, taking in the seven days of creation, the second creation story, and long genealogical lists. And in that first session, I set some rules for myself that I would come back to time and again in my reading.

First, I was not going to read the Bible as a Biblical scholar. By that I do not mean that I was going to throw all of my theological beliefs out the window. I could still read that story of creation and hold my feminist theological understanding of it at the same time.

Nor would I abandon my progressive faith principles. I knew the seven days of creation were part of a greater allegory pointing to God's work in creating us all.

Still, I was not going to allow myself to become so immersed in the academic and theological as to make the Scripture another piece of my ministerial work. Instead, I would read it as the English major I used to be back in college. I would let the words flow over me, and hear them being read in my mind. I would let myself fall back in love with the language, translated though it may be, and connect with the poetry of the Scripture.

Second, I made the reading a part of my spiritual practice. I committed to reading three chapters a day. This was an amount of reading that felt reasonable, and only took a small portion of my time each day. I added short prayers before and after, a step towards rebuilding an inner spiritual life that had been severely derailed by my workaholism the first few years in the parish. The whole routine took about fifteen minutes, at the longest. And yet, I could feel the difference in my day.

On those days when I forgot, though, or when I remembered late and picking up the Bible felt just too hard when I was half-falling asleep, I forgave myself. I did not want my reading to be guilt-based. I wanted to make a commitment, not out of sheer obligation but out of a desire to connect with the Word. Though my initial reason for reading the Bible came out of a competitive Facebook moment that stoked a sense of guilt, those feelings went away before long. The further I went into the world of the Hebrew Scriptures, the more my curiosity was stoked. That's not to say that it was not intensely boring at times. Really, have you read Leviticus? Leviticus had always been my stopping point in previous marathon Bible-reading attempts. I don't need to know how to properly make a grain offering or the proper proportion of flour to oil to frankincense. Nor do I regularly use the knowledge of how to stack bread on the tabernacle table: two rows of six loaves on a table of pure gold, by the way.

And the bad news is that Leviticus is not the end of the details. Once you've hit the finish line of Leviticus, you start the uphill climb of the genealogies of Numbers. Really, it's like reading names off a family tree with no context. And the truth is that those books aren't the only ones that will leave you longing for your Netflix queue. Even the prophets--for all the ways in which we love them in the progressive Christian tradition--can be sleep-inducing at times. In fact, if you are like me, by the time you are reading the prophets your patience with this whole exercise may start wearing thin.

At first I would catch myself trying to re-read the paragraphs that I wasn't immediately registering. I would think it was so important to pay attention to who begat whom that I'd get stuck on a page. But after a while, especially in the more difficult books, I came to see the words as a sort of tide that flowed over me. Even if I could not appreciate each individual drop of water, there was beauty in being immersed in the whole.

It was around that time in my reading that my ministerial profile began to make the rounds to churches looking for a new pastor. I was sufficiently happy in my current parish. Things were going well, and we loved where we lived. But my wife was graduating from seminary, and I knew I had done the work I could do in my current call. It was time to see where God was placing us next.

The search and call process is a lonely one for clergy. The necessary confidentiality can make it feel almost as though one is cheating on one's current church. To love one group of people deeply, while looking for the next church God is calling you to love, can feel like a form of infidelity at times. It's not, but it can feel that way.

Add to that the fact that you are competing with colleagues, many of whom may be close friends, for the same calls, and the isolation intensifies. How do you tell a good friend that you got called for an in-person interview with the church they really loved when they did not? How do you take it when that same friend gets an offer and you get a rejection letter?

It was a long winter that year, and the light was shut out for all but hours a day. It was a perfect setting for my spirit. The church that I had thought was "the one" had gone in another direction at the last moment. And so I started the search again, putting my profile in for consideration at a church where I didn't think I would have a chance.

I read 1 Kings around that same time. 1 Kings isn't Leviticus-boring, but it's not exactly a page-turner. In its pages, though, I found the story of King Solomon, and I embraced his prayer for wisdom as a sign of what I should be asking from God. "Grant me wisdom" became my prayer from winter to spring. I didn't need to "get the job." I didn't want a big call package. I didn't even ask for certainty. I just asked God for wisdom.

When that out-of-my-league church called for a phone interview, I prayed for wisdom. When they asked me to come in person, I prayed again. And by the day they called me after my neutral pulpit, and offered me the call, I had spent so much time in discernment, so much time searching for God's wisdom for me, that it took me a half second to say, "yes." I'm not saying that I ended up at my current call because I was regularly reading the Bible. I'm saying that my faith and my mental outlook were changed because I was reading. Knowing that my story is only one in millennia of faith stories, and drawing on the story of another, I found a peace I had never had before in the search process.

This has kept happening. When I was slogging through the Psalms, lovely on their own but less exciting 150 in a row, I truly understood that they were a prayer book unto themselves lying right in the middle of the Bible. Everything from joy to hopelessness, serenity to anger was given words.

When I was tempted, for fear of what it would mean for my career, to say nothing when I saw a potential ethical breach, I read about Daniel refusing to eat the king's rich food, and relying instead on plain vegetables to sustain him. And when I approached my first stewardship season with my new church, I found myself immersed in the Gospel of Matthew, and the parables about good seed and good ground.

Would I have been able to handle all of those situations without the daily influence of Scripture? Yes. Would I have responded to each the way I did? Probably not.

I do not hold the Bible as my idol. As I said, it is one more thing that points to the true Word, Jesus Christ. But it is a powerful witness to Christ. It is, I believe, the best we have. Sometimes it is contradictory. Sometimes it is incomplete. And sometimes it is exasperating. But it is ours, and it can sustain us as another form of bread for the journey.

So much of the work a pastor does is tied to our ability to be creative. That's particularly true for those of us who preach nearly every week. We look for inspiration everywhere. Still, I was surprised to find the subtle ways that the regular reading of Scripture made me more creative. The act of making time for this practice allowed my spirit time to be renewed each day. The diversity of forms Scripture takes, from the Psalms to the prophets, the Gospels to the letters of the early disciples, remind me that it is vital to proclaim the message in more ways than one. But more than anything, being reminded that there is a larger story that I am a part of, one that has been shaped over millennia, is a powerful catalyst for my own creativity. What I create now, in this life, will tell just a little more of that story. And, in the end, all of our stories are tied back to what is testified to in that book. Forming a sacred habit of regularly reading the Bible can be a deep spiritual resource for clergy as they interpret the Gospel in our ever changing twenty-first century.

It is now just about two years after I started my cover-to-cover read of the Bible. I am nearing the end of the New Testament. I've spent some time recently immersed in Paul's letters. And I'm being reminded once again that Paul, like all of us who confess Christ and wear the yoke of leadership, was a brilliant and fallible man. One who did the best he could to love God's people, even as he was figuring it all out. Even as the church itself was crawling out of infancy.

Paul's letters are not bad lessons for Christian leaders. The good, and the bad. In his self-contradictions I find comfort. In his failings I find solace. In his frustration I find community. And in his moments of joy and celebration, I find hope.

I am pressing on towards Revelation, that most misunderstood of Biblical books. I took enough seminary coursework to know the apocalyptic nature of the work is not meant to be taken literally. But I do take it seriously. I believe in the hope that strives for a vision of a new heaven and a new earth. And I believe that we all could stand to drink from a new River of Life. And I pray along with John of Patmos for the day when our prayer is answered: "Come, Lord Jesus!"

When I read those last lines, I wonder what will happen to my relationship with Scripture. I am hopeful I will not put the Bible aside; a reading assignment that has been completed. I hope that I will continue to dive daily into its waters, immersing myself even in the passages that pull the world I know out from underneath me, like a dangerous riptide. In fact, I hope I keep reading those passages most of all.

Making Scripture a part of my daily life, a habit, has changed me and I imagine that such a habit could change most clergy and those we serve. What is more, it has changed my faith. It has been said that God can use anything to create something good. Maybe that's even true of meaningless Facebook quizzes, and a stubborn competitive streak.

Chapter 5

May you be blessed!
Rev. Michelle L. Torigian

Worshiping in the Gaps: Developing Special Worship Services

Rev. Michelle L. Torigian

There seems to be a universal truth about people who attend church. Without a doubt, each person will face challenging and devastating moments in their lives. If this can be true for everyone on any given week, how then can the Church be attentive to such lived realities? For some, the ritual of Sunday worship feeds their soul. For others, Sunday worship becomes monotonous. Rather than feel inspired from weekly Sunday services, some may feel that spirituality can best be found outside of the church's walls or through other means.

In recent years, religious communities have seen the rise of the "spiritual, but not religious," the "nones," and the "dones." According to the Pew Research Center, "Between 2007 and 2014, the Christian share of the population fell from 78.4% to 70.6%, driven mainly by declines among mainline Protestants and Catholics." The study also indicated that the "unaffiliated" increased from 16.1% to 22.8% over the course of the designated seven years.[1]

Granted, some will keep connected with God even if attending weekly worship doesn't appeal to their spiritual side. In her book *Tribal Church*, Carol Howard Merritt states "While the frustrations with our institutions have caused younger generations to distance themselves from religion, they do embrace spirituality. They are more attracted to the discipline of communicating with God than getting the list of attributes of God completely correct."[2] Based on thoughts regarding the evolving religious landscape, change in the way churches connect with those who are unaffiliated is a necessity.

Leaders of the church must keep in mind the needs of all demographic groups, from various generations, theological perspectives, and cultural experiences. In reflecting on how to address the needs of many, some questions arise. When considering the demographic groups and their needs, one must consider who our weekly services reach and what potential worship experiences outside of Sunday mornings may be needed. Some questions include:

- Is holding a specific-themed service during Sunday morning worship experience enough?
- Which people within the church are not having their spiritual needs met and may need a special focused worship service?
- How does this service speak to those in our community outside of the congregation, both people of other Christian denominations and those currently not attending church?
- Does a special service reflect the true intention of worship?

Throughout these years of ministry, one of my clergy habits is seeking ways to address the spiritual needs of people in the "gaps," or those who are not churched or consider themselves "spiritual, but not religious." Some ways I take on that challenge is to have office hours outside of the church, writing for various outlets including the local newspaper, composing prayers for groups of people, such as teachers, and holding special worship services for people enduring particular ordeals in their lives.

What is worship?

Scripture does not necessarily have instructions for twenty-first century special worship services. The Bible does indicate that special instances of worshiping God occurred. For instance, in 2 Samuel 16, David calls for the ark to come into Jerusalem. As the ark enters the city, David and others dance before God. This special experience of celebratory worship includes shouting, sounding the trumpet, burnt offerings, offerings of well-being, blessings of his people, and meal sharing. In this experience, David is not alone but surrounded by others in this celebratory atmosphere.

James F. White notes in his book *Introduction to Christian Worship*, "We need to make a clear distinction between two kinds of worship: common worship and personal devotions. The most clear aspect of common worship is that it is the worship offered by the gathered congregation, the Christian assembly."[3] While personal devotions focusing on specific topics are vital parts of the Christian's life, experiences which unite people of faith over a topic of shared interest would be considered common worship.

Ultimately, whether or not a service is common worship comes down to Jesus' statement in Matthew 18: "For where two or three are gathered in my name, I am there among them." This is summed up in White's statement "We usually treat the act of assembling as merely a mechanical necessity, but it is itself an important part of common worship. We assemble to meet God and encounter our neighbors."[4]

Individual spirituality is only part of what a person of faith needs to feed their soul. Common worship completes the picture of what it means to be a Christian: we are not alone in our joys and concerns. God and neighbor are always a part of our journey. So, what if we joined with our neighbor in our common journey by offering sacred worship spaces that will provide us with support for our spiritual paths? What would those worship spaces look like?

Blue Christmas

During my second year of seminary, one of my closest friends and classmates informed me of a special worship service her church was holding the week before Christmas: Blue Christmas.[5] Since the days immediately before Christmas are extremely short, some are affected by Seasonal Affective Disorder. Additionally, many people are wrestling with the holidays for a variety of reasons, including grieving a deceased love one or broken relationship, facing financial troubles, and attempting to live into the societal expectations of the season. The pressure mounts for those celebrating the variety of December holidays, and space is needed to escape the anxiety and depression that comes with heightened holiday hopes and long nights.

Within a couple of years, I started offering the Blue Christmas service only days before Christmas. Candles were burned in the dimly-lit chapel. We sang hymns such as "In the Bleak Midwinter" and "Silent Night," reflecting on the solemn moments in the highly-anticipated holiday season. From my experience, this service tends not to draw a large audience. While only a few congregants and community members are in attendance, this service is one that is held very sacred to those present.

Armenian Genocide Remembrance Service[6]

While there are Armenian populations in many metropolitan areas around the country, some regions do not have an Armenian church. Because of this, there might not be a gathering of Armenians on or around April 24 to commemorate the atrocities of this holocaust. St. Paul United Church of Christ (UCC), Old Blue Rock Road in Cincinnati, the church where I pastor, has opened its doors to the Armenian community to hold this service.

My grandfather survived the genocide as a child, which makes this a service very close to my heart. During the service, we name those who survived, remember those who perished, and pray that atrocities like these will never happen again in our world. A service like the Armenian Genocide Remembrance Service is geared towards a certain cultural population. Occasionally, people from the host church or friends of those attending will be present to share their love and prayers with the Armenian community. Through their hospitality, the host church not only becomes more educated on justice and peace issues, but they also have the opportunity to continue to discern in what other ways God may be opening them to new mission experiences.

Facebook Worship

Social media has become another space for socializing with others. While social media often receives a negative reputation as a means of bullying and trolling, this medium also invites others to connect in deeper ways. In this virtual world, people will offer prayers, advice, fellowship, thanksgiving, and celebratory sentiments to many experiencing the mountains and valleys of life.

As part of my spiritual practices, I attended a few Facebook Parties that my friend the Rev. Nicole Havelka began to hold while serving in judicatory ministry for the United Church of Christ. She chose to hold these events to build community between churches across wide geographic areas. The basic format, which she borrowed from other organizations, was this: after creating a Facebook event for a one-hour "Party" on the organization's page, Havelka posted a question or prompt for conversation about once every ten minutes. Participants responded in the comments section below the question or prompt. The conversations went so well, she eventually reapplied the idea to a worship event, which she started calling Facebook Retreats.[7]

Havelka commented on the connections that are built through these online interactions. "What I found in leading online community building and worship was that it is actually more intimate than in-person worship," Havelka said. "When you're in traditional worship, you may hear prayers or even read them out loud with the group, but you don't have any opportunity to express your reaction to it. With Facebook worship, people are invited to respond in the moment about how they are being impacted by the prayer, story or song that's being posted. It helps the community know each other in a deeper way. Plus, if people miss participating in real time, they can always go back and read and respond to the posts and comments later."

At St. Paul UCC, we adapted Havelka's original Facebook Parties as Facebook Worship. These were first utilized during a tremendously snowy winter; Sunday worship was canceled on a few occasions due to inclement weather. As their leader, I desired to connect with people even though the roads did not allow for us to travel. Once I knew that worship was canceled, I notified people in the church of the service. After welcoming people to our Facebook group at 6p.m. on that Sunday evening, I posted a couple of videos, an opening prayer, a reconciliation statement with an assurance of grace, a photo with a quote, a reflection that I wrote which I had published on my blog, a few questions to ponder, and a blessing as we closed worship.

While the social media worship experiences I conducted were on a public Facebook page, Havelka discovered that the online gatherings worked better in Facebook groups (rather than pages) because it "fostered a greater sense of safety and community."

An online experience such as Facebook worship defies time and space. No matter where people are geographically or in their spiritual journeys, and despite if they log on while the service is happening or two days later, those who engage in social media worship can be a part of the experience from their exact location.

White claims that personal devotions "usually but not always occur apart from the physical presence of the body of Christ."[8] Yet now that the virtual world exists and gives us a different sense of the physical presence of the body of Christ, I would conclude that Facebook worship differs from personal devotions as there is the attendance of others present. Jesus' mandate of two or three gathering together can happen even in space of the virtual world. We often wonder what the next social media platform will look like and how we will utilize it to engage with those in our congregations and community. So, if Facebook and social media have taught us anything in the church it is that we must be attentive to whatever platform currently gives voice to our culture.

Things to Consider

Time. As church leaders, we often ask ourselves what times of day are best for various worship services. While evening seems an appropriate time for those working during the day, many others, including some elderly congregants, are not able to drive during night hours. Consider the context of those whom you may be trying to reach. If your context spans multiple groups and generations, create ways for those attending to carpool with one another if it happens to fall in the evening.

Space. Does the space seem too formal or casual for the worship? Offering the special worship services in a small chapel, fellowship hall, or repurposed classroom may add to the dynamics of the service. Spaces have the potential to bring a sense of added intimacy, formality, or other tone. Find the space that reflects the sentiments of the service.

Additional ways to offer the worship. How can another space and time for the service be added that invites more people into closeness with God and one another? Could this be an online space or another unique place? While reflecting on space and time, one may want to see if the service should be offered in another format at a different time. For instance, while we may have a Blue Christmas service at the church, what would it mean to also have a service on Twitter? How can we partner with the YMCA or other area organizations to have a special service outside of the church walls?

Offerings and special services. Some believe special services are appropriate times to have a collection, while others may nix the idea. Like the story of David dancing in front of the Ark of the Covenant, an offering was shared. Yet if the audience is primarily non-members, then maybe have a basket near the door for "free will offerings."

Ecumenical participation. Because churches and clergy have limited time and resources, each church opening their worship services to other congregations in the community allows us to work together to minister to all of God's people. Make sure to notify fellow clergy when holding these services. Some will pass the information along to other clergy or members of their congregations. Like those in our pews, often fellow clergy need spaces to process and grieve. Inviting them to sit in our pews during these services gives them a chance to process feelings outside of their church walls.

Creativity. Knowing that God is the creator of our world, and each of us is made in God's image, we are gifted with the power of creative minds. As pastors, we brainstorm ideas on how we can be pastoral to others in our churches and community. What special services will help people reconnect with God? How can we employ the resources we have to bring light to the needs of those in our congregations and community? What are ideas that will help our communities engage with the Holy Spirit? What is the one idea that you may think "This will never happen," and what will it take for you to try it?

Ways this will strengthen the Church

Special worship services have the potential to impact communities in the following ways:

Filling in the gaps: Hosting a special worship service is the equivalent to offering a one-day health clinic. As there will always be gaps in medical care in our communities, spiritual needs will always exist as well. In hosting special services, churches have the potential to reach the marginalized in communities who are hurting and may not have a church. With the presence of special services, more souls will find a place of healing.

Comfort: Many around us are experiencing a time of exile, much like those during the Babylonian Exile in the sixth century BCE. Just as comfort is needed today, writers of Scripture during the exile reflected similar needs. Isaiah 40:1-2 states, "Comfort, O comfort my people, says your God. Speak tenderly to Jerusalem and cry to her that she has served her term, that her penalty is paid, that she has received from the Lord's hand double for all her sins."

One of our jobs as clergy and church leaders is to comfort those in physical, emotional, or spiritual pain. The Isaiah text establishes the mandate to console the afflicted. Special worship services fill this mandate and serve as a blanket of comfort for those who experience the chills of life. We offer that unique wrap of care to those in pain.

Evangelism: While we are not attempting to proselytize or convert others to our view, our job is to spread the good news of God's love, grace, and peace. Whether we speak of hope coming into our shadow-filled world throughout the Blue Christmas service or we experience the companionship in a social media worship service, God's good news continues to spread in our communities.

Dreaming big: Through hosting special worship services, the Holy Spirit nudges us in new directions. By engaging in the "dreaming big" activities in our congregations, we can experience the presence of God in ways that we would never expect.

What possibilities will come next? In what new ways can we serve our community, and what may be the next special service we offer? In our efforts to expand the ways we experience worship, the walls are breaking down. God is calling us to new avenues. Through these encounters, we are able to allow the call of God to send us on new journeys in becoming the body of Christ that God needs us to be.

Conclusion

As Christian clergy, we are called to form practices and habits in our lives that will build up one another in the name of Jesus the Christ. Through these special worship services, we can offer places for people to be their most authentic selves while they explore their relationship with the Divine. Furthermore, by holding these services, we are developing the practices of evangelizing, pastoral care, and visioning in our own ministries.

There is no one set way or type of special worship service. Each context is different, and every church has their gifts, interests, and calls by God. Ultimately, our efforts should encourage the love we have for God, neighbor, creation, and ourselves to grow. If our efforts are given with the love of God and the passion to serve the Divine in mind, we will be able to shine the light of the kin-dom of God in our communities.

Notes

1. "America's Changing Religious Landscape." Pew Research Center, online, accessed 12. May 2015.

2. Carol Howard Merritt, *Tribal Church: Ministering to the Missing Generation* (Herndon, VA: Alban, 2007), 73.

3. James F. White, *Introduction to Christian Worship*. Revised ed. (Nashville, TN: Abingdon, 1992), 34.

4. Ibid., 35.

5. Some call this worship the Longest Night of the Year service. Whether they retain one name or the other, most of these services focus on the shadows of the shortest days of the year which, in the Northern Hemisphere, is right around the holiday season and a few days before Christmas.

6. The Armenian Genocide Remembrance Service commemorates the Armenian Genocide of 1915. During the massacres, Armenians of all ages were slaughtered under the Ottoman Empire. For more information, see John Kifner, "American Genocide of 1915: An Overview," (http://www.nytimes.com/ref/timestopics/topics_armeniangenocide.html).

7. Nicole Havelka. Personal correspondence (31. August 2015.)

8. White, 35.

Chapter 6

Young Adults and the Creativity of Local Churches

Rev. Ryan Byers

It should come as no surprise to clergy and leaders of the mainline protestant church that there are fewer and fewer adults under 40 in the pews on Sunday morning. I used to work as the full time Coordinator of Young Adult Ministries at a 4,000-member church, Second Presbyterian Church in Indianapolis. I started in 2008 a few days before the market crash. I had experience already with children, youth, and college ministries and I was intrigued by a position that dedicated its efforts solely to adults approximately ages 21–35.

The program had an existing foundation thanks to the work of the previous Lake Fellow[1] and a host of dedicated lay people. I jumped in and brought my knowledge of youth and college ministry skills to the program, which was a mistake for the most part. Adults 21–35 are sometimes quite similar to youth in terms of developmental needs. For example, the need for differentiation from their families of origin or their continued search for identity formation. However, they are nothing like college youth with whom they are often paired. Seven years ago when I started my position, young adults were of two generations: young Gen-Xers and older millennials and as Gen-Xers age into the 40s and 50s the only generation made up of young adults for the time being will be millennials. Thus, I discovered that young adult ministry was a multi-faceted work in ministry and not a work among an homogeneous people on the same journey or experiencing the same points of crisis.

I quickly learned that only the largest Presbyterian Churches had a position dedicated to young adult ministry and nearly all of these were paired with other responsibilities such as youth and young adults, mission and young adults, or college and young adults, for example. I also learned that denominational resources were sorely lacking. This particular age group had proved to be a conundrum to churches even as they continued to lose young adults. I set about to learn as much as I could about young adulthood: the sociology, the context, and the research by reading, listening, experimenting, and, as a young adult myself, I would reflect upon what I was doing and learning. Lastly, I wanted to share what I learned was successful and what was not. I wanted to share with churches of all sizes, especially small congregations, that young adult ministry demands outside of the box thinking and acting, creativity and entrepreneurial approaches. In my estimation, the future of the church depends upon this work.

The Research

According to numbers released in May, 2015, by the Pew Research Center, 35% of 18–29 year olds were unaffiliated with any religious tradition in 2014. Slightly more than half identified as Christian, of which 10% identified as mainline Protestant, 20% evangelical, 6% historical black Protestant, 16% Catholic.[2] The unaffiliated rate of 35% is an increase of four percentage points since 2007.[3] Overall the number of Americans who have since declared themselves unaffiliated since 2007 to 2014 is 7.5 million.

Based on the raw data this does not bode well for mainline churches that hope not only to grow numerically, but also hope to grow numerically with young adults. Since at least 1965 the denomination that I grew up in (Presbyterian Church USA) and the one that I am ordained into (United Church of Christ) have slowly been declining. These churches reached their peak of membership that year with 2.5 million for the UCC and 6 million for the PCUSA. 1966 began the slow decline as baby boomers were first starting to come of age and the tumultuous period of the 1960s was entering full swing.

What that means for many mainline churches is an over representation of members 65 years and older and an underrepresentation of those 65 years and younger, especially adults ages 18–29. A few data points: besides being more nonaffiliated than young adults 45 years ago, they are also less likely to be married when they exit their 20s. According to the Pew Research Center in an article from 2011 "… just 20% of adults ages 18 to 29 are married, compared with 59% in 1960."[4]

As a society we are dealing with a lot more single adults (and single parents) in their 20s than churches were a generation or two ago.[5] Such realities suggest a lot of ramifications for the sort of ways that churches ought to be engaging young adults. Churches hoping that their youth will return to church after they leave for college, graduate, find a job, get married and have children all before age 23 will be left wanting. No longer can young adult ministry be equated with married with small children ministry. The data does not bear this out.

According to work done by the National Study on Youth and Religion and also by Jeffrey Arnett, young adults (ages approximately 18–29) are in a period of possibility where they are exploring vocations, meaning, identity (including religious) unhampered by the tasks that young adults of earlier times were dealing with (such as marriage and children).[6] Yet, this period of unmooring can also be fraught with anxiety and depression made worse by crushing student debt, the worst economic crisis since the Great Depression, and the uncertainty of the future.[7]

It is easy to see why churches that were used to a "young adult" ministry model that hit its apex in the 1950s of young married couples bringing their small children to Sunday school[8] are having an incredibly challenging time adapting not only to the great socio-cultural changes of the past 50 years, but also to how that has changed young adulthood into something virtually unrecognizable.

What Can We Learn from Coca-Cola?

I have this thought experiment when talking with pastors, lay people, and church institutions about young adults and their increasing disengagement from church. What if in 1970 the Coca-Cola company had sent out its marketing people to measure what percentage of 18-to-29-year-olds consumed Coke regularly or occasionally? Let's say that the marketing people came back with a figure of 88% of 18-to-29-year-olds in 1970 (boomers) drank Coke regularly or occasionally. I have no idea how the executives at Coca-Cola would react, but I imagine that they would be pleased. Perhaps they would even have figured out ways to increase that percentage.

Skip to 1980 and the marketers come back with the same figure: 88%. No increase, but no decrease either. Then something happens around the beginning of the 1990s. The marketers notice that 18-to-29-year-old drinkers of Coke have decreased to 84%, not a huge worry perhaps in the eyes of the executives. Perhaps it is time to rethink strategy and see how the 90s unfold. In our thought experiment, by the 2000s the percentage of Coke drinkers ages 18 to 29 is only 77%.[9] By the year 2014 that number is now 65%. That's down from 88% in the 1970s. What do you think would have been the executives reaction and response to this decline?

In this thought experiment I have no conception for what percentage of 18-to-29-year-olds in any decade were consuming Coke, but I know this: if the data were true that Coke drinkers were increasingly drinking less Coke over the past four decades the executives at Coca-Cola would have done something about it. Perhaps they would have wrung their hands and made excuses upon first hearing the news. Then they might have garnered incredible resources, both money and brain power, to think of creative and innovative ways to get 18-to-29-year-olds to fall in love with a sugary drink that offers absolutely no health benefits.

In truth, if one substitutes "religion" for "Coke" and "religious affiliation" for the percentage of Coke drinkers, the data remains the same. In others words, in 1970 the percentage of 18-29 year olds who claimed religious affiliation was 88% and in 2014 the percentage of 18-29 years claiming religious affiliation is 65%, wouldn't it be wise for religious institutions to consider using their money and brain power to come up with a creative solution to making the church a relevant space for young adults?

The Reason to Engage

In the book, *The Orange Revolution*, the authors ask this question: "Would your organization, on the heels of its worst year ever, take their best people and put them on a team to design a product so outside your current business model?"[10] Would we? Have we employed such an approach in the church?

I remember going to college in the late 90s and seminary in the early 00s. Most of us had computers and none of us had an Apple product. Unless you were a graphic artist (and none of us were), Apple had become irrelevant. Apple products seemed too expensive and didn't meet our needs as casual computer users. Yet, all of us loved music. At the time there was no legitimate way to carry around all of the music we wanted or needed in our daily lives. Apple took this time or irrelevancy in their history and made it into an opportunity.

In *The Orange Revolution* the authors note: "On January 27, 2010, just nine years after its launch, Apple announced that the 250 millionth iPod had been sold—making it the fastest-selling music player in history. The initiative was launched in 1997, on the heels of a year in which Apple lost $816 million."[11] Apple had become irrelevant to many of us, but rather than bury their heads in the sand they got their tools of creativity out of the woodshed and got to work and it transformed the music industry and the way that consumers would utilize Apple. Now it is no longer just an alternative to the

PC, but it has become the all in one tool of the early 21st century for music, communication, and organization. I now have for work and personal use: an iPhone, an iPad, an iPad Mini, Apple TV, and a MacBook Air.

Admittedly, the church is not Apple nor is it a business, nor do we have a "product." Our bottom line is not profit. Yet, I sense that many of our congregations and denominations are hand wringing, worrying, and fretting about the sheer loss of members over the past 40 years, as Apple surely did in the 1990s. I listen to church members lament over the exponential decrease in young adults, and their children, from their pews and programs. There are a whole host of reasons, explanations, and theories for the decrease in religious affiliation, particularly the exponential decrease among adults ages 18 to 29 over the past two and half decades.[12]

This chapter does not seek to address such theories, but rather the practices and habits that creative organizations could teach the church about young adults. What are some of the innovative ways that leaders in the church are seeking to engage 18 to 29 year olds and other non-affiliated folks? Are we willing to commit resources— actual money, time, creativity, an openness to failing and trying again—to the lives of young adults? Perhaps more importantly, what are our ultimate reasons for engaging young adults? If it is to fill pews, choirs, offering plates, and committees then that is probably the wrong reason.

When I was working at Second Presbyterian Church in Indianapolis I reached out to other pastors and church leaders who were working with young adults. There weren't many; in fact, only a handful of the largest Presbyterian Churches (USA) in 2009 had a person dedicated to young adult ministry and most of them had other assigned areas. These areas would include college ministry, youth ministry, family ministry, and mission. I connected with the person at Fourth Presbyterian Church of Chicago (the second largest PCUSA congregation with just under 6,000 members): Liz Nickerson.

Liz had a variety of roles under the heading of young adults. We had conversation by phone several times and she articulated for me why we should be about the task of young adult ministry.

She suggested that as mainline progressives, liberals, or non-conservatives, we are not convinced that hell exists and that all "non-Jesus confessing as my Lord and Savior people" will be sent there. What she suggested rang true from my experience. Growing up in the deep South, many of my conservative Christian friends had an urgency about them. They literally believed that non-Christians would be sent to hell. That sense of urgency galvanized resources and creativity in service of a transcendent cause: evangelizing non-Christians so that their destiny was secure in heaven.

In the progressive mainline church, it seems our sense of urgency must come from somewhere else. One of the leading sociologists of religion, Robert Wuthnow, in his excellent book, *After the Baby Boomers: How Twenty and Thirty-Somethings Are Shaping the Future of American Religion*, suggests:

> Congregations could be a valuable source of support for young adults. They could be places where young adults gravitate to talk about the difficult decisions they are facing or to meet other people of the same age. Congregations could be guiding the career decisions of younger adults or helping them to think about their budgets and their personal priorities.[13]

I would take Wuthnow's conclusion further: if the reason we seek to engage young adults is not because of the fear of hell, or to increase our budgets, to staff committees, to have warm bodies in the pews, to sing in the choir, or save the institution of the church then our reason must be grounded in the witness of resurrection, the promise of forgiveness, and the hope of love that Christians have proclaimed over the centuries.

In spite of the stereotypes, for many young adults it is not an exhilarating period of identity exploration. From economic distress and crushing student loans, to the difficulty of finding meaningful and sustainable work, to political systems that seems largely disinterested in the needs and the dreams of young adults, the research shows that adults ages 18-23 are enmeshed in a culture of moral ambiguity and consumerism.[14] What is more, building meaningful communities and relationships are not sustained by the institutions around us: schools, colleges and universities, and religious institutions like the church.

Young adulthood is hard. Young adults are getting almost no institutional support or favors. Further, all young adults are not equal in privilege. It can be exponentially more difficult for black young men, young immigrants from Central America, young adults who identify as trans or queer, young adults with mental illness or disabilities, young adult women, and on and on.

And as if all of this were not enough, young adults are increasingly leaving the church. The church has almost utterly failed. Coca-Cola would not have given up on adults ages 18 to 29 without a fight and neither should we. We ought to seek out young adults not because we ourselves have arrived, but because our churches and our lives are not nearly as enriched without them. We seek young adults because they have gifts to share as they journey and they have gifts to share with us on ours. We seek young adults because Jesus would and did.

Visions & Dreams

When pastors and lay leaders have moments to collaborate about how to engage young adults—assuming that they wish to consider this topic—the end result will often be that religious communities are reluctant to dedicate the time, finances, and risk necessary to make an attempt. But if we could dream for a moment, a different vision could arise. If the church were to put together a team of its best minds and craft new models of engaging young adults in the 21st century, what would that look like? Denominations and churches cannot garner the sort of resources that an Apple or Coca-Cola can. Churches and denominations can't headhunt, create a collaborative brain trust, and pay high salaries for two or three years while a team tinkers and brainstorms about young adults and the church. Yet, we can dream dreams and cast visions.

In the fall of 2010 I was invited to a brainstorming session at Stony Point Conference Center in New York by Wayne Meisel. Wayne is the former president of the Bonner Foundation. The Bonner Foundation is a leader in developing college students through service learning. Qualified Bonner Scholars at colleges that have the Bonner Program receive college scholarships, engage in meaningful service each week, are developed as service leaders, and in my opinion become the go to students for community service on college campuses. Wayne called a meeting of about twenty-five people who care about young adults and the church from a variety of mostly mainline Protestant backgrounds. It was a creative brainstorming session with a particular focus: how the mainline church intersects with the lives of young adults drawn to community, intentional living, and service.

Wayne sketched out a vision that was big. He talked about hospitality, intentional community, service learning models, young adults, and the church. In the Presbyterian Church (USA), there exists the Young Adult Volunteers which is sort of the Presbyterian version of AmeriCorps or the Peace Corps. Young adults apply, raise money and support, have an orientation, and then are scattered to sites in the U.S and throughout the world. In my experience of encountering former YAVs (Young Adult Volunteers Alum) they are passionate, thoughtful, service and justice-orientated young people of faith. There are similar volunteer opportunities for young adults in other denominations such as the Lutheran Volunteer Corps, Episcopal Volunteer Corps, Young Adult Service Communities (UCC), Jesuit Volunteer Corps, to name a few.

Although each one is attached to a different Christian faith community, the mission of the Young Adults Service Communities sums up well what I see as the overall mission and intention of all of these faith-based young adult communities: Young adult leaders transforming communities through the faith-inspired pursuit of justice, collaborative action, and intentional living.[15]

However, I discern two problems with this model. First, there aren't enough service opportunities. *Time* reported in July of 2013, that "There seems to be a general hunger for service in the 30-and-under millennial generation; in 2011 there were 582,000 applications for 82,000 slots in AmeriCorps."[16] Second, a strange disconnect exists between service communities like Teach for America and mainline Christian communities. Wayne reported that when he lived in Atlanta, he went to visit the executive director for the Atlanta Teach for America. The director told him that in five years no clergy had ever come to his office. When I heard this I called up the Indianapolis executive director of Teach for America. Yet, this lack of engagement with service organizations is astounding given that Christians for centuries have been creative leaders in serving others, whether opening monasteries as places of rest for weary travelers, founding hospitals, or engaging in the full range of service to others as teachers, medical personnel and the like.

As a means of response, in 2013 the Aspen Institute and Franklin project put out a publication, *A 21st Century National Service System Plan of Action*. According to the document, the plan "…challenges all young adults to commit to one year of full-time service and proposes the infrastructure to engage one million young Americans in service to their country through national service."[17] It was signed by CEOs, college Presidents, former heads of the Department of Defense, State, Health & Human Services, and a whole host of civic-minded thought leaders. Wayne saw this as a need for the Church to engage.

In a July, 2013, Huffington Post article, Wayne laid out a vision in which the church can and should participate in such a bold plan.

Looking through the list of names attached to the Aspen Institute and Franklin publication I noticed only one signature from someone who had at one time worked in an official faith based capacity and it was that of Joshua Debois, Former Director, White House Office of Faith-Based and Neighborhood Partnerships. If mainline churches are consistently bemoaning the lack of young adults in their pews, perhaps they should seek them where many of them are. The Young Adult Volunteer programs host approximately fifty or so young adults in any given year, the YASC's about 20. All together faith based young adult service communities account for a tiny fraction of young adult service communities at large (such as Teach for America, City Year, et. al). Wayne argues:

The church has a critical role to play in achieving these social advances. It is time for the church to awaken out of its great slumber, to take notice of this important movement and to play an appropriate part.... I believe that faith-based service communities could collectively deliver 100,000 of the one million young adults the Aspen plan seeks to engage in full-time service per year.[18]

If there is one word that I urge churches to consider adopting it is agility. Churches need to be willing to draw upon tradition, the current context, and creativity if they are going to successfully walk alongside the lives of young people. We must listen to young adults and be receptive to the creative ways that they are trying to merge faith with vocation and vocation with meaning. Churches can engage young adults in ways different than I have written because how any church engages young adults depends on context. Ministering alongside young adults in downtown Chicago will be different than in a town in Iowa which will be different than a southern college town and so on. This is why a habit or practice of agility is needed in order to be creative in the church regarding young adults.

Conclusions

Mainline faith-based service and justice learning communities are only one way of creatively engaging the church and young adults. If we did take a serious look at Wayne's proposal to engage 100,000 young adults in these types of ventures, then I can only imagine the impact it would have on churches, communities, and young adults.

When I was living in Indianapolis I proposed to the leadership of the church I was serving that they take a look at crafting a young adult intentional community. Since my first meeting with Wayne in the fall of 2015, Second Presbyterian Church will have invited three young adults to participate in the Indianapolis Young Adult Volunteer program. In this particular YAV site, young adults live in intentional community, participate in a full range of Second Presbyterian Church missional activities, and engage in meaningful reflection alongside caring adults.

In my final year at Second Presbyterian I had nourished a relationship with the Indianapolis Teach For America chapter. I also became connected to an intentional community, the Open Hand, which is located on the near north-side of Indianapolis.[19] I approached Steve Reynolds, one of the main organizers of the Open Hand, about partnering with TFA and perhaps opening a few spaces in their homes for corps member. Steve took to the idea. His own daughter had just been accepted into TFA in Dallas and the sort of partnership that I was proposing made sense to Steve. Why not support TFA Corps members with an intentional community of care and support?

Steve ended up asking the owner of a very large house down the block from the Open Hand Community about opening her home to TFA Corps members. The neighborhood was very mixed economically with boarded up homes relatively close by, homes that were really expensive, along with everything in between. The owner of the home was skeptical at first about young adults living in community in her home. After warming to the idea, she agreed with wild enthusiasm by deciding to renovate her space, adding bathrooms for each room, and by the middle of June I went to the TFA Indianapolis orientation to recruit potential candidates on this new and creative venture with young adults.

The data around young adults within the church is a bleak picture at best, and yet, the Church can still play a role in the lives of young adults as they find themselves in periods of vocational and religious discernment. When the church takes the time to be creative in partnering with organizations like Teach for America and offering young adults sacred space to discern and discover who they are, an entire world opens up to the Church that would not have otherwise. Working with young adults requires habits of attention, agility, and accompaniment that the Church is missing by creating programming that all too often mirrors the youth groups of their teen years. Were we to utilize the habit of agility by listening and accompanying young adults inter-generationally as churches, an entirely new and creative path could be paved for the future.

Some time has passed since I left Indianapolis, and a few years ago I ran into Wayne at a Presbyterian gathering. He told me about the TFA home I helped sow a seed for, how young adults moved in, about how it became a hub of community with about 100 of them for events like a Christmas party. It was inspiring to hear that some of the seeds planted in my work came into bloom and it gave me hope that the church and people of faith who care about communities, service and justice, and young adults found the courage to cultivate creative ways of challenging the church to live out its calling to walk alongside all sorts of folks in changing the world. Do we have that same kind of courage?

Notes

1. Lake Fellows are Second's two year graduate residents in ministry program recipients.

2. Pew Forum Research Center, online, accessed 12. May 2015.

3. Ibid.

4. Pew Social Trends, online, accessed 4. May 2016.

5. For an excellent book on the adult construct of 18–29 year olds see Jeffrey Arnett's excellent book *Emerging Adulthood: The Winding Road from the Late Teens through the Twenties* (New York: Oxford UP, 2004).

6. *The New York Times*, online, accessed 4 May 2016.

7. Christian Smith and Patricia Snell, *Souls in Transition: The Religious & Spiritual Lives of Emerging Adults.* (New York: Oxford UP, 2009), 6–7.

8. Robert Putnam and David E. Campbell, *American Grace: How Religion Divides and Unites Us.* (New York: Simon & Shuster, 2010), 83–85.

9. Pew Forum Research Center, online, accessed 4. May 2016.

10. Adrian Gostick and Chester Elton, *The Orange Revolution: How One Great Team Can Transform an Entire Organization.* (New York: Free Press, 2010), 90.

11. Ibid.

12. As a side note of interest: Adults who were aged 18–29 in 1990 are now aged 42–53.

13. Robert Wuthnow, *After the Baby Boomers: How Twenty and Thirty-Somethings are Shaping the Future of American Religion.* (Princeton, NJ: Princeton University Press, 2007), 13.

14. Christian Smith, Kari Christoffersen, Hilary Davison, and Patricia Snell Herzog, *Lost in Transition: The Dark Side of Emerging Adulthood.* (New York: Oxford UP, 2011).

15. The United Church of Christ, online, accessed 4. May 2016.

16. *Time Magazine*, online, accessed 4. May 2016.

17. The Aspen Institute, online, accessed 4. May 2016.

18. *The Huffington Post*, online, accessed 4. May 2016.

19. The Open Hand Community had, for approximately ten years, invited young adults to live either in their homes or in a house that they had bought and renovated.

Part 2
Habits of community

Chapter 7

The Church *WITH* Christ:
The Practice of Building Community, Economy, and Mutual Delight

Rev. Michael Mather

Richard Florida once said to me: "You aren't talking about a school in the community, you are talking about community as school."

In 1986 I came to Broadway United Methodist Church in Indianapolis in order to be the neighborhood pastor; the pastor in the streets. Mrs. Miller down the street called me "the hoodlum priest." My job was to run the inner city programs of our metropolitan congregation. Broadway was an old mainline congregation that made a commitment to stay in their inner city neighborhood while many fled to the suburbs.

The most visible and leading program we ran was the summer program. It was basketball for the boys and cheerleading for the girls. It had been running for over fifteen years. Over my first few years at Broadway we changed the program. It was not an easy change. It was often painful, but we did it.

We built each week around a spiritual principle, beginning and ending every day with devotions. We expanded what was offered to include Bible Study, poetry, violin lessons, math, history, and science. We divided the program into two parts: Recreation for a Healthy Body and Education for the Human Spirit. There were two hundred and fifty young people around Broadway all day, every day. The program got a lot of attention, both close at hand and far away and we often were commended publicly. I broke my arm patting myself on the back I felt so good about what we were doing.

But the last nine months I was at Broadway in 1991 I did nine funerals for young men under twenty-five years old in the four block radius around the church. Many of those young men had grown up in the summer program. I thought we were helping to change the reality in the streets. But if nine young men ended up dead in nine months I realized that I was not nearly as helpful as I wanted to be. People would say to me: "Oh, but if you hadn't been doing this it would have been worse." I had two answers to that. The first one was "No." And the second one was "Even if you are right, it isn't good enough."

As the chorus of voices in this book express, the church is in desperate need of creative people who are willing to let go of programs, especially programs aimed to deal with poverty, and to form habits that will begin a new way of acting as the Church. In fact, perhaps our programs targeted towards "those in need" could take on the larger task of the elimination of poverty altogether. And if we were to do so, what would we need to change in order to reach that goal? The challenge is that we will quickly discover that the data suggests our endless food pantries, clothing drives, and poverty simulations do very little to actually eliminate poverty. Can we live into new ways of being and thinking that might allow us to use creativity as a habit to get at strategies that will actually work in eliminating poverty? We are fond of saying around Broadway that we don't want to just beat the odds for some, we want strategies that will beat the odds for everyone. To be sure, our communities and our churches will continue to face the enormous task of looking towards solutions to help end poverty. Broadway certainly felt like we were on the cutting edge of those solutions, only we discovered that perhaps there was something much larger to the picture that we were missing. It was right in front of our eyes if we would have had eyes to see. So many of us in the church have chosen not to be present to the abundant Christ at work in communities such as Broadway and the world and the church are poorer for it. I would not have known these truths had my bishop not sent me to another parish and community with similar challenges to the one I was leaving. I would soon discover a new way of acting, living, and believing and it would require my full investment in letting go of things in order to creatively take up the new. I began to leave behind the old wineskins for the new.

I left Broadway Church in Indianapolis to take a new appointment at a United Methodist Church in South Bend, Indiana. The church was a very small congregation located in the low income neighborhood of South Bend. We had about forty people in worship and we had a food pantry. When people came to the food pantry we would give people a survey from the government to fill out because we received a lot of government surplus food. The survey asked for the individual's income and expenses. Many times these forms told us that their income was half of what their expenses were. We were a small congregation so there was not much we could do with such information, so we put it in a file cabinet.

After worship on Pentecost Sunday in 1992 we gathered around tables downstairs for the weekly meal. A group of us were sitting at one of the tables talking about the sermon for the day and a woman said: "When you talked about the passage regarding Pentecost, you said that Peter read from the book of the prophet Joel and said that God's Spirit flows down on all people, young and old, women and men."

"That's right," I said. I was proud of myself. What a good preacher I was. It was more than half an hour after worship and she remembered what I said!

"Then why don't we treat people like that?" she asked. Ouch.

"What do you mean?" I responded.

She replied, "When people come to our food pantry we ask people how poor they are, not how rich they are. If we believe God's Spirit has flowed down on all people why don't we ask people about their gifts?"

Her words stung, and they were right.

Years before I had been given a monograph written by John McKnight entitled *The Future of Low-Income Neighborhoods and the People Who Reside There*. In the back of that monograph was a ten page survey of the gifts of people. It was designed by a community organization in the Lawndale section of Chicago and it was devised to take about the same amount of time it took clothes to get dry in the Laundromat in Lawndale.

We began to use that survey. We asked people if they had taken care of older folks or children. If so, had they done it as a job, for family, or helping a neighbor out. We asked if they could fix a toaster, drive a car, cook for more than ten people, clean up after more than ten people, paint a house, put up drywall, play a musical instrument, fish, and grow things (flowers or vegetables). At the end we asked three things: (1) What three things are you good enough at that you could teach someone else about it?, (2) What three things would you like to learn that you don't already know; and (3) Who besides God and me is going with you along the way?

One of the first people to come was a woman named Adele Almaguer who lived half a block from the church. She lived with three generations of her family and she worked part time as a cook at Notre Dame University. She told us she was a good cook. We asked her to prove it. She cooked for the custodian, secretary and the pastor (me) and it was great! Shortly after, the leadership of the neighborhood organization was meeting. We said, "don't meet somewhere else, meet here at the church and let Adele cook for you." She cooked for them and they loved it.

Over the next nine months she cooked for a variety of events around the neighborhood for which we recommended her. Studebaker Elementary School had a PTA meeting, she provided the food. The South East Side Neighborhood Health Center had an open house, she provided the food. Memorial Hospital held a press conference in the neighborhood and she provided the food. Then the Chamber of Commerce called. They wanted to do an all day meeting of their Leadership Program in our building. We told them we were happy to do it. They said since they would be there all day they would need to use our kitchen. We told them we would prefer they use our caterer. They agreed.

We made our only financial investment. We took twenty dollars and bought Adele a thousand business cards. They read "La Chapperita Catering: Spunky Tex-Mex Food." She fed seventy of the business and civic leaders in South Bend. Through that she got connected to the Michiana Business Women's Association and a year and a half later she opened up Adelita's Fajitas at the corner of 8th Street and Harrison in Elkhart, Indiana.

If we had asked Adele how poor she was, we would have all ended up poorer for it and we would have missed a lot of great food. It was a revelation to me. I had been running programs in the way they always had been run, but not in the way in which I believed God was at work in the world. Therefore, we began to build all of our work in the neighborhood on the gifts, dreams and passions of our neighbors and not on their "need" or what they didn't have. I realized that I had plenty of things wrong with my life too, but people around me used what I had to offer, not what I didn't and I should treat the people around me with the same grace with which I am treated.

When I was sent by my Bishop back to Broadway in Indianapolis in 2003 I discovered the summer program was going on just as I had left it eleven and a half years before. For several years we tinkered with it, making small adjustments, but it was still a program where we were offering classes to the poor people around us. No matter how many different ways we tried to do it we couldn't figure out how to do it in a way that would build on the gifts of the people around us. I have a friend who talks about "discernment by nausea." I was experiencing this as I thought about what we were doing. In March of 2008, I gathered together the leadership of the congregation and the staff of the summer program and I told them we weren't going to do the summer program any more.

"What are we going to do?" someone asked.

"I have no idea," I said, "but I know it won't involve 50 or 100 or 250 of the young people from our neighborhood, but all 4,000 people who live here. And none of it will involve registration forms." We spent the next two days praying and talking together about what we were going to do. In the end, we decided we would hire neighborhood young people to meet their neighbors. They would do three things. They would name the gifts, talents, dreams and passions of their neighbors. They would lay hands on them and bless them. And they would connect them with other people who cared about the same thing.

We called the new program "The Summer of Blessings" where the young people would "Name, Bless, and Connect." We hired eight young people and began the work that continues to this day. The shift did not come without complaint from neighbors, many of whom wanted the classes and babysitting we had provided. We encouraged all those who wanted that to make it happen. We simply said it was not our calling. The young people who were hired seemed to have real joy in discovering the gifts of their neighbors. We took an empty room in our building and converted it into what we called "The Loaves and Fishes Room." The young people would gather every day after their visits in the neighborhood. They would write down on large PostIt™ notes one gift and the name and address of the person with that gift and stick it on the wall. By using these notes we could mix and match ("connect") people and their gifts.

As the leader of a congregation, I certainly could have suggested that we keep on doing the same old thing, because it was the way we always did things. We changed so that we could do something that reflected what we saw in the lives of people in our neighborhood. Perhaps the habit that pastors and their congregations need to begin living into is simply to listen for and shine a light on where it is that God is at work in neighbors and those around them. In our context at Broadway we believe that God is already at work in people and that we don't need to bring God to them. In fact, we believe that one of our primary tasks and habits is simply to "have conversations and have faith." If we foster getting to know neighbors . . . their gifts, hopes, and dreams . . . this dynamic will create community, economy, and mutual delight. Our experience has been that old urban community programming and surveys focusing only on how poor people are do not transform communities. In this model, our neighbors are almost always identified by what they lack rather than by what they have. We don't treat people who have money this way, but we do treat the poor this way. In recovery movements it is said that we don't think our way into new ways of acting, we act our way into new ways of thinking. It is time for the church to act our way into new ways of thinking.

Now I had come back to the church where the nine funerals in nine months had haunted me; instead of using the same programs and getting the same results, we were now establishing practices that were consistent with the way God in Christ has acted in the world. Matthew 11:1-6 reads: "Now when Jesus had finished instructing his twelve disciples, he went on from there to teach and proclaim his message in their cities. When John heard in prison what the Messiah was doing, he sent word by his disciples and said to him, 'Are you the one who is to come, or are we to wait for another?' Jesus answered them, 'Go and tell John what you hear and see: the blind receive their sight, the lame walk, the lepers are cleansed, the deaf hear, the dead are raised, and the poor have good news brought to them. And blessed is anyone who takes no offence at me.'"

The question was whether we were going to be witnesses to what Jesus has done or whether we were going to pretend we were the ones who were doing things.

The great writer Flannery O'Connor created a wonderful character in her classic book *Wise Blood*—a preacher named Hazel Motes. "'Church of Christ!' Hazel repeated. 'Well, I preach the Church Without Christ. I'm member and preacher to that church where the blind don't see and the lame don't walk and what's dead stays that way.'"[1] I was Hazel. I was looking at things as if Jesus hadn't brought sight to the blind and hadn't raised us out of our deaths. What the woman at the church in South Bend did was give birth to my ministry. She opened my eyes when she asked me why we didn't treat people like we believed the scripture we had read in worship that morning.

As I looked, scripture helped me see this more and more clearly. In Acts 3:1-10 there is the wonderful story of healing that opened my eyes even further.

> One day Peter and John were going up to the temple at the hour of prayer, at three o'clock in the afternoon. And a man lame from birth was being carried in. People would lay him daily at the gate of the temple called the Beautiful Gate so that he could ask for alms from those entering the temple. When he saw Peter and John about to go into the temple, he asked them for alms. Peter looked intently at him, as did John, and said, 'Look at us.' And he fixed his attention on them, expecting to receive something from them. But Peter said, 'I have no silver or gold, but what I have I give you; in the name of Jesus Christ of Nazareth, stand up and walk.' And he took him by the right hand and raised him up; and immediately his feet and ankles were made strong. Jumping up, he stood and began to walk, and he entered the temple with them, walking and leaping and praising God. All the people saw him walking and praising God, and they recognized him as the one who used to sit and ask for alms at the Beautiful Gate of the temple; and they were filled with wonder and amazement at what had happened to him.

1. Flannery O'Connor. Wise Blood: A Novel (New York: Farrar, Straus, and Giroux, 1990), 101.

When people showed up for help with rent or a utility bill or another financial need this was not the way I had been reacting. I had (in effect) said, "Silver or God have we some. Here you go. See you later." The text instructs, rather, that "Peter looked intently at him, as did John, and said, 'Look at us.'"

Looking intently at people had not been my modus operandi, nor that of our neighborhood ministry. Instead, when I glanced their way I looked upon my neighbors as I had been taught to: these were poor needy people. I found it easy to forget that I had my own problems and weaknesses, and that others around me were also filled with the Holy Spirit. What Peter and John did on the steps of the temple was so much better than our usual responses.

We are on a constant journey to pay attention to the gifts of the Holy Spirit alive in the places where the world (and often the church) says there is only poverty, sorrow, and pain. Those needs are certainly real and true, but we have found ourselves a lot more effective when we have focused on building upon gifts and not trying to fix the need.

The work of building upon gifts rather than need is a place of creativity in the work of local congregations and matters of poverty. The overwhelming approach of churches in addressing poverty focuses upon need. It is our assumption that in using the creativity of neighbors and their giftedness that we can, in fact, play a role in the transformation of economy and poverty. But, such transformation does not occur because of our sense of programming. Such transformation occurs when we allow the creativity and gifts of neighbors to lead the way. The young people that we hire every summer, for example, bear witness to the resurrected Christ as they see and name the gifts in their neighbors. As they bless and celebrate those gifts, they remind people that their neighbors are not needy but needed. As they connect them to other people they become lights that open people's eyes to the abundant life that Jesus was constantly trying to get his disciples and the world around him to see. Do we have eyes to see and ears to hear?

Chapter 8

Doing Nothing Together: The Art of Getting to Know Each Other

Rev. Caela Simmons Wood

It was an introvert's dream schedule for an interview weekend. I could hardly believe my good fortune. After several months in conversation with a congregation in Kansas, we had reached the let's-fly-you-out-and-meet-in-person stage of the process. Plane tickets were purchased, a hotel room was booked, and as I opened the document from the search team's chair, I had a few butterflies in my stomach.

What if the weekend was jam-packed with *stuff*? What if I didn't have room to breathe? What if they kept me booked with interviews until 9:00 p.m. on Saturday night and then expected me to bring my A-game on Sunday morning? What if there was no time for me to unwind by myself or wander around town a bit on my own?

My butterflies were for naught. It was a delightful schedule.

One person—the search team's chair, who I knew the best at this point—was picking me up at the airport and taking me right to lunch. Then it was on to a quiet tour of the church (which I was dying to explore) and some downtime in my hotel room before another person from the search team picked me up to take me to dinner at someone's home. Aside from that first evening, I rarely had to interact with the whole search team at once. The rest of the weekend was one-on-one time with each person from the team. And they had selected activities that they thought I might enjoy. They knew I loved learning and the outdoors, so one person took me to the local museum about the prairie and another took me for a drive out to the local reservoir and dam. They knew I cared deeply about how my young kids might settle into this new town, so they reserved all of Monday morning for one of the moms on the team to take me to several preschools around town for tours. There was even time for a trip to the local co-op grocery because they had heard me talk about how much I was going to miss the fair-trade, local, and organic options in my current town. Plus, I still found time to sneak off on a long walk through downtown in the snow. Alone.

Through the careful attention to detail in crafting my schedule, the search team had set the tone for our developing relationship. We would take time with each other. We would slow down. We would spend time together simply for the sake of spending time together. We would see the business of "getting to know each other" as important and a valid use of our precious time and energy. That weekend was a gift. And, as we clergy often find to be the case, the congregation I would come to serve was beginning to shape and teach me in important ways.

Fast-forward a few months and I was packing up my boxes in Indiana as I prepared to make the move across the country to the new church on the prairie. To numb the pain of leaving people and places that I loved, I began reading books about beginning ministry in a new place; one of my colleagues recommended *A New Beginning for Pastors and Congregations* by Kennon L. Callahan. The book begins with the story of Tom, a pastor at a presumably-fictionalized church who astonished everyone by posting a sign-up sheet for get-to-know-you meetings on his first Sunday in the pulpit. Over his first few weeks he invited people to get together with no other agenda item except getting to know one another. Callahan's description of Pastor Tom hailed him as a hero-pastor …and it seemed to me like a pretty good idea.

Shamelessly ripping off Callahan's idea, I posted a sign-up sheet on the office door my first Sunday in the pulpit. Over the first three months in the new church, I met with over 50 people in one-on-one or one-on-two gatherings. We got together in parks, offices, coffee shops, and bars. We connected over brunch, margaritas, and iced tea served on porches. To this day, I feel a vivid sense of connection with particular places in my not-so-new-town. When I ride my bike through City Park on the way to work, I remember the sacred conversation I had with a particular woman as we walked and talked. My gym is right next to the office where I met up with another person, and I say a prayer for her each time I work out. I smile when I eat lunch at a place just down the street from the church and remember the odd diagram I drew on a napkin for one man as we talked about the challenges of staying cool in the midst of interpersonal conflict.

All told, I spent about 100 hours of those first 10 weeks on the job in these no-agenda meetings. Some people came to the meetings prepared. They had brought along photos of their families they wanted to show me. One or two people even typed up brief bios and handed them over ("Here, pastor. You said you wanted to get to know me. Read this and then we can talk."). Other people seemed unsure at first. It was difficult for them to wrap their heads around the idea of a meeting just for the sake of getting to know one another. They weren't sure where to begin. I usually said, "How about if we start with this: what really matters to you? What's important in your life?" Before long, they were off and running. We don't often have a chance to just tell another person about who we are and what's important to us ... heck, we don't often have time to think about who we are and what's important to us.

Of course, I don't mean to make it sound like the whole endeavor was roses and hearts. I held space for some difficult stories. There were plenty of tears. And when I got home at the end of each day, I was exhausted. I couldn't handle more than one or two of these meetings each day. As an introvert, the concentrated people-time was really a challenge for me. I have to admit that sometimes I would look at the schedule for the next day and wonder where I would find the energy to be fully present to those people I had been called to know and love.

After my first Sunday at the new church, I went home after worship and cried. I said to my husband, "It's just so weird, looking out at all these people I don't know and leading worship. I am used to looking around the sanctuary and seeing people I know intimately. How long will it take for me to fall in love with these people?" He said, "I don't know, but I'm sure it will happen soon enough. Don't worry."

I'm certain that falling-in-love period varies for every pastor. I'm also certain that, for me, the practice of meeting with people intentionally over those first few months helped speed up the process. Just as the search team had set the tone for me in our new relationship, I think those meetings continued a trajectory of Enough.

As we settled in together, there was a feeling that there was enough time to go around. We would take time with each other. We would slow down. We would spend time together simply for the sake of spending time together. We would see the business of "getting to know each other" as important and a valid use of our precious time and energy.

When do we stop hanging out with people just for the sake of ... being together? Does it happen when we're 15? 20? 30? 50? It seems that only a few of us are lucky enough to effortlessly hang on to this gift into our adult years. But you don't have to go much further than your neighborhood playground or local college campus to see that it is a gift that seems to peak somewhere in the childhood or early adult years ... and then gets bumped for seemingly-more-important things.

I spend a lot of time at playgrounds with our preschool-aged sons. When they were much younger, they were fairly oblivious to the other kids at the playground. They were focused on mastering the skills of scooting, crawling, walking, and climbing. If they noticed anyone at all, it was me. They would occasionally look up as if to say, "Are you still there, mama?" or "Look at me! I did it!"

As their social horizons have expanded, so, too, has their vision. No longer are they primarily focused on their own work and play. Now they run with each other and with new friends—inventing elaborate games of chase, daring each other to try new things, counting the number of times they can perfectly execute a particular feat.

Friends made at the park are usually hour-long friendships. The friendships are made effortlessly. As I settle onto my park bench, I see them running across the playground. Before long, I glance up and there is a whole pack gathered together. There are rarely formal introductions ("Hello, Ryder. My name is Madison. What brings you to the playground today?") At times they don't even seem to be talking to each other much at all. But it is clear that they are enjoying each other immensely. The day is improved by their time spent together. The sun shines a little brighter and the air is a little sweeter simply because there is someone to share the moment. And then, before you know it, it's time to go. A quick goodbye. ("Honey, tell your new friend goodbye. Thank them for playing with you today.") and then we disappear. Most likely, we will never see these playground friends again, but they have touched our lives and blessed us with their presence.

As we grow older, friendships change and develop naturally. We mostly move out of these hour-long friendships into relationships that are more nuanced, complex, and lasting. I minister in the same town where I went to college, so I am often transported back in time as I go about my business in our town and on the campus. It seems to me—both from mining my own memories and observing college students today—that people in their late teens and early 20s still seem to value hanging out simply for the joy of hanging out. A quick trip through the library on campus will almost always provide sightings of two friends sharing a table, both plugged into their laptops, textbooks, and earphones. But sitting there together, perhaps propping their feet on a shared chair. They periodically glance up and share a smile or slide their laptop or phone over to their friend to share something they find amusing. They could be studying alone, sure, but they'd rather be doing it together.

I can still easily remember getting together with my college friends to do . . . well . . . almost nothing. We would spend Friday night in the basement of our residence hall folding laundry or flipping through the channels on the television. We would get up on Saturday morning and eat breakfast together and then wander down to the mall to just walk around. We'd hop in the car on a Tuesday afternoon to drive out to Pillsbury Crossing—where we would stick our feet in the water, throw stones, and generally waste time.

Except none of that time was wasted. It was in the midst of all of those "doing nothing" moments that my very self was formed. Such down time was a time of critical formation. And those friends that I spent hours with are still my nearest and dearest today. They are the ones I would call if my marriage fell apart. They are the ones who would drop anything and rush to my side if my child were hospitalized. They are among the ones who will one day speak at my funeral. Those hours of simply being together were a gift. A gift that will sustain us throughout whatever life brings our way.

I'm not sure when, in my own life, my hours of doing nothing with friends started to slip away. I know it decreased significantly when I began full-time work. It seems like the real death knell was right around the time I had children. And if I'm being totally honest, I also know that part of the challenge for me is that I am often craving alone time at the end of the day. Getting together to "do nothing" with potential friends often seems like a luxury and it falls to the bottom of that long, adult to-do list that seems to have no end.

An element of this is my introversion. And, to be clear, I don't think extraversion is better than introversion. I think we actually experience a very similar tension in the time spent alone. The number of hours I spend simply being in relationship with myself and enjoying the gift of my own presence has also decreased significantly over the years. I don't think it is about introversion vs.

extraversion as much as it is about something else, something more worrisome.

Part of our difficulty doing nothing—alone or together—is that we've bought into the lie that the world tells us about the commodification of everything. We measure, we plan, and we scheme. We are always encouraged to work towards a goal. Even time spent doing nothing has to be done with a goal. Sometimes it is self-care: "Take time for you! Put on your oxygen mask so you can help someone else! Taking some down time will increase your productivity later!" Sometimes it is the goal of saving our relationships: "You have to make time for date nights. Go on a vacation with your partner. Your marriage depends on it!" or "Quality time with your children is a necessity. You have to spend that concentrated time together or they'll be in years of therapy."

We are taught that time is a precious and scarce commodity. The way we use it will make or break our lives. We give our young kids "agendas" for them to carry around in their book-bags—so they can learn to make to-do lists, schedule their assignments, and master their schedules. And adults spend all kinds of money (and time) searching for the perfect app that will magically manage their experience of time and help increase their productivity. Most people are not looking to manage their time so they can have more time to do nothing. We want to manage our time so we can DO MORE—get more work done, increase our net worth, and keep climbing that ladder.

It is only natural that this mindset extends into our relationships. Before we know it, we are treating everyone we encounter as a commodity. We are sizing them up, calculating how they can be useful to us. We look at the people who surround us and see them as a means to an end. "Is developing this relationship going to get me something I think I need? How might I leverage this relationship to get what I want?" The nice term for it is "networking." You could also call it "objectification."

While at the 2015 Festival of Homiletics in Denver, I heard Anna Carter Florence deliver a sermon on Judges 19. If that is not ringing any bells it is because Judges 19 is not a popular text for preaching or reading or ... well, just at all. It's not in the Revised Common Lectionary and unless you've recently read Phyllis Trible's *Texts of Terror*, you may have never paid any attention to it. It's the story of the unnamed Levite man and his unnamed concubine. The text is horrific, violent, misogynistic, and terrifying. This unnamed woman is abused, captured, raped and—finally—murdered. Cut apart limb by limb. You can see why it's not often tackled in a worship setting.

Carter Florence is not one to shy away from terror, though, and her sermon in Denver gave the hearers all kinds of ways to step into this ancient story and find truths for our own lives. At the core of that exercise, of course, is figuring out who our concubines are. We've all heard of sex trafficking, but most of us aren't sex traffickers. Most of us don't keep people and use them for our own sexual gratification (thanks be to God). But that doesn't mean we are off the hook. Because if we work with the definition Carter Florence gave for "concubine" as someone we use for our own purposes—outside of a covenantal relationship, without love—we quickly discover that we hold all kinds of people as concubines. We interact with people each and every day that we use for our own gratification, needs, and enjoyment. We all have our own concubines.

I felt a bit like a concubine recently. It didn't feel good. A few months ago a new business opened up just a few doors down from our church. After months of watching construction and hearing ads on the radio for this new neighbor, I noticed they were finally open for business. I walked down the street and introduced myself. I was hoping to strike up a conversation with the employees, maybe get a tour, maybe begin some new relationships. Mostly, though, it just seemed like the right thing to do to be neighborly and stop by and spend some time together. When I walked in there were two or three employees standing around, looking at computers, running from place to place, ironing out all the kinks on the first day. I said hello and explained that I was the pastor from the church a few doors down. It felt awkward. They didn't offer their names or tell me anything about their work. I asked how their first day was going and they said, "Really busy. We're slammed!" with a tone of pride. I didn't want to bother them by asking for a tour, so I saw myself out and thought I might try again once things calmed down.

About a week later, our office manager fielded a phone call from one of the staff members at the new business. They had a request: could they use our parking lot during the weekdays for their staff? I took the request to the appropriate committee at their next meeting. We wanted to support this new business because we appreciated what they were doing for the community and we wanted to be good neighbors. Unfortunately, we just didn't have enough parking to spare. We wrote them a letter explaining our rationale, sharing some ideas to help them with their problem, and wishing them the best.

Fast-forward a couple of months. The owner of the business had his secretary call our office and ask for a meeting with me. She said he wanted to "get to know me" and "build a relationship." I snarkily said to our office manager, "Ten bucks says this is about parking again." She laughed and said, "Surely not," but I had my doubts.

On the day of our meeting, the owner rushed into my office a few minutes late. He sat down, gave me the 30 second elevator pitch for his business and then started in on his request, "I handled this all wrong from the beginning. I should have come over here myself to ask you. But we desperately need that parking. I am begging for your help." It felt really awkward, having a complete stranger beg me for something I knew I couldn't even provide. I explained to him, again, that we simply didn't have the parking to give but assured him I would ask the trustees once again. I felt frustrated by the encounter. I was just a means to an end. He had no desire to "develop a relationship" or "get to know me." He just wanted access to our parking. I don't blame him for asking, but I do wish he hadn't done it under the guise of "building a relationship." Asking for something someone else has is not building a relationship. It is just asking for something you want.

The slope from networking to objectifying to concubining another human being is steep and slippery. Martin Luther King, Jr. spoke and wrote of "thingification."[1] In a nation founded upon the oppression of an entire race of human beings, where millions were enslaved and commodified and concubined and turned into objects for the service of those in control, I think we always need to be on guard against the tendency to thingify the other.

It is not possible, of course, to constantly enjoy another person's company just for the sake of enjoying our shared humanity. For starters, not everyone is enjoyable! That would simply be exhausting. There are some relationships and some interactions that are purely transactional. I think that's just how it has to be in order for us to make it through the day. But when the majority of our interactions with other human beings involve a track running in the back of our minds that's keeping tally of what this person might be worth to us, what they might do for us, or how they might help us? When that happens, it's time to take a breath, regroup, and hit the reset button.

This is one of the things I am trying to be mindful of in my ministry—both with the people in my church and the people outside the church walls. This tendency to commodify everyone around us and see them solely in terms of what they can offer us.

I've noticed that when I'm wrapping up a one-on-one conversation with parishioners they often apologize at the end of the meeting, "Well, I'm sorry I've taken up so much of your time. I'll let you get back to work now." I usually laugh a bit and say, "Well, the beauty of my life is that this actually is my work. I get to sit here and spend this time with you and it's not a waste of time at all." I often get a surprised look when I say that. But how great would it be if this wasn't a surprise? After all, we claim that we were created by a God who lives in relationship ... with the Earth, with all the creatures that share the planet, and with each of us. Our stories of Creation assure us that God created us and called us "good"—even before we had done a single thing to earn any accolades. We are "good" simply because we exist ... and God desires to be in relationship with us and desires for us to be in authentic relationship with one another.

What if we could all find ways to cultivate the art of "doing nothing" together? What if we could remember those lessons my church has been teaching me since before I came here? That there is Enough time to spend it with each other. To slow down. To spend time together simply for the sake of spending time together. To see the business of "getting to know each other" as important and a valid use of our precious time and energy. What a gift we could be to each other. What a gift we could be to the world.

Chapter 9

Creating Sacred Space for Those Experiencing Trauma

Rev. Dr. Andrew Hart

One Sunday after worship I was sitting on the sofa at the parsonage, when a member of the church ran over to the house panicked because an unknown person had come to the church looking for "a person of God." Returning to the church, I met a man who was probably in his late 50s or 60s. He would not look at me or go inside the church, and would not identify himself. His tattoos suggested that he was in the military; likely Army or Marines. We struck up a conversation and it became clear that he was wrestling with Post Traumatic Stress Disorder (PTSD). Sadly, he told me that no one from any church would help him or even talk with him; they would simply ask that he leave.

Months before this encounter, I was giving a talk about PTSD to a small group in Huntington, NY. Ten minutes into the presentation, a very thin woman walked in, wearing a dark trench coat, with a look of being very distant. She fidgeted more than a small child and I noticed that she was constantly scanning the room, especially the exits. When I asked for questions, she raised her hand, remarked that she was suffering from PTSD, thanked me, and ran out of the room.

Trauma can be invisible in many ways; we never know when we might encounter it, especially as it relates to churches. Often the existence of trauma is unexpectedly in our congregations and communities, including stories of war, rape, childhood beatings, and more. There are many people in our pews who have suffered from some sort of trauma. In fact, according to the CDC, one in five

Americans was sexually molested as a child, one in four were beaten
by a parent so bad that a mark was left on the body, and one out
of eight children witnessed their mother being hit.[1] Added to these
statistics is a large number of veterans who returned home from
war with the stigma of trauma and PTSD. What can we Christians,
both clergy and lay people, do for those who have encountered such
trauma? Is there a habit or practice that we can employ as we listen
to and journey with trauma victims?

The Habit of Sacred Space

Those who have experienced trauma, like persons from all walks
of life, often come looking for help in spiritual spaces. Of course,
trauma victims are not only those outside our churches; every
congregation has at least one person who has experienced trauma in
their lifetime. Yet clergy and their congregations are not therapists,
and neither are they trauma experts. They are, however, witnesses
to a healing Balm for scars and to a welcoming Presence of love. It
is my contention that one habit we must form in local churches is
the practice of creating safe and sacred space for those who have
experienced trauma.

For this habit, my guiding biblical story has always been Jesus
washing the feet of his disciples. In this spiritual act, Jesus does two
things: 1) he creates sacred space to acknowledge the hurt in another
person, and 2) he uses water to express the love of God in someone's
life. After Jesus gets up from this act of service, he tells the disciples
to go and wash the feet of other people, other people who likewise
need an acknowledgment of their hurt, other people who likewise
need the cascading water of God's love. Those who have experienced
trauma are such people the disciples were commanded to serve, in
need of listening and love. The act of washing their feet, whether
literal or figurative, provides a radically different narrative from
their trauma, a new narrative of hope. Because trauma can cause

isolation, creating sacred space by listening and loving imitates Jesus' act of washing another's feet and offers community rather than isolation, hope rather than despair. Before we can talk about the role of the church in creating sacred space for the trauma victim, we need to get a proper hold on a definition of trauma.

What is Trauma?

Trauma is an emotional or psychological response to a traumatic event in someone's life. There are many different events that cause trauma, some visible and many invisible or hidden. I am most familiar with two types of traumatic events: childhood beatings and war. As a child, I was beaten severely by my mother. As an adult, I worked as a chaplain for the United States Air Force Auxiliary (Civil Air Patrol). Working closely with many in the military, I came into contact regularly with those suffering with PTSD, such as the person who once, gripped my arm so strongly that it reminded me of wrestling with my friends in high school, and said, "Chap (Chaplain), we need help."

According to Judith Herman, a leading expert in the field, trauma is "when an event overwhelms the ordinary system of care or adaptation that give people a sense of control, connection, and meaning."[2] It is not just those who are physically and emotionally injured who are trauma victims, but also those who witness an overwhelming event that can suffer the psychological effects of trauma. For example, in New York City on September 11, 2001, it was not just those who were injured when the towers came down, it was also those who saw them fall, in person or even on television, who were traumatized.

Not necessarily everyone who experiences or witnesses a trauma will suffer any psychological effects from it. According to author Bessel Van der Kolk, "most people who have been exposed to traumatic stressors are somehow able to go on with their lives without becoming haunted by the memories of what happened."[3] Researchers are looking into the reasons explaining why some people suffer long term effects of trauma and some do not. Even among those who experience the effects of trauma, there can be different reactions such as "depression, phobias, and pathological grief."[4] For example, in one of the churches I served, there was a woman who came to me suffering from depression. She wrestled with depression her entire life, and discussion revealed she had been severely beaten by her mother. Her depression was likely one reaction to the trauma of being beaten.

For people involved in combat, whether on the battlefield or in a street attack (such as mugging), it is possible that they may suffer from a reaction called Combat Stress Reaction (CSR). Signs of CSR include "restlessness, irritability, apathy, depression, vomiting, aggressiveness, hostility, and confusion."[5] Perhaps the most well known reaction to trauma is Post Traumatic Stress Disorder (PTSD), a reaction often connected to the trauma of military combat and often portrayed in movies like American Sniper. Author James Meuer wrote, "It's like carrying around a glass jar filled with all the memories, dreams, faces, and fears. Every so often the lid gets loose and some stuff leaks out."[6]

Symptoms of PTSD include hyper-arousal, intrusion, social avoidance, and shattered meaning propositions.[7] In hyper-arousal, "the human system of self-preservation seems to go into permanent alert, as if danger might return at any moment."[8] Intrusion is the reliving of a traumatic event "as though it were continually recurring in the present."[9] Social avoidance is the limited attachment and severe avoidance of relationships or even interpersonal encounters.

Some who struggle with trauma find everyday stimuli to be triggering, which can unexpectedly and instantaneously shatter a person's sense of space and safety. While I was at home one evening on a Memorial Day, for example, I heard the sound of firecrackers coming from some folks down the street at 10pm. Imagine being a veteran with PTSD living nearby! Fortunately there are organizations that sell signs stating please do not launch fireworks and letting people know that a combat veteran lives nearby. We must always be aware of the spaces we are creating, both in the church and in society, so that triggers do not cause the problem to be made worse. So now, having defined trauma and coming into awareness of its effects, how do we embody a habit of creating and practicing the type of sacred space that offers healing?

Sacred Space Begins with Awareness

Sacred space is not simply something to be created in a vacuum; it is created through awareness. One critical piece of learning received from the Gospels is that Jesus was very aware of the people that he was ministering to. From the Samaritan woman at the well to the disciples afraid in their boat on a stormy lake, to his stopping to care for someone in the crowd who had a physical ailment, Jesus was continually aware of those around him.

Awareness is a critical element for ministry with people who have suffered trauma. No two people experience trauma in the same way, not every veteran is the same, not every survivor of abuse is the same and so we must, like Jesus, be aware of each trauma victim as an individual. Also important is an awareness of different demographic factors that impact someone's experience of and reactions to trauma. For example, take a veteran who was in World War II, part of the greatest generation, who is now suffering from PTSD. It is likely that this veteran is not going to talk about his experience because of the way that generation responds through silence; the veteran is likely to be in church and to rely on the church for support and comfort. On the other hand, a twenty-five year old veteran who served in Afghanistan and also experiences PTSD is probably more willing to talk about the PTSD and may actively seek help in other places. It is unlikely that this younger veteran will seek comfort from the church; however it is very likely that they will turn to their sense of spirituality, perhaps as a part of the millennial "spiritual, but not religious" crowd.

Given the importance of awareness, the church must answer the call to create sacred space that is listening and loving, where veterans and other trauma victims can be welcomed as they are. In my experience, ministry with those experiencing PTSD has occurred most often beyond the church, perhaps on the basketball court or at a funeral, and through the power of awareness I was able to create sacred space.

Because sacred space can be offered anywhere at any time, we can draw from the well of creativity to find unique ways to be in ministry. Our listening is not limited by a certain place and the balm of God's comfort is not restricted to the church. Our awareness of each person and our willingness to provide creative sacred spaces can lead to some amazing ministry opportunities. After all, we do not need to possess answers or healing ourselves; simply our awareness can be like the gift of water to a runner during a race. Having spent time in awareness with the veteran who showed up at church in the opening of this chapter, I am certain that taking on the habit of creating sacred space can heal. After some discussion with the veteran, I prayed with him and then provided a Bible, suggesting he read the Psalms in all of their honesty and brokenness before God. He broke down crying, saying that no church had treated or cared for him like this before. This is what it means to create sacred space.

Creating Sacred Space

It is clear to me that once we have developed relationships with people who have experienced trauma, it is our creativity in cultivating sacred space that can lead to opportunities for healing and connection with others in the community. The three sacred spaces I know and recommend are not the only examples, of course, but I have seen them be a space of healing for people who need it. Three sacred spaces that we as the Church can offer are yoga, rituals, and small groups.

Yoga: Yoga is an excellent method for helping someone deal with trauma. In a recent book,[10] Bessel A. van der Kolk, a leading expert on trauma, makes the argument that practices like yoga can greatly assist someone with trauma because yoga leads to better self-awareness, as well as regulation of emotion.[11] In my conversations with veterans, it is clear that yoga does help. In fact, author and fellow veteran Brian Castner affirms this assumption as he says, "It holds the symmetry and release I crave."[12] He continues, "I am Warrior (a yoga pose) and my crazy (a reference to PTSD) has melted under the radiant vinyasa."[13] Churches can provide yoga classes at discounted rates to trauma victims and veterans, which is a visible way to create sacred space for people to heal.

Ritual: Another act of the Church that helps with trauma is ritual. Jesus blessed us with the two rituals of baptism and communion, indicating the importance of ritual in spirituality as acts that provide familiar, repeated assurance of God's presence and that affirm a sense of community. Soldiers have shared stories of rituals performed when they are deployed such as a group placing their hands on top of each other and praying before a mission, or making the sign of a cross over a Humvee. This is why David Hogue reflects, "rituals are critical to healing and transformation."[14]

One service that I have used over the years comes from the Presbyterian Church's (USA) Book of Common Worship and is entitled Service for Wholeness—Congregation. Within this service, there is a ritual of anointing someone's forehead with oil. This age-old practice is helpful in reminding people of the healing balm of God's love as we struggle with our ailments whether they are physical or emotional. At the end of the service we gather together at the front of the church, form a circle, hold hands and pray The Lord's Prayer together. Many other rituals can also be used, such as rosary beads for those from the Catholic and Anglican traditions, but no matter the religious tradition, ritual is an important aspect of recovery.

Small Groups: Some churches may feel called to establish small groups for trauma victims. St. Paul reminds us in his letters that when "one member suffers, all suffer together with it; if one member is honored, all rejoice together with it. (1 Corinthians 12:26)." Clearly as part of the body of Christ we are called to support each other, and this support can take the form of a small group that creates sacred space together. Small groups can be a place for trauma victims to get together and talk about their experiences in safety, which is especially critical for someone suffering from PTSD. In my experience, it is imperative that veterans or survivors of trauma lead the group, as veterans in particular tend to respond better to invitations from other veterans, as opposed to folks who have no experience of military culture. A model like that of Alcoholics Anonymous, Narcotics Anonymous, or Overeaters Anonymous can be helpful so that the small group's feeling is warm, open, and non-judgmental. However, if the group's plan includes or desires actual counseling, then a licensed therapist who deals with trauma should be present for the meetings.

Conclusion

It is entirely likely that what is needed among trauma victims will emerge on its own as we create sacred spaces and practice awareness in our encounters with all people. The creativity involved in this work assumes that, with each group of people, with each individual, a new way of responding may be necessary and we may need to adjust our habits of ministry, learning to wash one another's feet in new expressions of service and healing. Because I believe in the power of the Holy Spirit at work in the world, I have no doubt that the Church can and will rise to the challenge of creating sacred space for those who have experienced trauma. It might be yoga, rituals, small groups, or something altogether creatively different, but we are capable of addressing this challenge in our world.

The hope of the Gospel can move mountains among those who feel pushed down and create community for those who are isolated. Come, let us work alongside the Great Healer, for those who have experienced trauma are in our pews, in our families, and in our communities. God does not leave trauma victims alone and neither should we.

Notes

1. Besser A. Van der Kolk, *The Body Keeps the Score* (New York: Viking, 2014), 1.

2. Judith Herman, *Trauma and Recovery* (New York: Basic, 1992), 33.

3. Van der Kolk. *A Traumatic Stress* (New York: Guilford, 1996), 5.

4. Ibid., 94.

5. Ibid., 104.

6. James Muerer, *Damaged* (New York: Westbow, 2013), 20.

7. Judith Herman, *Trauma and Recovery* (New York: Basic, 1992), 12.

8. Ibid., 35.

9. Ibid., 35.

10. Van der Kolk,

11. Ibid., 63.

12. Brian Castner, *The Long Walk* (New York: Anchor, 2012), 158.

13. Ibid., 80.

14. David Hogue, *Remembering the Future, Imagining the Past: Story, Ritual and the Human Brain* (Eugene: Wipf and Stock, 2003), 120.

Chapter 10

A Table by the Window
Public Office Hours as a Central View into
Contextual Ministry

Rev. Zayna H. Thompson

My very first day in parish ministry was a Wednesday. Wednesday October 16, 2013, to be exact. I remember because I have carried out the exact same routine every Wednesday since. After a morning spent in what I consider my introvert-haven, also known as a home office, I girded my loins and stepped into the center of the public square: a locally owned, centrally located coffee shop, for what I had advertised to my new congregation as "public office hours." Settling at a table in the back promptly at two in the afternoon, I pulled out my calendar and commentaries and began planning worship for the coming weeks. I had every intention of staying until five. I had little expectation anyone would take up my invitation to stop in and introduce themselves. Pleasantly surprised, I was visited by three members of the search committee that had recently called me, an older retired couple out running errands for the afternoon, and a stay at home mother who brought in her youngest son just to say "hello" and drop off a welcome gift. When I stepped into the pulpit on my first Sunday, there was already a sense of familiarity from the faces that stared back.

The second week went much like the first. Folks trickled in, stopping for a quick cup of coffee and a hello. The third week was when I met Will. Will was a native to our small town, but new to the church. His first Sunday visiting was my first Sunday preaching. Will, who found me at the back table amidst the after-school crowd, is an older man with dementia and a life-long learning disability. I had remembered him from worship and as I looked up and caught his eye, it dawned on me that his smile must be permanently plastered across his face. The fourth week I arrived to find Will was already at the coffee shop, sitting at a small table elevated by the platform in the front window. He waved emphatically through the glass as I approached the front door. As it turns out, Will was appalled by my seat at the back of the shop the week before. "You're the pastor! How can anyone see you if you are way back there? I just can't stand the idea of that, Reverend. I just can't stand it." He has been saving me that table, the one up front, right in the window, ever since. This is Will's ministry.

I wish I could claim the creative idea of public office hours as my own, but as many new innovations are, this was shamelessly stolen. While attending an urban seminary I watched as several of my colleagues were awarded internships at one of those new almost-non-denominational congregations that managed to worship without a building, deploying ministers into the world where God's people actually lived. They met with their overwhelmingly millennial members at Starbucks, or whichever generic Irish pub occupied the corner closest to their home. They held staff meetings in city parks and worshiped in conference rooms regularly found empty on non-business days. And while I had little interest in urban ministry, this practice was fascinating.

Little has changed in my two years of practicing public office hours. From the beginning I made this block of time a priority, hoping to establish a consistent presence in the community square: every Wednesday from two until five in the afternoon. I'm always at the same spot: that small coffee shop serving as a cross section of our diverse community. This is a sacred time and place in my weekly schedule. I'm committed to making my presence as reliable as possible. Of course, I still take vacations and advertise when I'll be absent, but most likely, if it is Wednesday, my congregation knows their pastor is available to talk. The number of visitors varies from week to week. While it is not unheard of, I rarely spend three hours alone. I average between two and five individuals each week. And each person who comes to see me comes for a different reason. Public office hours are for no one thing.

Roger comes to talk business. He serves on our governing board and is a faithful servant in all things financial. Last year he took on the challenge of creating a colorful, clearly articulated narrative budget, outlining the missional use of our annual funds. On the side of this major project, he works a full time job and is the proud father of three young boys. He is a prime example of this generation's working parents. I stand in awe when Roger and his wife are able to synchronize their five schedules filled with sports, parent meetings, play dates and family outings often enough to also be active participants in our church life. For Roger, public office hours create flexibility for meetings. It means he doesn't necessarily need to plan ahead and if he finds himself free, he always knows I'm available to touch base on font choices, pie graph colors, or theological language.

Melanie first came to see me in the depths of winter, and in the depths of her own doubts. She had walked away from the church over a year before, and had since struggled with what to do with her lingering questions of faith, spirituality, and suffering. She brought her family to worship every once in a while, but it was clear that she was still searching. What is a modern woman to do with these questions? She knew all the "answers" church had given her in the past. And she knew the answers were simply not working for her anymore. I received a one-line email earlier in the day: Can I see you at the coffee shop this afternoon? Melanie needed a place to hold her questions and she needed that place to be away from church, and I would venture to guess she needed that place to be away from the authority of the pastoral office.

Jane came in once with claims of just stopping by. She told me she was downtown running errands and saw me sitting in the window. I bought her a cup of coffee and she spent a good twenty minutes catching me up on her grandkids and the novel they were reading in book club. And then she grew quiet. And then she confessed. She confessed she wasn't out running errands but had just come from a support group for families of people suffering from Alzheimer's and apparent dementia. She had just gotten up the courage to go to this support group and now she was working up the courage to go back home. We sat quietly for a moment, and then she pulled out pictures of the puppy her grandson had just adopted. For Jane, that place in the window was a sanctuary. It was holy ground standing between the care she needed to give herself and the care she needed to give her husband. It was a chance to breathe.

Then there are the dozens of community members I see coming and going, stopping in for their afternoon caffeine fix. Sitting in my window, I see students, teachers, city workers, retirees and business people stopping by or staying for a meeting or to catch up with a friend. I see book studies and first dates. My habit is to sit and watch. Jesus had a thing or two to say about paying attention to the comings and goings on around our ministries. Speaking of God's coming promise, he warns for the necessity of watchfulness:

> But about that day and hour no one knows . . . . For as in those days before the flood they were eating and drinking, marrying and giving in marriage, until the day Noah entered the ark, and they knew nothing until the flood came and swept them all away . . . . Keep awake therefore, for you do not know on what day your Lord is coming. (Matthew 24: 36-39a, 42)

Progressive Christianity calls followers of Jesus to join in kingdom-building through community-building, working for justice, and speaking the truth about God's inclusive love. We never know when the opportunity to join this work will present itself. The temptation to spend our days eating at the women's fellowship potluck, planning weddings and funerals, organizing capital campaigns and rally day parties might easily distract us from the world God is building right around us. The business of everyday ministry, I'm afraid more often than not, blocks our view of God's people living and walking right around us. What better place to keep watch than in a front window in the center of town?

My keeping watch in that front window brought me a sacred encounter one winter. It was the coldest day of the year, the first winter I moved back to Wisconsin when I met Leon. I was only thirty minutes into my public office hours when a disheveled man, clearly underdressed for the brutal weather, came into the coffee shop asking for the pastor who hung out here. I introduced myself, bought him a hot chocolate and invited him to sit down. Leon had gone to my office just a few blocks away prior to this encounter and was told where he could find me. Later, when I spoke with my secretary, I came to learn that our church was actually his fourth stop that day. The first three churches did exactly what I would have had I encountered Leon at my office. They brought him in, they attempted to listen to his story and after not getting anywhere, they handed him a few bucks, wrote him off as another transient passing through on the bus line between major cities, and sent him on his way.

I, on the other hand, was trapped by my commitment to public office hours for at least another two hours. And so I listened. I sipped my freshly brewed peppermint tea as another layer of fresh snow fell just outside the window and I listened. And in those two hours I heard the story of an honest, genuine, but broken man, crippled by hunger and anxiety searching for someone, anyone, to hear his story and to respond. I don't blame my colleagues for not hearing Leon. He was hard to hear. He talked in circles, several circles that never quite connected. I asked him where he was coming from. I asked where he was trying to go. I asked what he needed from the church. He wasn't able to give an exact answer to any of these questions. Instead he would talk nonsensically about planetariums, and Paul's travels to Berea in the New Testament, and the Quad Cities and Aunt June who had sent him a birthday card six months ago. It was exhaustive and exhausting. Finally, he said something that made sense to me. The conversation went something like this:

Leon: "Have you ever been to Alaska?"

Me: "No, but I'd love to go someday!"

Leon: "You don't say? Well, I imagine my current situation is comparable to being in Alaska."

Me: "Well, it is cold out there!"

Leon: "I have never been to Alaska, so I have no idea how cold it is. I don't know anything about Alaska. I can't imagine it. Going to Alaska would be like going to Mars or even Jupiter. If I go to Alaska, I might as well go to another planet. No, Alaska is completely foreign to me. I'd be paralyzed."

Me: "And you feel like you are in Alaska now?"

Leon: "Yes."

It took 143 minutes of listening for me to hear Leon tell me he was lost. His speech was so discombobulated by fear and anxiety it took 143 minutes for him to connect that circle. We took Leon in that night, and I contacted the other congregations in town.

We put him up in a hotel and arranged for a warm dinner. With every good night's rest and balanced meal Leon looked more alive. By the third day he was able to tell me the story of how his father had died the year before, how his step siblings had gotten most of the inheritance, how he was traveling to see the keeper of his trust in hopes of moving somewhere he could escape the anxiety of the group home he came from. He told me that when he arrived in our town, he didn't know where his next meal would come from and when he has to worry about where he will find his next meal he finds it impossible to find housing. And when he doesn't know where he will sleep one night, he certainly can't be bothered to figure out where he will sleep for the next week. It all became too much and when he walked into that coffee shop, his body, mind and soul had been completely overrun by anxiety.

Slowly, day by day, as Leon was able to gain control over his most basic necessities, he seemed to come to life right before my eyes. By the fifth day, through the veil of his anxiety, I came to know Leon as one of the most intelligent, sensitive, and kind men I have ever met. Leon is no longer in Alaska, in fact he settled in the next town over. I am glad to call him friend.

I often wonder if I had been in my office that day, if I had limited my time with Leon to the twenty minutes I had free between administrative duties, would I have missed this resurrection miracle? Would I have missed the chance to not just witness it, but join in?

Every once in a while a church member will ask, "Now, what exactly do you do down there on Wednesday afternoons?" I usually tell them that I just "hang out, and wait for whoever comes by." I'm not sure I could fully convey what all is present in those three hours a week. Those three hours are for study, marriage counseling, fellowship and laughter. They are for check-ins and committee meetings. They are for evangelism and church growth. They are for keeping watch, for being sure I don't miss Jesus or Leon passing through. Whatever God uses this time for, you can be sure that next Wednesday I'll be at the table by the window promptly at two. You can also be sure Will has probably been there since noon.

Chapter 11

Real Presence: Clergy and Community in the Age of Social Media

Rev. Elizabeth Dilley

"I don't understand *why* you need to go," my husband said on that humid day, "but I do understand that you need to go." It was May, and I had just explained to him that I was taking two days off from work to drive five hours to attend the funeral of a man I'd never met, all to support his widow, a woman I'd be meeting for the first time at the visitation. And yet, these people were not strangers to me. How could they be, when I had walked with their family through the ravages of cancer that left my friend a widow before she was forty, with four children under the age of four? How could I say that I did not know this woman, when for years we had checked in with one another at least every few days, commiserating over politics and parenting?

Community is a holy gift. We think that we are choosing it, by selecting neighborhoods we like, congregations where we find a "fit," the perfect schools for our children (itself a complex matrix of decisions that reflect broad values about education balanced with individual needs), and gyms where we exercise. We think we are choosing these things freely, but in the choosing, we find ourselves bound to crazy strangers and beloved pilgrims, steeped in traditions of various longevities, and intertwined in one another's stories. We find ourselves caring about the old man who always rides the recumbent bicycle for far too long in the morning, perhaps even daring to ask the Y staff about him if he's been gone awhile. We find ourselves connected to strangers, who have become beloved sojourners.

All of this is by Divine creation. We do not choose a community, but the Spirit guides us into community. From the very beginning of creation, God spoke of a Divine relational "Us," not of a solitary heavenly existence. "Let us make humankind in our image," the book of Genesis says, and from this moment, we begin to see not only the relationality of God, but also the special relationship that God and humankind share. From Genesis to Revelation, the Bible speaks of God in relationship with humanity, and of humanity in relationship with God and with one another.

What we often see is the struggle for these relationships to find order in ways that are harmonious and life-giving. Wars, genocides, rape and murder all shape the experience of people living together on this planet, with denial and rejection of the Holy as being far more the norm than the exception. We may have been made and shaped for community, but it is seldom easy.

For most of the 2000s, I served a theologically (and politically) progressive church in a theologically (and politically) conservative part of rural Iowa, and the vast majority of the people who shared my political beliefs were my parishioners. It was rewarding, but also isolating as a politically progressive Christian. Community was often difficult as I struggled to pastor with integrity and maintain appropriate boundaries with parishioners. In the years following the 2004 elections, I yearned to know how others struggled through the deep political depression I was experiencing. I wondered how to organize and shape the future in healthy, holistic ways that reflected my progressive values. I found myself languishing for a community in which I could simply be a part, rather than the leader. I also wanted to know how to do this as a parent, which I deeply longed to become.

At just the right time, I came across a web community for politically progressive parents. Politics and Parenting1 is mostly comprised of moms, all of whom felt gutted by the 2004 national elections and were galvanized to make a difference in 2008. There were a few dads and a few who, like me, were not yet parents but wanted to be a part of a community of like-minded adults raising compassionate children.

I lurked for several months, reading posts regularly but not posting anything about myself or the topics at hand. I wasn't sure if I belonged. I wasn't sure how the group would welcome a non-parent who really wanted to learn how to live as a politically engaged, progressive sort of mama in the midst of pretty polarizing parenting "camps" in the community where I lived. Finally, however, I shared a bit about my life on an introductory post, and found that this group of politically active, generous-hearted women welcomed me joyfully.

Over the years, we argued over Democratic presidential nominees, celebrated or lamented our state governors and assembly leaders, welcomed new babies, sent love and prayers to hospitalized children, and found ourselves heart-deep in community that only deepened as we migrated from our own website to a secret Facebook group. Some days we just gossiped about celebrities, or shared perspectives on different parenting issues we were experiencing.

One of the core values of Politics and Parenting is, "Do what works for you." Some of us came to parenting by adoption, others by accident, still others by plan. Some of us are Bradley parents, some of us gratefully used medical interventions in childbirth, some of us had little choice in how the births took place. So, some of us breastfed and some of us formula fed. Some of us use birth control, some of us hate it. Some of us work outside the home, some of us work from home, some of us make parenting our sole work. Some of us send our kids to private schools, some to public, and some participate in homeschooling. Some of us are married (to men or women), some of us co-parent with an ex, some of us are single by choice or circumstance (some of us fit into more than one category here). Some of us have blended families. We have mamas of singletons to mamas of seven, with the ages of kids ranging from newborn to in their thirties.

Most days, Politics and Parenting is the closest thing I experience to church—the good and the bad. We are bound by core values that shape our life together, including a commitment to that diverse understanding of what constitutes "good parenting choices." We check in regularly with one another, especially if someone has dropped off the radar recently. We have a common fund we use to spread "sunshine" when someone needs it. When we argue, it can get ugly, causing people to leave either permanently or for a season. We are pretty racially homogenous, although our children are less so (and the few grandchildren even less so). Our inside jokes are comprehensive enough to require a lexicon that is constantly being updated. We don't actively evangelize; a certain possessiveness leads many of us to proudly declare this is our space and we aren't sharing it.

Like all communities, Politics and Parenting requires love, genuine affection for each other and our quirks, a willingness to stick it out through the tough times, and a commitment to the values that have shaped us over time. We have cultivated a place where we do not claim to have all the answers, but we are committed to asking good questions, keeping each other accountable, and supporting one another. We are vulnerable, and we hold each other's vulnerability with tender and sometimes rough hands. We rage, we weep, we celebrate, we apologize, we forgive.

And while I experience this as holy space, I hesitate to actually call it "church." We are not all religious, for one thing, and not all of us who are religious are Christian. The atheist moms are some of the best at cultivating values of wonder, awe, inquiry, and mutual respect. Knowing the ways that Christianity occupies such a privileged place in our nation, I feel I would dishonor the non-Christians among us by calling this place "church." I do call it community, in the deepest sense of the word.

What is most odd to outsiders is that this community occurs almost exclusively online. Politics and Parenting began as an offshoot of a politically progressive online space, and over time it migrated into a closed Facebook group. Unlike many of my other friends from social media, where our digital encounters supplement our in-person relationships (whether from high school, college, or among colleagues), the real friendship among my community at Politics and Parenting primarily exists digitally, only occasionally being supplemented by in-person visits among a few of us at a time.

The habits that cultivate digital community are surprisingly common to the ways that one would participate in an in-person community. The most important is showing up. Someone always posts a daily "open thread" to get a conversation started, but there's never a requirement to stay on topic. We start our own conversations related to the core values that have drawn us together (politics and parenting), and we show everyone pictures of our kids on the first day of school. When someone is experiencing a crisis—a painful divorce, a difficult pregnancy, frustrating in-laws, health diagnoses, job changes—those who have "been there" share their wisdom and act as a sounding board for the one in crisis.

We also have the habit of checking in with one another. Some recent arguments have left some of us feeling bruised, and a few folk stepped away for a time. Some of us stayed in touch, and those regular check-ins helped those folk to know their pain had been heard, so that when they returned, it was to joy and reconciliation.

I've heard people say that online community is not real community, but after all that I've experienced in Politics and Parenting, I can't imagine anything more real. When we do meet in person, most of us describe it not as "meeting" as if for the first time, but "finally seeing each other in person." We are indeed old friends.

A particular joy for me is that I provide no role in shepherding this group, other than through my active participation. It is an enormous relief to me and a gift from this community that I am not primarily responsible for how the group continues to be shaped and changed, nor for calling out destructive behaviors. As a member of the group, I do share a stake in this work, but it does not depend on my leadership to have it happen. I am free to bring my full self to these parents, to reveal my personal and private self to them, and to receive with vulnerability their wisdom, counsel, and love.

I've come to believe that every clergyperson needs a space where they can be present as a not-leader, and to cultivate an active presence in such spaces through our daily and weekly habits of presence and care. We are called to be full persons with a life beyond our vocation as clergy, and we need space that is "ours" without it being "our responsibility." More than ever, technology, the internet, and social media offer clergy a chance to experience such authentic community without expectations of leadership. Some might suggest that community in such a context is not truly community, but I have found the complexity of community quite naturally embraces diverse mediums for healthy relationships.

I am a strong advocate for clergy peer support and learning groups such as communities of practice where clergy can both deepen our spiritual practices as we grow in the craft and practice of ministry. I am also a strong advocate for community where we can bring not our ministerial presence, but our full, vulnerable selves to receive love and care. The Church benefits from my participation in Politics and Parenting, because that is a place where I can share my vulnerabilities and receive the deep care of friends. It is a place where my needs for community and care can be met in ways that would be inappropriate for me to seek in my congregation or other ministry settings. By cultivating an active and honest presence in this community, I am continually refreshed for my ministry.

To be honest, this group also helps me see the ways that human dynamics and group function or dysfunction are not limited to religious communities. I am able to practice other ways of self-differentiated behavior in the group and test the effectiveness of these strategies. When successful, I can creatively apply what I've learned in this space into my leadership in ministry.

I joined Politics and Parenting because I wanted to be a better parent to my (then-future) children. What I've learned is that I am a better Christian and a better minister by the creative habit of friendship and care that I experience through my participation in a community that has not called me as its leader, a community that is facilitated, in this case, entirely through technology and social media. While I am never "free" of my obligations as an ordained clergyperson, my role in that space is not primarily one of chaplain. When I take on that role, it is by mutual request and assent, and only for a short time.

Which takes me back to that May afternoon in 2013, when an old friend I'd never met was preparing to meet hundreds of family, friends and strangers as they paid their respects to a husband and father gone too soon. I would not have done this for just anyone. But this woman was not just anyone. She was the mom who helped create a book of stories, pictures, and advice for our family as we prepared to welcome our first child. She was the mom whose faith and love provided me with an example of what it meant to parent in accordance with one's Christian values. She was the mom who, as a church musician, "got" my work better than any of the other parents.

What can you do in such a time? Well, you can point your car east, bearing the love of the Politics and Parenting collective, a sack of doorknobs (an inside joke) to swing at anyone who told our friend she was grieving wrong, and your own flesh to offer in embrace and lamentation.

Because sometimes, real presence looks like a physical body. And as a Christian, sometimes I just need to offer my physical body to those I love.

Chapter 12

Synergy in Ministry: Pastoral Excellence Groups as a Catalyst for Creative Transformation

Rev. Dr. Bruce G. Epperly

Susan was a fountain of creative possibilities for congregational growth and transformation.[1] Good ideas came easily to her and she wanted to act on them without delay. She regularly shared her insights and program ideas with her church leadership and outreach teams. Her congregational leaders nodded their heads, affirmed her creativity and commitment, but seldom did anything to implement her innovative projects. Susan felt like she was alone in ministry and was growing increasingly frustrated by her congregation's failure to respond to her creative ideas. She planned to chide her congregation's leaders for their apparent apathy at the next board meeting.

The day before the board meeting, Susan attended a gathering of new pastors, sponsored by Lancaster Theological Seminary's "Wholeness in Ministry" program, aimed at helping new pastors make the transition from seminary to their first congregational call. She shared her story and after a few minutes of silence, her colleagues in ministry began to ask questions about her approach to congregational leadership. Their queries included: "Do you have a team of creative thinkers from the church with whom you regularly meet? Do you think your initiatives fit the congregation you are currently serving? Do you ever solicit ideas from your members? If not, what possibilities might better suit your particular congregation's history, demographics, traditions, theology, and energy level?"

Susan left the ministers' gathering with new insights on her leadership style as well as a more realistic sense of her congregation's openness to change. She also identified a handful of persons who might be companions in transforming the church. Susan left the gathering recognizing that pastoral creativity is a communal process and not just the result of a pastor's solitary imagination and initiative.

A few weeks later, Susan e-mailed me with positive news. She identified a few "congregational creatives," who were steeped in the traditions of the congregation but also excited about new ways of doing ministry. Together they crafted a menu of possibilities in the areas of faith formation, outreach, and mission and gathered a larger team to help implement them. Susan discovered that imaginative and creative ministry is most effective when it emerges from an ongoing dialogue with the congregation as well as insights from supportive colleagues in similar congregational settings.

Susan's story could be repeated scores of times in colleague group gatherings, sponsored by Lancaster Theological Seminary, as well as many local and regional denominational ministerial groups.[2] It takes a village to inspire ministerial creativity. While pastoral ministry, especially in small towns and rural areas, is often a solitary enterprise, ministers can test new ideas and discover new perspectives on ministry as a result of participation in intentional clergy groups.

Theology of Ministerial Small Groups

Healthy and creative ministry joins theology and practice. Our beliefs about God, the world, human existence, and our ministerial vocations shape our pastoral practices. Conversely, our pastoral practices test and transform our theological affirmations, whether these involve the nature of divinity or our vocation as pastors.

Our theology of ministry can influence our creativity in ministry and our willingness to take on partners in imagining new possibilities for our congregational and professional life. As we reflect on our understanding of ministry, do we see ourselves as isolated individuals, whose success depends entirely on our own efforts? Or, do we understand our ministries as part of a dynamic web of relationships, in which pastoral excellence emerges from the interplay of personal creativity and community support? Do we embody our theology of ministry and relationships in our day to day practice of ministry?

It goes without saying that ministry, especially solo ministry, often promotes a sense of isolation. Much of our work is done in the privacy of our studies with little or no initial input from others. On their own with few ministerial colleagues and modest administrative support, pastors are tempted to become "lone rangers," accountable only to themselves in terms of their programmatic initiatives and theological reflection. Solitary pastors seldom consult others regarding their ministerial foci or the quality of their preaching, teaching, leadership, and pastoral care. This is especially true for small town liberal and progressive pastors, who may find themselves surrounded by more conservative colleagues and congregants, with whom they have virtually no spiritual or theological common ground.

Many pastors resonate to a statement made by Julia, a single pastor of a Lutheran Church in a Central Pennsylvania village, an hour's drive from Harrisburg. She confesses that "I'm on my own out here. I don't have anyone to talk with and feel that I just have to make it up as I go along. I feel the pressure to succeed in a difficult congregational and community context, and work night and day with modest results. I'm never quite sure I'm doing it right." After joining a ministerial excellence group, Julia was able to affirm, "I feel more connected now and much less guilty about my struggles in ministry. I'm letting go of my feelings of failure. I've come to realize that my church is not unique in its challenges and responses to issues of stewardship, denominational identity, and change. I've been able to test my innovative ideas with other pastors, get their input, and avoid some pitfalls on the way. Knowing that I'm not alone, and that I have colleagues who share my journey gives me hope."

Tom, a Western Maryland United Church of Christ pastor, most of whose congregants get their information on Fox News, added, "My colleague group has shown me how to share a more progressive message in ways with which my congregants can resonate. I have learned from the group that I can affirm my concern for justice and belief that God is still speaking in ways that connect rather than alienate me in terms of the congregation." He added, "My colleagues' experiences have helped me in translating my ideas in ways the congregation will understand. They've kept me from burning bridges that would have alienated me from more conservative members and diminished my effectiveness as a pastor."

Healthy and creative theology is synergetic in nature. It is grounded in the grace of interdependence and the reality that our lives emerge moment by moment from a dynamic network of relationships. Ministerial creativity involves the synthesis of many factors in the context of our particular pastoral context. None of us is successful or creative on our own. Our achievements result from our response to persons around us, our sensitivity to God's presence in our particular congregation and community, and our willingness to listen to the divine call in our personal and professional life. Colleague groups play an essential part in revealing how we can best respond to God's vision for us and our community.

Even though I have been ordained for over thirty-five years, I still consult with colleagues through questions on Facebook, in a group of Cape Cod pastors that meet on a monthly basis, and with the smallest clergy group possible, the day to day synergy of marriage with my wife of thirty-seven years, a local church pastor on Cape Cod. I also send regular e-mail messages to my congregants, soliciting their input and guidance in congregational initiatives that I am imagining. These interactions ground my creativity in the practicalities of congregational life and the experiences of other pastors as well as provide me with insights that shape my creative ideas in new directions.

Clearness Committees and Wisdom Sharing
in Creative Ministry

The ministerial colleague groups that I led for nearly eight
years at Lancaster Theological Seminary were grounded in a
flexible integration of the insights of process theology and Quaker
spirituality, especially as it is embodied in the practice of clearness
committees. At the heart of Quaker spirituality is the affirmation
that God's light shines within every person. There is a spark of
divinity in each of us. Accordingly, we can, through times of silence
and encounter, access God's wisdom to face the challenges of daily
life and ministry. When groups gather in prayerful dialogue, the
divine sparks can ignite and persons can experience greater insight
and wisdom.

In a similar fashion, process theology asserts that God is
present as the source of possibility and inspiration in every
moment of experience. Divine wisdom is always contextual and
always lures us toward new horizons in ministry, personal life,
and communal well-being. The aim of the universe is toward the
evocation of beauty, a harmony of harmonies, inspiring imaginative
experience and creative transformation, whether in a sermon, bible
study, church newsletter, or congregational strategic planning and
problem solving.

Process theologians affirm that God presents us with visions
for our time and place, particular to our congregation, and its
unique gifts, rather than abstractions irrelevant to our daily lives
and ministries. God's vision for us involves an array of possibilities
aiming at growth, wholeness, and beauty of experience appropriate
to the highest good in our particular context.[3]

As pastors, we can access divine wisdom and possibility
in a variety of ways—prayer, meditation, *lectio divina* (holy
reading), spiritual direction, counseling, and coaching. We can
also experience God's vision more clearly through colleague

groups, committed to flexible adaptations of the Quaker clearness committee. Quaker spiritual guide Parker Palmer describes the theology and practice of clearness committees:

> Behind the clearness committee is a simple but crucial conviction: each of us has an inner teacher, a voice of truth, that offers the guidance and power that we need to deal with our problems. But that inner voice is often garbled by various kinds of inward and outward interference. The function of the clearness committee is not to give advice or "fix" people from the outside in but rather help people to remove the interference so that   they can discover their own wisdom from the inside out....if we respect the power of the inner teacher, the clearness committee can be a remarkable way to help someone name and claim his or her deepest truth.[4]

The Lancaster Theological Seminary "Wholeness in Ministry" program was, above all, prayerful in nature. Daylong sessions began with silent and verbal prayer, a time for checking in, the practice of *lectio divina*, a prayerful process of encountering a biblical text with an openness to God's creative wisdom inspiring individual and group reflection, and a theme for the day. Our themes were tailored to each clergy groups' needs and included topics such as: preaching in the Advent season, dealing with conflict, discovering your spiritual gifts as a pastor, pastor as spirit person, the role of pastor as teacher, and stress reduction and self-care. Most often, our clearness committee approach to professional guidance occurred during the time of checking in, during which participants were invited to share where they were in ministry and any issues that were challenging in their current ministerial setting.

Dean, a North Carolina United Church of Christ pastor, describes how our flexible approach to group theological and spiritual direction was helpful in his own quest for ministerial creativity. "I came to the gathering wanting something more from Holy Week and Easter. I wanted our congregation to experience Holy Week and Easter more personally and not just as events they already knew by heart. I had some ideas related to music, poetry, and film I wanted to use. I also thought doing the Stations of the Cross in our downtown neighborhood would heighten our church's sense of the way of the cross in their own lives. Frankly, I also wanted to experience Holy Week in fresh ways myself. I was tired of being the leader and nothing more; I wanted to be present with Jesus on Good Friday and Easter."

Dean shared his liturgical vision and then asked for the group's response. After a few moments of stillness, members asked clarifying questions and then shared their own Holy Week ideas. The energy of their liturgical synergy was palpable. Dean reflects, "I got more than I anticipated. I gained greater clarity about my own vision and what would work in my congregation. I was happy that my concerns inspired the group to think more creatively."

Prayerful Synergy

Ministerial creativity is nurtured by prayer and contemplation that enables us to more fully encounter God's whispered word in the course of our day to day ministries. When we take time for stillness and prayerful dialogue, we can experience divine wisdom coming in the Spirit's sighs too deep for words.

Ministerial excellence groups are a creative synthesis of listening and sharing, wisdom giving, practical application, and spiritual formation. In the groups that I led at Lancaster Theological Seminary, our day-long sessions began and ended with spiritual practices tailored to the group's personality and needs, including lectio divina, centering prayer, breath prayer, anointing with oil, and prayers of thanksgiving and intercession. A particular practice with which we often concluded our sessions occurred as we shared our joys and concerns and prepared for the celebration of communion.

After a time of intercessions, I asked the group to be silent for a few minutes as a way of embracing God's still, small voice for the journey ahead. I lifted up each member's name in the silence and invited the group and each of its members to bless and be blessed. When I mentioned a particular name, members focused prayerful blessings on that person. The person receiving these blessings was invited to embrace and receive the blessings given, and experience the deep connectedness of life. In the spirit of Jesus' affirmation of the relationship of the vine and the branches, these moments enabled members to experience greater divine energy and relational support, often issuing in a sense of God's presence and wisdom and a release of blocks to ministerial creativity. As we gathered for communion, we felt more deeply the graceful interdependence of life that joins us in God's Spirit regardless of distances in time and space.

I believe that these closing prayers enabled the participants to experience creative visions for their ministerial contexts. Prayer is an act of creative transformation that opens us to our connectedness to God and creation. Awakened to the graceful interdependence of life, we are able to access the infinite resources of divine creativity and share these resources with others. While we can never fully measure the impact of our prayers on others, I believe that within the causal relationships of life, our prayers and contemplative practices open us to deeper manifestations of divine possibility and energy and enable God to be more active in our lives. Our prayers create a field of force which opens us to quantum leaps of energy and creativity.[5] We become more attuned to God's creative visions, which are always more than we can ask or imagine.

Participants in our groups commented about the importance of these prayers in deepening their sense of connection with God and their colleagues. They no longer felt isolated and alone in ministry. They experienced a unity with others that they count on between meetings and the energy of love that inspired imagination and action in their ministries.

More Than We Can Ask or Imagine

Creative theology is affirmative in nature. While theologians recognize the brokenness of life and its tragic impact on individuals, congregations, communities, and nations, healthy theology places sin in the context of what Thomas Merton describes as our "original wholeness." Our creativity is grounded in God's generous and graceful involvement in our lives and the world. Creative wisdom gives birth to the universe, spins forth galaxies, and gently guides our planet's evolutionary process, through all its hits and misses. In companionship with God, grace is creativity and creativity is grace. The apostle Paul captures God's abundant creativity moving in and through our lives in Ephesians 3:21-22:

> Now to [God] who by the power at work within us is able
> to accomplish abundantly far more than all we can ask or
> imagine, to [God] be glory in the church and in Christ Jesus
> to all generations, forever and ever. Amen.

Our personal and professional creativity emerges out of this dynamic grace of interdependence and has as its fulfillment in sharing that creativity in ways that bring glory to God and the community of faith. Synergy in ministry takes us beyond ourselves to give life and light to others. Our creativity becomes catalytic in the creative transformation of our congregations.

Today, congregations and their pastors need to tap into all the creative and imaginative resources they can find. Many pastors perceive a future of scarcity, manifest in declining memberships, budget shortfalls, and growing irrelevance in our increasingly pluralistic culture. Once vital, many congregations measure their futures in shrinking endowments and doomsday forecasts. Yet, God constantly makes a way where there is no way by bringing forth new possibilities in the apparent dead ends we face.

Process philosopher Charles Hartshorne described "reality as social process." While honoring our personal initiative, Hartshorne recognized that none of us is self-made in life and ministry. The communities of which we are members provide the womb of possibilities from which creative ideas and transformative practices emerge.

Colleague groups are communities of imagination and practice that enable pastors to test their creative ideas, challenge their ministerial practices, and open to new horizons of spiritual transformation. The graceful interdependence of supportive colleague groups opens us to new ways of doing ministry and enables us to act rather than react to the challenges of twenty-first century ministry.

Notes

1. I have chosen to use pseudonyms to honor the confidentiality of our ministerial excellence groups.

2. From 2003–2010, I led ministerial excellence groups aimed at responding to three seasons of a minister's life: (1) the first three years of ministry, (2) pastors with five or more years' experience in ministry, and (3) pastors considering retirement. These groups inspired several books on pastoral excellence and well-being: *A Center in the Cyclone: Twenty-first Century Clergy Self-care* (Lanham, MD: Rowman and Littlefield, 2014); *Starting with Spirit: Nurturing Your Call to Ministry* (Herndon, VA: Alban, 2010); *Tending to the Holy: The Practice of the Presence of God in Ministry*, written with Katherine Gould Epperly (Herndon, VA: Alban, 2009); *Feed the Fire: Avoiding Clergy Burnout*, written with Katherine Gould Epperly (Cleveland, OH: Pilgrim, 2008).

3. For more on process theology, see my *Process Theology: A Guide for the Perplexed* (London: TT Clark/Continuum, 2012) and *Process Theology: Embracing Adventure with God* (Gonzales, FL: Energion, 2014); Catherine Keller, *On the Mystery: Discerning Divinity in Process* (Minneapolis: Fortress, 2008); and Marjorie Suchocki, *In God's Presence: Theological References on Prayer* (St. Louis: Chalice, 1996).

4. Parker Palmer, "The Clearness Committee: A Communal Approach to Discernment," the Center for Courage and Renewal, online, accessed 12. March 2016.

5. For more on the theology of prayer, my *Process Theology: Embracing Adventure with God* and *Process Theology: A Guide for the Perplexed*; or Marjorie Suchocki, *In God's Presence: Theological Reflections on Prayer* cited above in note 3.

Part 3

Habits of Spiritual Discipline

Chapter 13

Prayer by Painting
Tracing Over the Daily Office in Pastoral Life

Rev. Dr. Rick McPeak

"Pray as you can, not as you can't."
— Brother Samuel Weber, St. Meinrad's Archabbey

In nine years we have not missed a morning of praying the daily office at our church. Each morning we pray the ancient words of the Book of Common Prayer and take the Eucharist and in this ancient way of praying we become aware of and attend to the world God has given us. The praying that happens within our walls becomes a way of paying attention to the world, offering us insight into where God is at work outside of our walls. Prayer is not just words, however, but a posture for how we approach who we are, whose we are, and who God is in the world.

I have come to understand that posture of prayer, not so much in words or in speaking, or interceding or prescribing, but rather in seeing, in painting, receiving, and describing. I discovered that while we have been praying the words of the BCP something else was also happening. The narthex to our little sanctuary was being transformed into a baptismal mural. The walls, the ceiling, and the floors became a visual testimony to the power of Jesus' words, "Out of the believer's belly shall flow rivers of living water. (John 7:39)"

In retrospect I have asked, "How did the place of spoken prayer also become a canvas for a visual expression of the same impulse? Why would my congregation curiously allow me to keep the entry to our church in a perpetual state of chaos for over five years? Why was

I so drawn to applying paint to the trite wood paneling that covered the walls of the space? What did the words of Jesus that my mother wrote in the flyleaf of my first Bible have to do with how I found myself praying today? Why was my church starting to look more like a Roman Catholic church than a radically protestant chapel?" In answering these questions I repeatedly return to the experience of an unexpected encounter with a monk.

In the early 1980s I first met Brother Sam. I received a call from a member of the religion department faculty at Greenville College to see if I could travel to St. Louis and pick up a guest speaker who would be addressing the college community over the next few days. It was a Saturday and though I had a lot to do to get ready for the Sunday evening youth meeting, when I heard that he was a monk from a monastery in southern Indiana, I could not resist.

We had some difficulty finding the bus station where we were to pick him up and after arriving late we encountered transmission problems right in the middle of downtown. Our guest showed no aggravation at our inefficiency as we found a place to park the car, located a pay phone, and made arrangements for someone to come and get us. Over lunch at the Spaghetti Factory, Brother Samuel shared that he had come to Greenville College to talk about prayer and that he would be available for several days. I immediately scheduled him to speak with the church youth group that I was leading. My Sunday Night program had taken care of itself. Over those few days, I heard Sam speak several times and then scheduled to drive him back to St. Meinrad's in southern Indiana because my wife and I were making a trip to Lexington, KY that Wednesday. After lunch at the monastery and an extensive tour, we bid farewell to a strange new friend who was beginning to feel quite familiar.

Over the years I have visited St. Meinrad's on numerous occasions. Rather than experiencing it as a strange place it now feels more like a home away from home. The brothers now feel like brothers, and I have come to share in their curious vocation—prayer.

While it is tempting to think that my first introduction into prayer as a habit for a minister came from Brother Sam, I now recognize that he actually presented a reminder of something I had known all along, but had become unaware of. Over the years I had often expressed the "thoughts of my heart" (see the Collect for purity), but with limited understanding. It was Samuel's enduring perspective on prayer, however, that gave me insight into the lenses through which I have come to see my life and ministry within my churches and now with my students in the classroom. Another leg of my journey began through the enduring message of the monastic community in the words of Brother Sam: "Pray as you can, not as you can't."

Prayer by Painting

No minister needs to be convinced that his or her calling in some way is a call to prayer. However, most find that call exceedingly difficult to follow. It has taken most of my adult life for me to learn how I pray and to begin mastering it. I pray by painting. Though I only became aware of that in the last couple of decades, it has become apparent to me that I have always prayed by painting, coloring, cutting, cleaning, mowing or in some other kinesthetic way. In sharing my journey, I do not seek to instruct anyone in the art of prayer but perhaps to give some sort of permission for disciples to embrace the unique gifts that God has given for the purpose of intimacy with the Divine.

In 2 Peter 1:3 we hear, "[God's] divine power has given us everything needed for life and godliness, through the knowledge of him who called us by his own glory and goodness." The author continues in verse 4 that through "God's precious and great promises" you may escape the corruption that is in the world because of lust, and may become participants of the divine nature." In these words we see the secret to a life of sustainable spirituality: participation in the divine nature. We participate in God when we recognize that we already have all that we need in order to enter into a life of spiritual intimacy that endures. In verses 5–7, the writer declares that when one becomes aware of what God makes available it becomes reasonable to "make every effort to support your faith with goodness, and goodness with knowledge, and knowledge with self-control, and self-control with endurance and endurance with godliness, and godliness with mutual affection, and mutual affection and love."

This simple but profound formula for life and spirituality presented itself to me first when I was still a teen. The language is straight forward and the logic clear. It was easy for me to understand. We have what we need; if we accept that truth then we have a reason to give effort, and that effort should display a sequence and an accumulative effect. The lack of effort can only be explained by the fact that someone has become short-sighted and forgetful. The person of faith needs to remember and observe that she does not need to get God to do something more. By practicing the moral effort to build upon one's faith the disciple confirms her calling and insures that she will not stumble. Because this is true, the writer "keeps on reminding" the followers of Christ. He is not telling them something new but reminding them of something they already know.

Though this passage of scripture impressed itself on me at an early age, I found it easy to forget as I entered the professional ministry. My prayers and my effort were connected more to desired outcomes and professional success than to participation in the divine nature. Sure, God wants me to participate in God's nature, but I had work to do, places to go, ministry to fulfill, people to see and promises to keep. I wanted God to pitch in, to do God's part, to get on board. This attitude created for me a prayer life in which I was the mastermind and God a sort of necessary genie in the bottle, and not a very good one at that. Without realizing it, I had embarked on a journey that would take a deep well of spirituality to sustain me, but I had, in the words of Jeremiah the prophet "dug out for myself cisterns that could not hold water. (Jeremiah 2:13)"

Thanks to the fact that I am created in God's image, I was a hearing, seeing, thinking person who could and would see the obvious if I took a minute to pause and attend to my life. Hearing myself pray alarmed me! I had made myself the Lord and Christ my servant. And I had been shaping myself in this mold for years. I couldn't seem to open my mouth to pray without uttering blasphemy. In the angst of such awareness I did something unintentionally wise. I simply quit praying. At least that is what I thought. Really I had simply quit talking. Later I would remember Paul's words in Romans, "there is no fear of God before their eyes" (Rom. 3:18). In response, God gives the law, "so that every mouth may be silenced, and the whole world may be held accountable to God" (3:19). Had I remembered this I would have known earlier that my silence demonstrated not the end of my prayer life, but the beginning.

A new life of prayer emerged and it differed considerably from the former. The difference was simple. My new life of prayer was description where my old one was prescription. In other words I quit telling God what to do and I started seeing myself, others, and what was going on around me. I didn't really think that was prayer at the time, but because I had been rendered mute by seeing my prayers as blasphemy, I had time and the mental vacuum to actually start listening and seeing. And so, I started doodling.

One of the ways I doodled consisted of tracing over the letters of a phrase, sentence or paragraph that I found important in my reading. This method was introduced to me years before by an eccentric retired minister who most found overbearing. He had shared with me how he had quit underlining in his Bible and started overprinting instead. That method struck a chord with me. I simply liked doing it. But I didn't realize at the time-over fifteen years ago-that I was practicing art.

Prayer as Attending

Art is simply a tangible concrete expression of the practice of attending to something. As such, art is a vehicle for the activity of attending and it leaves a trace of the presence required for attendance. The "activity" of the artist is first dramatic before it becomes creative. By that I mean the artist, as attender, first enters the dynamic interchange of image and imagination (by looking, listening, choosing, and tracing) before she starts producing an image. In my case, for instance, I first practice careful attending by looking and listening to whatever is right in front of me. Often the pen or pencil becomes the tool that helps me do that. If I am sitting in front of something or someone it doesn't mean that I will actually see or hear them. So I trace over their image by drawing, recording, coloring or photographing them. Once the initial imprint is made I review it by tracing over it again and again this time noticing the color, shape or texture. After that the line between idea and activity becomes blurred. My mind vacillates between intense focus and carefree imagination while my hands carefully follow the script.

This experience is best understood as improvisation. Theologian Samuel Wells discusses the life of spirituality in terms of improvisation when he writes:

> The improviser has to realize that the more obvious he is, the more original he appears. . . . People trying to be original always arrive at the same boring old answers. Ask people to give you an original idea and see the chaos it throws them into. If they said the first thing that came into their head, there'd be no problem.
>
> An artist who is inspired is being obvious. He's not making any decisions, he's not weighing up one idea against another. . . . How else could Dostoyevsky have dictated one novel in the morning and one in the afternoon for

three weeks in order to fulfill his contracts? Experienced improvisers know that if they have attained a state of relaxed awareness, they can trust themselves to be obvious.[1]

My experience of painting mirrors the improviser's state of "relaxed awareness." I can relax because I am following a script and I increase my awareness by doing it very carefully. Then the mistake appears. My image does not perfectly correspond to reality, my tracing goes off line a bit, my photo reveals something I had not intended. This is a point of crisis wherein the artist recognizes that she has now created something or she tries to "fix" the mistake. The mistake must be seen as a gift if the artist is to become creator as well as recorder.

When I am a true artist I continue to follow the process by attending to the mistake with the same effort that I attended to the original image that impressed itself on me. I recognize this as a continuing expression of value, or love. My initial choice of what to paint or draw indicates my valuing of it and my continuing attention to the mistakes I impose on it indicates my valuing of the attending over simply reproduction. It is also an affirmation of myself as an attender.

Let me illustrate this by describing how I attend to drawing a line. First, I choose what I need to attend to, then I focus on a particular part of the object by seeing the line which is almost always created by two or more shapes butting up to one another. I can do this free-hand or use tools if I so desire. Once the line is drawn I do not erase, instead I accept whatever imperfection it presents. Then I trace over the line knowing that I will not be able to stay exactly on the same trajectory. Because I know this, I intentionally err to the side of centrifugal force. That is, I let the momentum of my stroke carry me off the script.

When tracing letters, I began to recognize that this process made them calligraphic. With numerous tracings the now-calligraphic

lines begin to give the impression of intention and the lack of proportion and incorrectness in shape seem less important. Normally
the image is still recognizable but it bears the signature of an artist.
The reproduction of the image is actually enriched and it provides
insight. For instance, when another artist recognized my work in a
mural because the lines were becoming calligraphic, I realized that
my art had its own style or slant. The term "slant" reminded me of
a line in a poem by Emily Dickinson: "Tell all the truth, but tell it
slant; success in circuit lies."[2] That statement gives me courage as an
artist, theologian, pastor, and a follower of Christ. Our approach to
life will always bring a peculiar slant which, if repeated, along with
the truth-telling of others will weave a much more profound fabric
than any one stroke or statement can.

This form of mental and physical attending takes faith in the
process. I know that my on-going attention to the image through
medium and material will, in the end, produce something of beauty,
but probably not the beauty that I would have intended. In this way,
the painting becomes a gift I receive, not a gift I give. Often it takes
the response of a viewer to help me see the beauty and value in the
image that has now become a script that I have in some way both
perverted and sanctified.

Intuitively, I have always known my artistic activity to be as
spiritual as it is material. My practice of the Christian faith in worship
continues to affirm this insight and to enhance the experience. Again
and again, I have seen or heard an echo of my experience as an artist
in worship and my experience of faith in the production of a work
of art. For instance, I have come to see that my reception of Christ
as Savior has a spiritual dimension mediated through memory and
imagination, but it becomes very material when I eat the body and
drink the blood of Christ.

I have also found that the daily office and the prayers of the
people form analogs to my artistic experience. In praying for others,
I am first prompted by the script given to us through scripture and

tradition. When I recite the Lord's Prayer I am choosing a script to which I will attend. When I join in the traditional prayers of the people, the Book of Common Prayer gives me lines to pray such as "for prisoners and captives and for all who remember and care for them,"[3] . . . Lord have mercy.

In this traditional form of prayer I see a shadow of the same elements that I encounter in the artistic endeavor. I attend to that which has been put in front of me by my community (the Lord's Prayer for instance) just like I choose to attend to what life places in front of me. This seems obvious, but can be so easily missed. When the disciples asked Jesus, "Teach us to pray," in Matthew 6:9, Jesus responded saying, "When you pray, say this, Our Father who art in Heaven . . ." It is obvious what we are to pray, but most often I prefer to be original. I find as a pastor and professor, if I don't pray original prayers my students often infer that I don't have an authentic relationship to God in Christ. Analogously, I find that if I drive into town from my small piece of county without seeing the landscape at all, I am virtually blind.

In times of communal prayer I have learned to practice something similar by bringing whatever has dropped in my lap to God and the community. The key has been to do it without prescription, without originality but with careful observation and description. If I am scheduled to begin a new semester at school, I trace that in prayer. "For Greenville College beginning another semester. Lord have mercy." Tracing prayer is a simple act of attending to the obvious, however, it is also a call to bring even greater awareness. I can bring that awareness by describing the situation more fully. "For Greenville College beginning another semester wherein she requires 19-year-old students to take a class with 63-year-old Rick McPeak. Lord have mercy." I can embellish my observation by adding a descriptive clause after the word students or after my name. In doing so I might receive an insight that will become transformation. For instance, after my name I might say "who now has eight grandchildren" or "who has taken on so much this summer that he is completely unprepared" or "who after all these years is still energized by teenagers." The descriptive statements often reveal the obvious prescriptions, while beginning with prescriptions can often blind the pray-er to the obvious problem at hand. Asking God to open students' minds or soften their hearts or provide resources might take away from the obvious need for me to stop whatever I am doing and prepare myself to receive these students.

In the last year a particular situation presented itself. A community in Ferguson, Missouri erupted in racial disharmony. Normally, I would remember an event like this in prayer: "For the citizens of Ferguson Missouri, forced to process the death of Michael Brown at the hands of the police. Lord have mercy." However, this prayer would not have displayed adequate attention in my case. It might have been adequate for me to pray if I still lived out in Seattle; however, I live less than fifty miles from Ferguson. If I go to the airport I drive within a mile of the site where Michael Brown died. My descriptive prayers had to include more when it came to Ferguson. "For Rick McPeak and the St. Paul's Free Methodist Church, living in the shadow of the violence in Ferguson and feeling fearful and inadequate to know how to respond yet forced to think and talk about it every day. Lord have Mercy."

I was scheduled to teach a course in the fall semester entitled "Topic in Ministry: Power, Politics and the Pope." Could I faithfully engage that topic without reference to Ferguson or without exposing myself and my students to the real world of power and politics right at our doorstep? I could not. Our first class session that August met at the Burger Bar on West Florissant Avenue, the epicenter of the conflict in Ferguson. I did not know what to prescribe for this situation, but it was obvious to me that I had to recognize that it had been dropped in my lap. My job as artist, improviser, pastor, disciple, would be to attend.

Attending, I have come to believe, is the foundation of sustainable spirituality. When I say "spirituality" I do not mean something immaterial, I mean something all-encompassing. True spirituality includes everything; nothing is left out. As such it demonstrates integrity; in other words, wholeness, and wholeness makes sustainability possible.

Psychologist and author M. Scott Peck devotes an entire chapter of his book *The Road Less Traveled* to "The Work of Attention." He first posits the activity of attending under the category of love. Most of us recognize love as the key category for both religion and spirituality. When our religion becomes something less than an expression of love all religious traditions and communities condemn themselves. Love is a universal value. For "love" to truly be love it must possess integrity. False concepts of love abound and Peck seeks to dispel any inadequate understanding of love from the start by offering the statement, "I define love thus: The will to extend one's self for the purpose of nurturing one's own or another's spiritual growth."[4] Building on that foundation, Peck turns to the "work of attendance" by showing its connection to love in that attending requires an extension of the self, which is work. He writes:

> The principal form that the work of love takes is attention. When we love another we give him or her our attention; we attend to that person's growth. When we love ourselves we attend to our own growth. When we attend to someone we are caring for that person. The act of attending requires that we make the effort to set aside our existing preoccupations (as was described in regard to the discipline of bracketing) and actively shift our consciousness. Attention is an act of will, of work against the inertia of our own minds.[5]

I have found the simplest forms of art (tracing for instance) to have inestimable value because they demand my attention and the sort of attention they demand is in some way natural to me. When I am an artist, I am attending in a way I can rather than in a way I cannot. Brother Samuel's teaching on prayer applies here. It applies because attending is prayer.

Once we are praying we find that the ancient understanding *"Lex Ordani, Lex Credenti"* begins to be applied. This Latin phrase translates, "The law of prayer is the law of belief." What this means is that as we pray we will come to believe. In other words, our prayers shape our theology, and they are in fact our theology. In my spirituality, prayer finds its analog in tracing. They both function like calisthenics, producing in me a sort of muscle memory that trains my mind to default to attending. That kind of training requires regular practice.

It could be asked, "Why practice attending in art rather than simply attending to people?" It is my contention that attending requires us to, as Peck says, "set aside our existing preoccupations (as was described in regard to the discipline of bracketing) and actively shift our consciousness."[6] When I am dealing directly with people, I tend to be so invested that I cannot give up my agenda for them. I find it nearly impossible to drop my preoccupation of fixing or directing them and shift my consciousness to purely attending to them. Painting a landscape, a line, a wall or a ceiling allows me to attend and shift my consciousness. Prayer, then, is an act of being trained to attend without judgment or control. I am learning to describe rather than prescribe. When, after hours of tracing, I turn my attention to a person, my love for that person can more easily become unconditional. The paradox seems to be that as I learn to care less I can attend more fully and thereby actually care more.

Pastor as One Who Attends

The paradox of art as prayer functions, like faithful living, both intuitively and counter-intuitively at the same time. I practice reciting the script until it is time to go off-script. I attend to a painting until it is time to stop painting and attend to a loved one.

In the meantime, whether in art or life I keep learning to attend. If pastors have a role with members of their congregation it is to attend to their lives and stories. If pastors can take on the art and habit of prayer as attending, then this opens up doors to ministry and transformation in ways never imagined were we to remain in the slumbers of traditional prescriptive forms of prayer. The pastor praying in such a way as to attend to the world as art is the transformation that makes all others possible.

And these transformations are not abstract or conceptual, they become very concrete. I found this out in a very particular circumstance this last year in teaching that class on "Power, Politics, and the Pope." Learning to attend allowed me to see the obvious fact that Ferguson, Missouri was less than an hour away from my home. Knowing how to describe and pray, my life reminded me that I make six to eight field trips into St. Louis every year. On these trips I expose students to experiences that will give them a proper context to deal with the content of my courses. It became obvious that we had to start this new course in Ferguson.

Being present in Ferguson amidst street organizers, Black Panthers, Nation of Islam representatives and my young friend, Fareed, who was there as a free lance documentary film-maker gave new meaning to a ministry course. It was easy to say "Yes" to Fareed when he offered to give us a tour of the area and tell us how he received his bandaged wounds. It wasn't long before we pulled up to the homespun memorial for Michael Brown on Canfield Boulevard.

The memorial consisted mostly of stuffed animals, candles, and notes. The bulk of it formed a sort of island in the middle of the street causing traffic to slow and briefly navigate around it. Often a conversation between someone in a car and a pedestrian pilgrim would hold up traffic briefly. No one seemed to mind. The site seemed strangely peaceful compared to the activity of the Burger Bar. No one was strategizing down here, just attending.

A man from Detroit began standing watch by sitting in a lawn chair. I didn't see this as necessary until a police car came by and after slowing to observe the pilgrims rather than the memorial, the officer stepped on the engine and sped off. The apparent hostility was met with shrugs and grimaces. The peace was not broken.

Shortly, a young woman, maybe twenty, arrived and began sobbing. Deep guttural sounds emerged as she first knelt and then prostrated herself at the site. I wondered if she might be related, but it seemed like everyone was related there. My whiteness and the whiteness of 10 of 11 students seemed less and less apparent. Quiet conversation developed. We learned who was from the neighborhood and who had come distances to stand vigil or to pay respects. No one asked why we were there or what we thought, and our names and where we were from did not seem to matter. Soon the sobbing turned from background noise to a wailing that demanded everyone's silent attention. It forbade us to leave and left me feeling completely helpless. Rising to her knees the mourner turned toward the crowd of us-twenty or so-and asked, "Does anyone know how to pray?" Instantly my lone African-American student, Paris, spouted, "Dr. McPeak knows how to pray."

I had been standing in silence, glad that I was not lecturing, preaching, or facilitating conversation. Knowing what to say or how to teach someone in this moment was the furthest thing from my mind. But Paris was right, I did know how to pray. That knowledge has come from years of tracing over the prayers of the Church. As all eyes turned to me I opened my lips in a prayer that has been etched in my consciousness,

> Almighty God, unto whom all hearts are opened, all desires known and from whom no secrets are hid, cleanse the thoughts of our hearts by the inspiration of the Holy Spirit that we might (in this time and in this space) perfectly love you and worthily magnify your Holy name, through Jesus Christ our Lord. Amen.

The sobbing ceased, no one said "thanks" or "nice prayer" or anything like that. An anonymous voice had simply brought a classic prayer of the church to a very specific context. This encounter was made possible because such a prayer had been learned by rote in the Daily Office morning prayers in a small church an hour away. More than recited or spoken, however, I felt that prayer was painted onto the memorial at Canfield Boulevard. It became a work of art, like the notes attached to the stuffed animals, giving deeper meaning to the mundane, sanctifying a time, a place, and persons through the use of both improvisation and tracing.

As we pray every morning at St. Paul's, the words of the ancient church's Daily Office call me, and all pastors, to a life of careful attention to the world. I did not know how to pray on Canfield Boulevard because I had all the right words or had some sort of special connection to the divine. I knew how to pray because I had been taught how to paint by my friend, Guy Chase, and I had been given permission by Brother Samuel to pray as I can, not as I can't.

Notes

1. Samuel Wells, *Improvisation: The Drama of Christian Ethics* Kindle ed. (Grand Rapids, Michigan: Baker, 2004), 59.

2. Emily Dickenson, *The Poems of Emily Dickenson: Reading Edition* (Cambridge, MA: Belknap Press/Harvard, 1998), poem 1265.

3. *Book of Common Prayer and Administration of the Sacraments and Other Rites and Ceremonies of the Church* (Seabury Press, 1979), 384.

4. Peck, M. Scott, *The Road Less Traveled*, kindle ed. (New York: Simon and Schuster, 2012), 81.

5. Ibid., 120–121.

6. Ibid., 120.

Chapter 14

Incarnationally Experiencing the Divine—One Mile at a Time

Rev. Dr. Jeffrey M. Gallagher

I made the quick right from Commonwealth Avenue onto Hereford Street and started the daunting, though by all accounts fairly meager, climb up towards that final left onto Boylston Street. With the smiles and cheers of my family at mile 25 propelling me on, I was now less than a mile away from the finish of the Boston Marathon. My legs were aching. My lungs were strained. I was simply putting one foot in front of the other. Slowly. Very slowly, by this point. I could barely hear the shouts from the deeply-packed crowds lining that historic straightaway over the voice in my head: "Finish. Just finish."

That blue and gold painted line in the street—holy ground to marathon runners even before the attacks rendered it so in 2013—appeared to be on the back of a flatbed truck inching away from my grasp, as I struggled to catch it. The race was not going nearly as well as I might have liked. But that didn't matter. Much more was accomplished than a 26.2 mile trek from Hopkinton to Boston that April day.

That race began for me some five years before I laced up my shoes that morning.

~~~

Unlike many clergy in today's ministerial landscape, I began seminary in my early 20s. Without any children yet I was blessed to be able to attend school full time. That worked out well for finishing an arduous degree; but not so well for my waistline. Living such a sedentary lifestyle, reading way too many theological tomes, and often eating on the go, my physical health suffered. I stopped exercising in college and now I was beginning to pay the price for my inactivity.

My habit of a sedentary life, unfortunately, did not end when I attained my degree and started at my first call in Maine. With the demands of a brand new parish—and me trying to prove myself as the new, young clergy in town—exercise was an afterthought. I focused on work. My wife and I started a family. And my health continued to suffer. It wasn't until I looked in the mirror one day after attending my yearly physical that I realized something needed to change. My son was now six months old. I needed to set an example for him. So I decided, that day, to start eating better. And I began to exercise again. I started with cycling and then turned to running—a sport I competed in during high school.

Only this time, instead of running to stay in shape for soccer, I began to enjoy running for its own sake. I would lace up my shoes at lunchtime, or early in the morning, and just hit the streets. I noticed things in town I had never seen before while careening by in my car. I heard the sounds of nature that often escaped me while in the office. The smell of the ocean woke up my senses better than even the strongest cup of coffee. Parishioners waved to me on their way to work—an intimate form of connection I began to forge. People outside of the church started to notice me in the grocery store or at Town Hall. "Aren't you that minister who runs?" they'd say.

I was beginning to become healthy physically, but much more than that, I was becoming healthy spiritually. Running was quickly becoming a part of my identity.

~~~

I will confess to you that I have never been much of a person for prayer. This isn't to say that I don't pray; I do. Up until this point I never found a discipline that "worked" for me. Quiet meditation was out with the racing mind God has blessed me with. Even sitting and reciting rote prayers just didn't seem to fill a need in my soul. I found that I would engage in little moments of prayer often throughout the day, but I was never able to sustain anything prolonged. That is, until I began to run.

Once I overcame the "my-lungs-and-legs-are-burning-and-I-think-I'm-going-to-die" feeling, something inside me started to change. My mind was focusing less on the physical action I was undertaking. I was thinking about people in the church who were having surgery. I would run by someone's house and say a prayer for what they were going through. An idea about how to handle a pastoral care situation would arise. A sermon illustration would pop into my head. A glimpse at the painted skies of a sunrise would fill me with awe and thanksgiving for all that God has made. Each step I took and each breath I breathed in and out—rising like a visible word to God on a cold winter's run—became a prayer. I was finding God in nature; I was finding God in sport. I was finding God right outside my door and throughout the streets of my neighborhood. Right before my eyes, running was becoming an integral part of my calling as a pastor. This was the spiritual discipline I didn't know I needed.

~~~

My new discipline shouldn't have come as a surprise to me, Jesus was always walking with the disciples, teaching along the way. I have to believe that some of his best ideas came while walking (or as I imagine him in the evening, after the disciples are asleep, running) along those dusty roads. And even Paul likens the journey of faith to that of a runner in his first letter to the church in Corinth: "Do you not know that in a race the runners all compete, but only one receives the prize? Run in such a way that you may win it. Athletes exercise self-control in all things; they do it to receive a perishable wreath, but we an imperishable one" (1 Cor. 9:24–25).

Physical activity and faith provoke a profound power that binds them together hand in hand. Both require practice. Both require discipline. Both require patience. Both require believing in something unseen, perhaps the possibility of crossing a marathon finish line. Both are easy to give up on when flat streets turn into steep mountain climbs; both can also reveal moments of immense beauty and grace when seen through to the end.

I believe that God speaks to us in the language we're most apt to "hear" God in. For some that is a beautiful play or waltz danced. For others it is the last moment of lingering light when the sun dips below the horizon. For others it is the laughter of their children on a backyard swing. For me it is running, because it represents the time in my life when I am least distracted and most focused on myself. Running is the time when I am most apt to hear what God has to say. I believe this is so because running is the language that I understand God best in, and the one in which, I believe, God understands me best.

Running is a thin place for me, as Celtic Christianity might call it. Thin places are those spaces where the veneer between God and I seems quite nearly translucent. Running, therefore, is where I feel the most fully known by God, and where I am reminded, most clearly, who I am and whose I am. I do not believe it too much to say that running reinvigorated my ministry. I was feeling my relationship with God strengthening and experiencing more connection to my parishioners. I was feeling more in touch with my community. I was feeling more creative and energetic in my work. But the benefits were not solely my own—the church also began to reap the rewards.

~~~

"Let's run from Maine to Jerusalem during Lent," I remember saying to a parishioner one day, waiting for the uncontrollable laughter to begin, or the "you're not Jesus, so how do you plan to run on water?" question to emerge. But it didn't happen. She actually liked the idea. And so we floated it to the congregation. "Let's run the 5,400+ miles together as a church," we said and, sure enough, people responded. Each week, runners (and we included walkers and bikers) would report in how many miles they had covered and each week I would offer an update in our church's weekly email. Would we get there, I wondered, as those days of Lent rolled on. Or would

I have to undertake my own laborious Good Friday trek, running hundreds of miles on Holy Week to finish the journey?

Not even close.

Not only did we make it to Jerusalem, we also covered enough miles to make it back! From the elderly woman who would proudly write in about the mile she did each day while on her treadmill staring out at the ocean, to those training for marathons, we covered the distance, and then some. It became clear, this experiment was not just about the miles. A community started to form between those who were making the journey. People started talking about experiencing God while running in the snow on a quiet morning, or walking by the woods and seeing God's creation frolicking by. People were having their own spiritual experiences—drawing closer to God and each other, by simply picking up one foot and putting it back down again. Running was transforming our church community.

As the transformation continued to take place in our church I began to wonder if we should take it a step further. Conversations around the church started to produce taking our transformation to the next step. In a conversation with one parishioner and fellow runner I said "Let's start a church running team," not thinking it would get any traction. "We could call it 'Church to 5k,'" I said, playing off the popular "Couch to 5k" running training plan. I, once again, waited for her to start laughing uncontrollably. But there was no laughing. So, we set up a training plan. We sent out emails and notices in the church publications. And we gathered one evening hoping someone might show up and they did. Lots of them. All ages and ability levels gathered, and the church running team was formed. We met all summer long, weekly, and encouraged each other—no matter what our level of fitness—to achieve our goal: a 5k race in the fall. We made up church running shirts (even though, sadly, my "Run Like Hell" tagline on the back was voted down), and on race day we all crossed the finish line.

Much more was achieved than a mere 3.1 miles along the Maine coastline that summer. We had become a community. We had become a family that cared for and supported one another. We had become the most unconventional church group I had seen before, and it was beautiful.

Running was changing our church community. But in a few years it would do much more than that.

~~~

April 15, 2013

My oldest son and I had just buckled into our car in Newton, Massachusetts. We vacated our spot at the foot of Heartbreak Hill, having just seen the last of the runners we were cheering on in the Boston Marathon pass. The day was beautiful and sunny—perfect racing weather. All morning long I had been thinking of how nice it would have been to be running the race myself that day. Then my phone started buzzing and call after call, text after text, kept coming through. I was trying to enjoy the ride with my son, but then I just had to answer to see what was happening.

"Are you ok?" were the first words out of my friend's mouth. "Of course," I said, "we're in the car on our way home." "Thank God you weren't at the finish line," she said.

And then I turned on the radio and heard the news of an explosion. Two of them. Bombs shattering a picture-perfect Boston day as runners ran those same final steps I struggled down a few years before. As of yet the cause was unknown, but soon all would be clear: terrorism. A few were killed and many more were injured. Runners became paramedics. Spectators became heroes. Volunteers became part of a triage operation. Everything about Boylston Street changed that day. When we arrived home we found out that all of our church members running and spectating were safe. But for many others the news was not so positive. We knew we needed to do something to show that we cared. So we cared the way we knew how: we ran.

We sent out emails and Facebook messages the night before

arranging a meeting time and wondering whether anyone would show. Over 100 people did—many of whom were not church members, or runners. Even camera crews came to cover our little memorial run. Dressed in Boston Marathon blue and gold, we ran and walked 2.62 miles up and down the streets of our town. We listened to a woman who had been stopped—mid-race—when the marathon was cancelled. We saw tears stream down her face as she recalled wondering whether her husband, also running, was still alive. We held her grief as we shared our own. We talked, we cried, we ran, and we began to heal.

And we prayed. We prayed for healing for those who had been injured and we prayed for peace for those who had lost loved ones. We prayed for those who committed the heinous violence. And we prayed in part:

> May each step we take bring us that much closer to a world where peace and love reign and violence is no more. And may each breath we breathe be a prayer—a prayer of remembrance for those who died, a prayer of healing for those wounded and recovering, a prayer of thanksgiving for the first responders and all those who showed such great courage in their response, and a prayer of hope that this will not happen again, that our actions of peace and love can be enough to banish the evil and violence from this world.

Once again, on that night, running had proven so much more than just a physical activity.

~~~

Today, running remains my most important spiritual discipline. Clearly, every run doesn't yield profound insights, nor is every step laden with prayer, but lifting one foot in front of the other across pavement is still a spiritual experience for me. Sometimes the prayer is simply one of gratitude for being able to get up and move my arms and legs in God's creation—however fast or slow that might be. The process is sacred.

Ten thousand miles later, running has transformed my life and the churches I have served in ways that I never thought possible. Running has opened up doors for me to converse with people at the bedside. Running has brought new people into the church who initially came just to be a part of a running group and has provided numerous sermon illustrations and children's messages. Running has deepened relationships and formed bonds between people that will not be broken.

There is no doubt that running has deepened my relationship with God. I am healthier spiritually and physically because of it. I am a better pastor, a better father, and a better husband. And it has shown me that if you want to see humanity at its best, then participate in a marathon. Run or spectate, and see thousands of people united around a common goal, with thousands of others cheering them on and doing everything they can to support their efforts. God's kingdom, I have to believe, will look something very much like a marathon community.

~~~

So what will the twenty-first century church look like? The future is uncertain, to be sure, but I think running could be a pace-setter. I believe the church will be less intellectual and more incarnational— more in line with the original sense of the church as "the way," as the movement with movement that it was in Jesus' day. Of course, this doesn't mean we will do away with theological or intellectual inquiry, but that doctrine will become less and less important than doing. Gone are the days of parishioners simply coming to church to sit in pews as "observers" of worship. People want more experiential, embodied, incarnational, hands-on experiences of God—both on Sunday mornings and beyond. If churches are going to survive we need to find a way to offer such incarnational experiences. The church will, naturally, need to move, then, beyond the four walls of our venerable buildings.

We will see more service Sundays, where congregations gather to help out neighbors and beautify their community, in lieu of traditional morning prayers and sermons. We will see more experiential service projects and mission trips, where people will live out their faith with their feet and hands. We will see more intergenerational gatherings where young and old alike engage a lesson as a multi-sensory worship experience. We will see more of a sense that worship extends to the soup kitchen, the soccer field, and the cubicle at work. Prayer stations, tactile blessings, rituals to mark life milestones, will all become ways in which we seek an incarnational encounter with the divine.

And certainly when running is viewed as the type of body-prayer that it is, running fulfills this incarnational desire to experience God in a way that is not purely intellectual. Experiencing God becomes arms and legs in motion, the feel of the wind on our face, the smell of spring flowers bursting into bloom, color explosions as the natural landscape emerges from its winter hibernation, the sounds of nature rustling and foraging in the woods, and even the taste of salt on our lips if we're lucky enough to run by the ocean. It doesn't get more incarnational than that.

The church will also, likely, continue to borrow from other faith traditions. As the global community becomes smaller and smaller—and we are exposed to more ways to connect with our Creator—people will continue to borrow from other traditions which, quite honestly, have incarnational spirituality figured out much better than Christianity. The rise in popularity of yoga among Christians is a perfect example. People are realizing that perhaps Hinduism and Buddhism understand something more clearly than Christians: God can be encountered in movement and body. As Christians we need to embrace this borrowing and admit that we do not have the market cornered on doorways to the divine. We need to embrace new practices and believe that God may speak as loudly through them as through the most well-loved selection from the Pilgrim Hymnal. Running may not be for everyone, but it may provide an alternative for those who find it near impossible to connect with God while wearing a suit in a nearly un-sittable 17th century pew.

As a clergy I believe it's important to understand that people are seeking new ways to connect with the divine. We must consider it important to understand the need to encounter God with our senses. And Christianity is going to need to borrow from other traditions to stay relevant as others uncover that God can be found outside of Sunday morning, outside of worship, outside of sanctuaries, in a created world that can become a Sunday morning sanctuary of its own.

I know what it's like to experience God while running, and I believe that can only help me reach out and serve those who choose not to worship, but rather run by the sanctuary on Sunday morning. There is a way to help such roadside pilgrims to name the movement of the body as an incarnational experience of God. Perhaps running alongside them just might be the 21st century preacher's task.

While I cannot foresee the future, I believe we are in for quite a ride because the church is changing. Paul understood the ever-changing nature of the church in the early period, which is why he drew upon running as a metaphor. Paul taught that running is a description of what Christian faith-and the faith practiced in community-can be. That is, focused upon a goal. Connected to God. Working together. Incarnational. Believing in something unseen. Getting the best out of ourselves and each other. Achieving things that some may never have thought possible. Caring for one another along the way. Running just might be the most creative image for describing the church at its best. And for me that is a powerful image for what creative ministry is all about.

Chapter 15

The Heart of Silence

Rev. Dr. Sarah Griffith Lund

As the youngest of five children, I don't recall experiencing silence during my childhood and adolescence, unless it was when we were all unconscious, that is, asleep. Either we were all making our own racket or hootenanny or the television was blaring or the boom box (a rectangular sound making machine popular in the 1980s), or all three of these at once. Our world seems filled with constant noise, distractions, and a clamoring for our attention. I stand my ground on this truth: my siblings drove me to God. Alone with God was the only way I could hear myself think. This was the truth I discovered my first year in college, far away from home: silence was not the absence of sound, but the presence of mind, and the presence of God.

Discovering Silence

After graduating from Princeton Theological Seminary and my ordination into ministry, good fortune led me to participate in an experimental program sponsored through the generous support of a major initiative of the Lilly Endowment born out of concern that young clergy were dropping out of ministry at an alarming rate. Two programs supported my development in the early years of ministry in the local church. First, the twenty-four month residency Transition into Ministry Program modeled after the medical school residency program. The second was the peer based program called Bethany Fellows. Of the two programs, the peer model offered the most impactful experience on my ability to flourish in ministry and here is why: every six months for five years, I met with my clergy peer group for five days of retreat. At the heart of the Bethany retreat was a period of twenty-four hours of silence.

As a solo church pastor at the age of 26 and serving a 200-member financially struggling congregation, I began to mark my life in six month periods of time. No matter what difficulty I faced leading the congregation (a music director that didn't want to play an instrument Sunday morning for worship other than a trumpet. No piano or organ. Just a trumpet. Or fear of becoming "Open and Affirming" in our welcome of gay, lesbian, bisexual, and transgender Christians), I knew I could survive for six months. Because at the end of six months, I knew I would be back with my peers, seasoned mentors, and sitting with that sacred time of silence.

I came to view my time of silence as a fasting from outside noise. For me, this meant no communication with others in any form and turning off communication devices. To not check email, Facebook, Twitter or text messages for twenty-four hours altered my reality. It forced me to cast my gaze inward and to connect with my inner spiritual voice. In the silence, I could listen to my mind's unspoken dialogue with God. At first there was nothing there. I was so accustomed to filling my head with noise from the outside world that I didn't yet have an ear for what God might sound like. At first I seemed afraid that God's silence was a signal of God's absence. Maybe I couldn't hear God because God wasn't around. I didn't question God's existence, but I did question God's presence. The question for me was not, "Does God exist?" Instead I asked, "Where is God now?"

So in my first experience of extended silence on retreat, I laced up my sneakers and went looking for God. The desert location of the retreat center provided miles of trails to guide my silent, walking meditation. The sound of the gravel crunching underneath my feet echoed inside my head, clearing my thoughts, and making space for me to find God. This process of walking as a way to prepare myself for encountering God became my ritual for entry into silence. Walking warms up the physical and spiritual muscles. Once I become fully present to my body, I can more deeply engage my mind and spirit.

The second half of my silence (apart from a good night's sleep and meals) is then spent in concentrated seated prayer. I locate a sacred space that speaks to me, whether seated on a cushion on the floor in front of a religious icon, or a warn bench in a cathedral crypt, and I stay there for several hours. In this time I form no complete thoughts, I ask no questions, I seek nothing. I simply focus my attention on being with God, for I have decided that God is with me, all this time, anyway.

The very first retreat with the twenty-four hours in silence baptized me in salty tears. I wept for the hardness of ministry and for my feelings of inadequacy, frustration, and fear. How was I going to pull this church up out of debt, grow the children's ministry and build a new Christian Education wing all at the same time? How could I lead this church, reflective of a southern cultural context different from my own, without compromising my values? How was I going to survive? Would I be happy serving this church for the long run? Who will my friends be in this small town?

To my great surprise and relief, at the end of the twenty-four hours of silence, while sitting in the chapel, a small inward voice said to me, "Remember your ordination vows? You promised to give yourself to me in service and I promised to never let you go." I'm confident that the only way I could hear this divine reminder of who I was and who God was, resulted from this reoccurring time set apart from what my United Methodist minister friend calls "the relentlessness of Sundays," for silent, uninterrupted and deep contemplation.

Silence as an Ancient Tool

Thankfully, I discovered that this uninterrupted deep contemplation, or silence, was not something I had to create. Silence, in fact, finds its roots deeply held in the history of the Christian faith from its origins to the Reformation to spiritual movements today. We read scriptural references to the significance of silence as the portal to God in the words of the Psalmists and the Gospel writers. Psalm 62 begins with the confession, "For God alone my soul waits in silence" (Psalm 62:1). For Elijah, the voice of God was heard not in the wind, earthquake or fire, but in a "sheer silence" (1 Kings 19:11–13). Out of this silence, Elijah recognized the voice of God. In the life of Jesus we read accounts of him leaving the crowds to find a place of solitude to be alone with God. Jesus says, "Come away to a deserted place all by yourselves and rest a while" (Mark 6:31–32). Once Jesus led his disciples into this place of silent retreat, he himself "went up on the mountain to pray" (Mark 6:45). Scripture teaches us that God enjoys having our undivided attention. The God who whispers into the ears of the ancient prophets is the God who meets us in the heart of silence as well.

Mystics of the church confirm God's desire to deepen relationships with those made in the divine image through the spiritual practice of silence. Thirteenth century mystic, Meister Eckhart, said that "nothing is so like God as silence."[1] Sixteenth century mystic, St. John of the Cross, wrote that "silence is God's first language."[2] Twentieth century scholar of death and dying Elizabeth Kubler-Ross said, "Learn to get in touch with the silence within yourself and know that everything in this life has a purpose. There is no need to go to India or anywhere else to find peace. You will find that deep place of silence right in your room, your garden or even your bathtub."[3]

Transformative leaders in Christianity point to the spiritual practice of silence as a grounding force at the heart of their relationship with God. Dietrich Bonhoeffer adopted a daily practice of honoring silence because he was convinced that it was valuable in helping him to listen to God's Word and center his mind on God. Bonhoeffer said, "We are silent at the beginning of the day because

God should have the first word, and we are silent before going to sleep because the last word also belongs to God . . . Silence is nothing else but waiting for God's Word and coming from God's Word with a blessing. But everybody knows that this is something that needs to be practiced and learned."[4]

Henri Nouwen changed the landscape for the ability of clergy to claim their roles as "wounded healers." Nouwen's profound experience with silence as a spiritual practice highlights the transformative power of the ancient spiritual practice. Nouwen writes, "Solitude is not a private therapeutic place. Rather, it is the place of conversion, the place where the old self dies and the new self is born . . . The wisdom of the desert is that the confrontation with our own frightening nothingness forces us to surrender ourselves totally and unconditionally to the Lord Jesus Christ."[5]

Silence as Preparation

This ancient rhythm of silence was first introduced to me as an ancient spiritual discipline during my seminary years when I attended a weeklong retreat at Holy Cross Monastery in upstate New York. It was my last semester of seminary and I wanted to prepare myself for whatever it was God was calling me to do. I had no idea. Brother Bede led the retreat and instructed us to experiment with silent walking mediation. At the end of the retreat, when it was time to return to campus, it pained me to turn my cell phone back on. I had left it in my car the entire week. As I sat in the driver's seat and turned the phone on, it lit up with message alerts. One was from my sister telling me that our cousin Paul was scheduled to be executed in thirty days.[6] Little did I know just how much the spiritual practice of walking silent meditation at the monastery prepared my spirit for one of the most disturbing experiences of my life: serving as my cousin's spiritual advisor on death row and witnessing his execution. The thing about a spiritual practice is that we have no way of telling what we are being prepared for and readied to do.

As a result of this initial experience in silent retreat I have been living now into this pattern of silent contemplation for twelve years, experiencing at least one if not two extended 24–48 hours of silence. I know that the spiritual practice of silence is why I remain committed and energized to fulfilling my vocation as an ordained minister of the church. God's invitation to serve has taken me on an incredible journey since my ordination on October 27, 2002. The practice of silence deepens my ability to discern where, what, and with whom God is calling me to serve. It is coming out of silence that I have had the clearest sense of direction, knowing what decision to make about an upcoming opportunity.

The spiritual experience of silence can be enhanced through intentional spiritual discernment with a trusted mentor. Bethany Fellows provides young clergy with several leaders with whom to engage in conversation related to life and vocational discernment. When I engage in silence and have a brief, thirty-minute spiritual mentorship session as part of my period of silence, my time in silence deepens and the outcome is richer. It is not that the spiritual discernment provides a much needed chance to "talk." Instead, the short session with a spiritual mentor forces the hardest questions to emerge: Who am I? What is God calling me to do? What makes my heart sing? It is questions such as these, uttered aloud in the presence of a trusted mentor, which takes seed in the soul. Entering back into silence with such clarifying questions leads into profound insights awaiting to be discovered upon emerging back out of silence at the end.

Silence is an ancient spiritual practice that leads us to deeper, more authentic relationships with God, our neighbors and ourselves. I recently had a conversation with Dick Hamm, former Minister and President of the Christian Church (Disciples of Christ) about the Bethany Fellows model of small, peer groups together practicing silence. He recounted to me that this model emerged out of the belief that "a mature spirituality was a key element in the health of pastoral leaders and, in turn, in the health of congregations." Hamm further reflected that silence is the heart of the Bethany Fellows, which seeks to "bring the resources of intellect and Spirit together in lively interplay, creating a community of mutual support and discernment."

Silence as Pastoral Practice

In a time of institutional crisis and heightened anxiety, the spiritual practice of silence can provide religious leaders with a tool to tap into the deep well of wisdom and inner peace. At a time where denominations are scrambling to restore a bygone era, young clergy are faced with challenges that no other generation in the history of Christianity has faced. We are the ones for whom the institutional church is crashing down around. In this season of dramatic change, the church needs emerging leaders who have deep, authentic spiritual lives.

Creating space for extended silence amidst demands of the church may seem ridiculous to most clergy. Who has the luxury to take twenty-four hours of silence? Is spiritual care a luxury? Or is it a requirement for the kind of leadership our church longs for? I find tremendous hope in the number of young clergy who have been and continued to be shaped by the Bethany Fellows model of peer support, spiritual retreat, mentoring, and extended time in silence. For me these spiritual practices, especially silence, within a spiritual community has made all of the difference, kept me in ministry, saved my marriage, and made me a better mother.

The impact of retreat and extended time of silence is not by chance. It has been tested and proven to be beneficial, and therefore, become a proven method for spiritual vitality. The retreats are strategically scheduled every six months, a total of eight retreats over four years (40 days!). During these years, Fellows build upon their seminary experience and theological education in prayer practices and spiritual disciplines, which sustain the soul for a life-time of parish life. Each retreat experience contains worship, solitude, and multiple learning components tailored to the emerging needs of their congregations. The retreat includes a site visit to cutting-edge congregations that stimulates fresh creativity for at-home ministry. Monthly coaching sessions hone their ability to read congregational systems, make appropriate interventions, sustain inner vision, and inspire those around them while discovering effective networking skills.

The truth is that when we engage with the spiritual discipline of silence, our lives are interrupted. In sacred silence, space is created for the Spirit to whisper to us, lead us, and guide us. In such uninterrupted space, creativity can flourish. This is the creative energy and vision that is needed to lead the church in the twenty-first century. Founding Director of the Bethany Fellows Don Schutt shared with me in a conversation that "silence/stillness/quietness tends to move one away from the head toward the interior (as the Quaker/Friends have espoused since their inception several centuries ago and many Catholic orders have practiced for millennia). The Bethany retreats have had silence at the center since the beginning."

The Bethany Fellows model has emerged as one of the most successful of the Transition into Ministry experiments, with a success record of 99 percent retention of clergy in ministry who participated in the program. Of the nearly 150 Bethany Alumni, 90 percent remain in local church ministry, and nine percent are serving at different levels of church leadership. According to Kim Gage Ryan, Bethany Fellows Director, the reasons why this model works so well is "through the collegial support of peers and mentor/ leaders, young ministers are better able to navigate the beginnings of a vocation and young adult life transitions. While on retreat the Fellows are engaged in spiritual practices as well as visits with dynamic congregations, fueling creativity and insights to share with their congregations, building confidence and strengthening their leadership."[7]

After serving the local church for nine years, several years in judicatory leadership, and now on staff at a seminary, I currently serve on the leadership team for Bethany Ecumenical Fellows. I walk alongside newly ordained young clergy in their first call. I hold space for them during the silent retreats. I provide one-on-one spiritual mentorship. And I witness the significant growth of each person who engages with this ritual of silence in the pattern of retreat every six months in their first years of ministry. The success of this model speaks to the power of spiritual practices at the heart of the transformation of young religious leaders. If rising leaders of the church need to be able to deeply discern the future vocation of the church, then what spiritual disciplines will sustain this discernment process?

At the outset of this book, Chad Abbott refers to what John Philip Newell describes as asking "What is trying to be born that requires a radical reorientation of our vision. What is the new thing that is trying to emerge from deep within us and from deep within the collective soul of Christianity?"[8] The conclusion posited here is that creativity will be a requirement for those wishing to positively influence the future of Christianity. My contribution to this work is to suggest that the spiritual practice of extended silence is not only an ancient tool, but a healthy model for our work as clergy, creating the space for us to tap into the sacred energy that fuels spiritual creativity. In sacred silence, we hold space for divine light to shine forth. Silence wraps our hearts in light. From such a light, powerful leadership can emerge with insights and energy to join in God's transforming of the world.

Notes

1. *The Christian Century*, Silence blog, online, accessed, 5. May 2016.

2. The Society of St. John, "The Sound of Silence," online, accessed, 5. May 2016.

3. The Elisabeth Kubler Ross Foundation, quotes tab, online, accessed, 5. May 2016.

4. Dietrich Bonhoeffer, *Life Together* (New York: Harper & Rowe, 1954), 79.

5. Henri Nouwen, *The Way of the Heart: Connecting with God through Prayer, Wisdom, and Silence* (New York: Ballantine, 1981), 27–28.

6. You can read more about this in my book *Blessed are the Crazy: Breaking the Silence About Mental Illness, Family and Church* (Chalice Press, 2014), where I go into great detail regarding my own family journey with mental illness.

7. The Bethany Fellows, online, accessed, 5. May 2016.

8. John Philip Newell, *The Rebirthing of God: Christianity's Struggle for New Beginnings* (Woodstock, VT: Skylight Paths, 2014), xi.

Chapter 16

The Labyrinth as a Clergy Practice

Rev. Dr. Kay Mutert

"Solvitur ambulando." [It is solved by walking.]
Diogenes, later attributed to Augustine

The work of a clergyperson functions under the lived complexity of a congregational life demanding attention in vast areas ranging from administration, pastoral care, budgeting, public speaking, and community presence. In some cases, such a scope of clergy responsibilities can cause churches to function less like a worshiping congregation and more like either a non-profit organization or a business. As a result, clergy can often feel pressure to be a jack-of-all-trades. Moreover, clergy speak frequently of the many tasks that their seminary training did not actually train them to do. In looking at the tasks of a clergyperson it seems evident that most clergy spend the bulk of their time functioning from the left side of the brain wherein the analysis, intellect, and language of the church becomes expressed. Our worship services are overwhelmingly word and language driven, which leaves very little room for creativity. Additionally, when we think of clergy playing the role of administrator through the analysis of their church systems via church councils, by-laws and constitutions, the oversight of staff, or the attention to budgets, the work of clergy can feel cumbersome and out of balance. If the work of clergy is so imbalanced, where do they find room for creativity? How does the context of the church offer clergy the space to use their imagination in connection with the Spirit to hope and dream for a new future?

While there are many ways to foster creativity, one way that a handful of vital faith communities have been doing so is through the ancient spiritual practice of the labyrinth. The labyrinth provides the capacity to bring back into balance the work of clergy by offering a kinesthetic experience of imagination, silence, and meditative awareness to God's work in our midst. While labyrinths have pre-Christian origins, the church of the middle ages utilized labyrinths to centralize the work of holy pilgrimage and prayer with walking meditation. The labyrinth is not a maze. In a maze, those who walk have the potential to lose their way, especially because of dead ends. In a single path labyrinth, the pilgrim finds their way. A labyrinth is one circuitous path to walk, with twists and turns leading into the center, a place for quiet reflection. The pilgrim then returns by the same path, moving back out to re-enter the world they momentarily left behind. Given our word-laden, continually hectic and judgmental world, the practice of the labyrinth offers a different experience.

The labyrinth is non-judgmental, peaceful, with no words, and offers those who walk the opportunity to find balance, nurture creativity, and bear witness to the work of Spirit within. Clergy struggle to nurture within themselves a sense of balance or creativity because they are so entirely immersed in the world of words, analysis, institutional structures, and finances. Are we not limiting the work of the Spirit in our midst by narrowing the work of clergy in such a world? How might we free our clergy so that they may pay more attention to their imagination and creativity?

Many years ago I was serving as a minister in the United Kingdom. During that time I was invited to be a part of a leadership team for a remarkable program offering sabbatical retreats to honor the significant benchmarks of ministry service: five-year, ten-year, twenty-year, thirty-year periods. I stepped into working with those completing thirty years of ministerial service. We expected them to participate by clearing their calendars for a ten-day retreat, with no phone calls, funerals, or emergencies. Churches were expected to support and allow their clergy this time away. The event was held at the lovely Ammerdown Retreat Centre, outside of Bath, England; the Centre describes itself in the following manner:

> Imagine a Conference and Retreat Centre nestling in woods next to a Stately Home, surrounded by beautiful landscaped gardens and parkland, with an exquisitely beautiful chapel in its midst. The whole place is steeped in peace and tranquility. No traffic noise, only birds singing![1]

In that idyllic natural setting, we designed a part of the retreat activity as a daylong "gentle" countryside walk of ten miles. Other activities included bread baking, times for art expression, singing, flower collection, and arranging for worship setting- things that revitalize the spirit and heart. We worshipped, sang, held silence, laughed, and prayed. There were no church budgets or questions of finance. We did not engage in discussions of how best to increase the numbers of people worshipping in the pews. No one was asked about their church newsletter. Instead, our retreat leaders envisioned activities that possessed the power of a recovery and renewal of spirit among clergy. Since this was a time with thirty-year-ministry British clergy, there were no women present. The men who attended went into the vulnerable and sacred places of their hearts in this refreshing and renewing experience. It was a time to acknowledge the struggles faced in their journey, a time to renew friendships, to rekindle creative fires, and in that one day, a time to walk.

Impressed by the fact that these clergies could walk ten miles easily, I thought of myself and my clergy friends at home, as I tried not to presuppose judgment on our physical condition. I prepared for the occasion, hoping that I could last the journey. The walk was significant in creating an experience of retreat that was a beautiful time of shared story and experience, renewal and refreshment, heart and expression, imagination and creativity.

About that same time, the labyrinth, a walking path of prayer and meditation, became a part of my practice and work. As this ancient pattern became a part of my own spiritual practice, I introduced it to my congregations and those attending retreats as a natural metaphor for the spiritual journey, the life path. I then began to include the labyrinth in my teaching and vision for community and clergy, later incorporating it into my ministry work offering renewal of spirit and creative expression to others. I realized that it was my greatest desire to see others experience the benefit of the practice of meditating/praying while practicing the movement of walking. And as I began introducing this ancient practice, a new vibrancy of faith was awakened not only within me, but within the clergy under my care. Clergy came to our retreats so distressed over the work of their congregations that the labyrinth became a place of refreshing and imaginative sacred space where God could speak and they could listen.

While many clergy may already be using the labyrinth as a part of their personal spiritual practice, whether regularly or occasionally walking a full-size creation, sitting and tracing a smaller form with finger or stylus, or following the path with the eyes, for those who have not yet experienced or embraced the labyrinth, perhaps there is an invitation present here for clergy to open themselves to such a sacred habit.

In her benchmark book *Walking a Sacred Path*, the Rev. Dr. Lauren Artress—who is the founder of Veriditas, the worldwide labyrinth organization—writes of her personal discovery of the Chartres labyrinth, which led to the new calling in her life and ministry of offering the labyrinth to others. Those who traveled to the famous Chartre Cathedral with Artress did not expect that when they arrived they would find chairs on top of the labyrinth, seeming to suggest that it was a gift to the church long forgotten. Artress and her fellow pilgrims began taking the chairs off the labyrinth one by one and uncovering this ancient path that has since shaped so many fellow pilgrims seeking out a spirituality unconfined to the walls of the church.

In uncovering the labyrinth as a spiritual practice in her own life, Artress writes, "The labyrinth is a spiritual tool meant to awaken us to the deep rhythm that unites us to ourselves and to the Light that calls from within. In surrendering to the winding path, the soul finds healing and wholeness."[2] In the lives of clergy, what speaks to such deep rhythms of light that call within? Certainly not church budgets. Clearly not overseeing a staff. The deep rhythms of light within us that call not from the levels of analysis, church structures, or words alone, but from the space of imagination and creativity found in the labyrinth has the potential to offer us sacred space to encounter God's call of the church into the future. As the church continues to encounter decline and change in its midst, we need more tools like the labyrinth that will ignite and center us in our faith.

Labyrinth historian Jeff Saward writes that "throughout the long history of labyrinths whenever and wherever society is going through rapid change and development the labyrinth has blossomed."; so today "humanity is seeking the sure path of the labyrinth in an uncertain and confusing world."[3] In the great pressure of the calling to serve others in this day and time, the life of the clergy can be a word-laden, action-filled life offering little time and space for one's own renewal, reflection, sometimes without the inner realization of the need for time-out or time-in. Clergy would be wise to use the labyrinth in the transformation of time and space from all the anxiety and pressure and into renewal and new life.

As I write this essay, I am ending a week on the small Isle of Iona off the west coast of Scotland, leading a group pilgrimage titled Journey to a Thin Place. In my time there I have been mindful anew that the labyrinth journey is much like the pilgrimage journey. There is an intention to go, to set time apart, to take the walk, to enter the path. Then begins the journey itself—the movement toward the center, which is a time of releasing, letting go, as the destination, the center is approached. As in a pilgrimage, the time in the labyrinth center opens one to a place of reception, reflection and growth, and listening for the still quiet presence of the Holy. The journey outward from the center in the labyrinth is similar to the returning pilgrimage journey toward home. The returning is just as significant as entering the threshold into liminal numinous time. And for both, the pilgrimage and the labyrinth, we return from our time apart at the journey's end.

When we step back into our life and work, we are somehow back but not the same. The intentional time apart of pilgrimage, the intentional spiritual practice of reflection as offered in a labyrinth walk or meditation is needed to face the daily stress and challenge of our life journey, for clergy, for all who are wanting transformation or a deeper walk in faith on the road of life.

In the week's time I spent with my fellow pilgrims in that ancient Celtic spiritual place of Iona, we created seaweed labyrinths on the sandy beaches to walk and witnessed the tides wash them away. Together we traveled to the south shore of Columba's Bay and walked the stone labyrinth there guarded by the sheep, facing out to the beautiful bay where St. Columba set foot long ago to start anew his work and ministry of spreading the story of God's love. Later we laid out a canvas labyrinth in the village hall for a closing ritual at the end of a meaningful week. Walking on ancient land which still holds the presence of Holy Mystery for today's pilgrims, we reflected on what we could learn from that early Celtic spirituality. In our reflections, we discovered the value not only of walking alone but walking as a community. As one participant said, "I had walked the labyrinth alone, but never in community. Wow, what an experience!" For clergy, who by their very calling, work in community leading others, it is vital to walk together. The labyrinth offers us opportunities for both: we walk alone for contemplation, meditation, we walk together as we pass on the path, in solitude yet in community.

In the introductory chapter to this book, Chad Abbott asserts "[W]e form creative habits that embody deep listening, letting go, compassionate relationships, and creativity. In these we find a new old way of being that can open our lives to God and what God has in store for our future." The labyrinth is indeed a new old way of being, a sacred habit, an ancient walking meditation offering a practice for experiencing spiritual contemplation and renewal. Whether the reader is a clergy looking for a vital spiritual practice or a layperson looking to deepen their spirituality, there is an invitation in the labyrinth to experience the rejuvenation of creativity, a safe place of silent holding as a path of prayer, and an awakening to the world of imagination and inspiration. May walking this ancient pattern offer our clergy a new vision for a sacred habit by awakening creativity to the work of the pastorate and new directions on the spiritual path.

Medieval Chartres Labyrinth pattern, found on the floor of Notre Dame Cathedral, Chartres, France, placed there circa 1200–1210. (This labyrinth is printed with permission by Veriditas from their website, www.veriditas.org.)

Notes

1. The Ammerdown Centre, online, accessed 4. May 2016.

2. Lauren Artress, *Walking a Sacred Path: Rediscovering the Labyrinth as a Sacred Practice*, 2nd ed. (New York: Riverhead, 2006), xxii.

3. Labyrinthos: Labyrinths and Mazes Resource Centre, online, accessed 4. May 2016.

Part 4

Habits of Self Care

Chapter 17

The Practice of Sabbatical as Renewal[1]

Rev. Callie J. Smith and Rev. Dr. Robert Saler

The work that we do at the Center for Pastoral Excellence at Christian Theological Seminary in Indianapolis is a fostering of clergy and pastoral habits of excellence and health. Clergy thrive in their ministries because they develop and form strong practices that shape a lifetime of ministry. As the wider scope of this book argues, it is these practices used creatively that will shape the future and transformation of the universal church. One of the ways that we shape that future with clergy and their congregations is by extending an "invitation to step away," or better stated, renewal and sabbatical leaves. Because sabbatical leaves tend to be infrequent (about once every seven years on average, for that minority of parish pastors that even takes them!), it is easy to dismiss "sabbatical" (as opposed to "keeping Sabbath") as a clergy practice in and of itself. However, as we hope to show in this article, both the pastoral imagination and the congregational realities surrounding successful sabbaticals suggest several key frameworks of practice before, during, and after the leave itself. Thus, sabbatical itself is a kind of matrix of practices (self-care, congregational communication, dreaming in community, honoring our whole beings) that can both clarify and amplify excellence and health in ministry.

The Invitation to Step Away

Consider these stories.

A local pastor of a mainline Protestant church was aware, as were her congregation's leaders, that the church was in a neighborhood of changing demographics and that the congregation would need new models of being welcoming. So, she secured funding for a three-month sabbatical and traveled, with her family, to a context where she had never been (Namibia, in her case), for the primary purpose of experiencing what it would mean to have to be "hosted" in a situation of depending on others. Her congregation, while she was gone, invited Bible professors from a nearby university to come and speak about the importance of hospitality.

Another pastor found that his greatest font of creativity came, not when he was reading formal theology texts, but when he was woodworking—the sermon ideas would come fast and furious on the occasions when he could be in his shop. So his congregation granted him three months to be at home, with only modest expenses, so that he could have uninterrupted time at his shop. He came back with renewed energy such that the vigor and creativity of his sermons was noticed by the entire congregation.

Another clergyperson commenting on his final reports to the Lilly Endowment Clergy Renewal programs, wrote: "We traveled to two different continents, spent time at a ranch, fulfilled lots of dreams—but you know what the most transformative part was? Having every single meal together as a family for three months. That was the revelation."

The invitation to sabbatical as renewal is an invitation
to imagination

People of faith across generations have persisted in spiritual practices they believed would sustain and bless life over the long haul. Like prayer, like community, like Sabbath and sabbatical, some practices spread through a person's soul or a community's life and, in one way or another, bless us profoundly for the long-haul.

In the case of pastoral ministry, regular renewal and sabbatical times are opportunities to receive sustenance for the long-haul.

Renewal leaves help leaders with uniquely demanding schedules carve out time to renew their resources for that ministry. These leaves express a community's commitment to faithfully structure itself in ways that will sustain life for all its members. While not all businesses and institutions in our culture prioritize sustaining and blessing structures, the church has prophetic opportunity to embrace exactly this sort of blessing process, for its leaders and for itself.

Another way to think about this is around pastoral passion: at some point in a pastor's discernment regarding call to ministry, she was able to tap into a wellspring of joy around the calling—however inchoate at the time—that led (in most cases) to her taking on the challenges of eschewing a more financially lucrative career, obtaining theological training and ecclesial vetting, and forming herself as an emerging pastor. Sabbaticals are times to re-tap into that vein of connection with God and with God's people so that joy in the calling might reenergize the work of the calling.

If a pastor were to walk into her office after a few months away feeling energized and refreshed for ministry, ready to step back with vigor into her pastoral duties, then what might she have been doing for those months prior? The answer, of course, varies radically among pastors, and that is a good thing. Renewal leaves should be designed so that an individual pastor in all her individuality can live into the joys of her particular avocations, spiritual disciplines, relationships, and so on in ways that will be vitalizing beyond what any one-size-fits-all program can hope to achieve. The same holds true for congregational activities undertaken during the pastor's leave period.

Chairpersons of renewal leave planning teams have told us that collaborating with their pastors to prepare a Lilly Endowment Clergy Renewal Grant proposal was a learning experience for the whole team. Whether or not they actually received a grant, congregations with no history of sabbatical leave policies have developed and implemented those policies as a result of thinking through their renewal proposals together. Indeed, a number of congregations report that the very process of dreaming together about what shared renewal between the pastor and the congregation might look like is a benefit in and of itself, regardless of the final outcome of funding possibilities.

What's it For? Who's it For?

What precisely is a pastoral sabbatical "for?" We're very familiar with making a case for something that results in a valued product, but what about making a case for something whose results are not so easily recognized?

Sabbath itself challenges many cultural contexts, ancient as well as contemporary. Whether it's a Sabbath day after six days of labor or a Sabbath year after six years, the concept pushes us to expect, both for ourselves and for our neighbors, periods of time when we will not necessarily expect the production of tangible results. Practicing Sabbath provides a divinely-sanctioned opportunity to value the lives of entire communities based on grounds other than productivity and usefulness for work. However, somewhat paradoxically, precisely this "stepping away" from day-to-day productivity can be the catalyst for greater excellence in a congregation and a pastor's ministry.

Indeed, a key thesis that we would commend to you is as follows: the pastoral practice of sabbatical is best imagined, not as a benefit primarily for the pastor as individual, but as a process of shared benefit between the pastor and the congregation.

This thesis has several implications. One has to do with terminology: while the notion of "sabbatical" has deep roots in the biblical notions of "Sabbath," in our experience the term "renewal leave" is more effective for connoting (to congregation members especially) the holistic impact of a successful pastoral sabbatical. The stepping away from day to day routines on the part of the minister, with the support of a congregation, is ultimately meant to facilitate an influx of vitality to the congregation and its shared ministry with its pastor. This is not to say that pastors and congregations should not use the term "sabbatical" if they find it helpful; only that sometimes more neutral language is helpful, especially to the extent that it also dispenses with some of the less helpful associations of sabbaticals in, say, academic contexts (we don't want congregation members to expect the pastor to have written a book while away!).

The other has to do with honest assessment of a given congregation's health as it relates to the timing of the renewal leave. Put bluntly: pastors should only consider taking sabbaticals, and congregations should only consider supporting them, if the situation between the pastor and the congregation is healthy. If the pastor is truly "burnt out," if the sabbatical is meant to be a time-out (or worse, trial separation) between the pastor and congregation, or if the congregation is in latent conflict that has the potential to erupt while the pastor is away, then sabbatical is not the appropriate intervention to address those challenges; more systemic and less disruptive interventions would be needed in that case.

Emphasis on pastoral sabbaticals as benefitting the entire congregation drives one of the great strengths of the Lilly Endowment Clergy Renewal Programs' structure, which is its collaborative grant proposal process that involves more than simply pastors and their families. Clergy Renewal leaves seek to involve congregations and pastors together in the process of exploring what rest and renewal may look like for the pastor. From early brainstorming to collaborating on actual grant proposals, congregations support pastors on this journey and partner with them to structure ways for the congregations to both function and thrive during the leaves, which often includes the congregation spending time in intentional study and reflection while the pastor is away. We regularly remind those involved that the primary "product" of a successful leave is a refreshed and renewed pastor, and that the key to a good renewal leave is the whole congregation's enthusiasm about the possibilities that such re-energizing of ministry might provide.

Pastors and congregations, however, do not need the occasion of a grant proposal to begin engaging in theological reflection on the values of Sabbath-related spiritual disciplines like pastoral sabbatical even when they might not produce clear, tangible results. Far from raising a taboo question, engaging each other around these topics can be an opportunity to have critical discussions within congregations about health and mission. After all, if the goal is for a renewal period to "renew" a congregation in its health and mission, then the congregation needs to have a general sense of what health looks like in the first place!

Pastors and Communities

In 2014, the Huffington Post featured a striking article by Beth Sirull. This article explored the concept of sabbatical leaves for nonprofit leaders, describing them as beneficial for not only the leaders but also for the organizations and communities they serve.[2] This connection between the well-being of leaders and that of their communities is an intangible that warrants the attention of faith communities, as well.

Sirull cited a 2009 study on the impact of nonprofit sabbaticals. The study showed improvement in leaders' work/life balance, health, and work performance. Most remarkable, though, were the benefits to the organizations themselves. Almost two-thirds of respondents saw organizational boards becoming more effective, and over eighty percent of leaders reported increased comfort delegating responsibility as a result of colleagues having planned for and provided leadership during the sabbatical time.

On the one hand, these findings may be no surprise to those catechized into the Christian imagination. The book of Revelation, after all, pictures God's final redemption as an entirely new heaven and earth (21:1). We who think in terms of Christian faith may well expect redemptive things to affect not simply individuals who experience renewal but entire communities and eco-systems in which they are involved.

"The observance is a theological act," Walter Brueggemann reminds us about Sabbath practice in Reverberations of Faith. He identifies the impulse to "redefine human society in terms of production and consumption." Sabbath's orientation to another value system, he explains, "provides a visible testimony that God is at the center of life—that production and consumption take place in a world ordered, blessed, and restrained by the God of all creation."[3]

Sabbath-related practices testify to a divinely-sanctioned story of human worth apart from production and consumption. Practices like renewal leaves and pastoral sabbatical enter a realm beyond the benefit of only a few individuals. It makes theological sense that we enact these practices on behalf of many more lives than simply our own individual selves or our own immediate communities.

Many of us may be on board with the idea that we are intricately connected with one another. Still, to name practice of pastoral sabbatical as a form of testimony takes relational perspectives even further. Brueggemann's Sabbath-as-testimony challenges us to build regular rest and renewal into our schedules as active expressions of the gospel message. Imagine the testimony of an entire community of people finding regular ways to practice Sabbath and sabbatical in the midst of their busy lives.

In our work, congregations have shared poignant stories of pastoral renewal leaves sending ripples of insight and health into their communities. Creating space for even one leader to step away has invited others to pause and listen to their own lives and world with new attention and a fresh sense of grace. Lay leaders step up to take on new roles—roles that they often don't want to give back once the pastor has returned, often to the joy of the pastor! As one congregation member whose congregation received a Lilly

Endowment grant reported: "Any time people work together to deepen their obedience to their own faith callings, and to allow lay leadership to grow—both through a central leader taking intentional rest and refreshment time, and through leadership gifts being recognized and strengthened within the body—the result is positive and instructive."[4]

Vacation or Renewal?

The most common obstacle that laity and pastors face in helping their congregations discern the wisdom of sabbatical is the objection that the pastor taking significant time away (our recommendation is three to four months) is simply giving the pastor a "long paid vacation." What are the best ways to respond to this concern, non-defensively and theologically?

Put simply, pastoral sabbatical means more—much more—than simply taking extra vacation time. Renewal periods are times for the pastor to step away from the persistent obligations of parish life to engage in times of intentional exploration and reflection. Moreover—and this cannot be emphasized enough—renewal leaves are not solely for the benefit of the pastor; from the beginning, they should be understood as a shared enterprise between the pastor and the congregation for the benefit of both.

The nature of this benefit trades on the paradox highlighted above: ultimately, the pastor's brief hiatus from the daily work of the congregation has as its goal a renewal of pastoral vitality so that the shared ministry between pastor and congregation can benefit. Far more than Marx's famous derogation of leisure time as simply "renewing oneself for labor," this is a question of how pastors sustain excellence over the long term.

Pastors have worked with their congregations in many and various ways to craft leaves that remove them from their daily contexts enough to become opportunities for renewal. However diverse the kinds of renewal may be, a couple themes are helpful for thinking about how renewal plays out in pastoral sabbaticals: refuge and sustenance.

Far from simply "checking out" or escaping briefly, as we might do during a vacation, sabbatical times and renewal leaves actively set apart certain kinds of space in the rhythm of our lives. "One of the most precious gifts we can offer is to be a place of refuge, to be Sabbath for one another," writes Wayne Muller in *Sabbath: Finding Rest, Renewal, and Delight in Our Busy Lives.*[5]

One story may illustrate this: a woman wrote to our program saying that she had grown up as a pastor's daughter, and had frankly "hated" the church for all of the evening meetings, weekends, and vacations that her father had to work. But when this pastor's congregation sought funding to send the family on a renewal leave, she felt that the congregation was deeply honoring her father AND his family (and that the funding agency was honoring them as well). The activity not only rehabilitated the image of the church in her mind, it also helped improve her relationship with her father (and thus her father's vocation).

The companions we seek during intentional spaces of sabbatical or renewal may very well comprise part of the "refuge" blessing. In their book *Clergy Renewal: The Alban Guide to Sabbatical Planning,* A. Richard Bullock and Richard J. Bruesehoff note the significant role that well-selected companions may play during a pastoral leave. Holding space open for engaging mentors or spiritual companions during a leave can help one maintain focus, metabolize insights, and shape that experience "for the deepening and renewal of one's relationship with God."[6]

The refuge of well-chosen companions, in fact, may extend even beyond particular sabbaticals or leave-times, becoming part of our life's rhythm. The Lilly Endowment Clergy Renewal Programs, for instance, invite congregations to set aside a portion of their grant budgets for pastors' post-leave activities, including counseling or spiritual direction. Planning and implementing, working and resting, journeying and returning—the fellows we choose to help us actively create spaces of renewal can help us continue claiming that transformation for which a pastoral sabbatical lays rich groundwork.

Obstacles into Opportunity

When thinking about stepping away for a pastoral sabbatical, it's valuable to note the obstacles which arise. Renewal times are not all rosy. Stepping away from ordinary rhythms can be a mixed bag. On days when we tell ourselves we will rest and not work, our minds may fill with urgent-seeming reasons to sneak in a little productivity or consumerism (i.e., have someone else produce for us). Time designated for "renewal" can seem refreshing, but it can just as often seem a battle with obstacles, impulses, or fears which would keep us from it.

But consider: what if obstacles are actually part and parcel of observing pastoral sabbatical? Stepping away for wilderness renewal is part of Jesus' own transformation into a figure of public ministry who challenges the very value systems he first resists in the wilderness. Those temptations are obstacles. They are also indicators casting light on what in his community would turn a person away from God's priorities.

In a similar way, the individual habits and community assumptions which tell us we cannot possibly step away for a sabbatical or renewal leave may highlight the very systems and priorities which we are gifted with a calling to challenge. Those temptations to bypass Sabbath-related rhythms may be part of our own transformation process as we mature in our current forms of ministry and embrace new visions of ministry for the future.

Those who have participated in the Lilly Endowment Clergy Renewal Programs have shared in honest reflection over the years about their concerns before as well as during a renewal leave. One pastor desired being needed and resisted the idea that what he devoted his days to could be done by others. Another pastor feared not wanting to return to her pastoral role. One congregation relied on a senior minister's presence for the community's motivation. Another anticipated loss in attendance and giving. Potential reasons abound to avoid pastoral sabbaticals. A recent book about her clergy renewal leave by one of the first recipients of the Lilly Endowment Clergy Renewal grants, Laurie Haller, describes how painful it was to realize that she truly would have to "recess," that is, withdraw any illusions of her essentiality to the community's functioning, if her leave was to have a transformative effect on her ministry and that of the congregation's; such "recession" can be painful in its own right.[7]

What habits, arrangements, or commitments have kept you from planning a pastoral sabbatical or renewal leave? What congregational dynamics or leadership assumptions discourage you from imagining 3–4 months away? These obstacles may point to areas of transformation which sabbatical practice could shape you to address in the future.

They also point to the need to be intentional about crafting a renewal leave that takes seriously the fact that it usually takes a while for pastors on leave to get into the "zone" of quality renewal time; in general, it is advisable to plan a time period that is sufficiently lengthy (3-4 months is ideal), to build in at least a week on the front and back ends of the sabbatical to transition in and out of routine of ministry gracefully, to limit contact between pastor and congregation (using social media asynchronously rather than synchronously is advisable), and to identify pastoral care resources that the congregation trusts so that the congregation is less tempted to contact the pastor while away.

Transformed Leadership

Crucially, practicing pastoral sabbatical does not mean having a "one and done" experience, after which life goes on as it did before.

The very term "practice" points to something that happens regularly, which has broader impact and longer-term implications. A pastor can take a sabbatical leave and then dive right back in to the life she left. However, in exploring sabbatical as a practice, we are much more interested in considering the influence that a successful leave time might have on the long-term health of the pastor and the congregation.

Practicing the pastoral sabbatical can mean planning for a major disruption of leadership patterns in a congregation. As intimidating as that sounds, such disruption could very well be an investment in the future of that congregation's ministry. In these days of significant change across the congregational landscape of North America, the Sabbath-related practice of disrupting habitual patterns can invite us into fresh perspectives on leadership for the twenty-first century.

Disruption, after all, is a powerful part of the biblical concept of Sabbath. Sabbath practice calls us to the sometimes-sweet, sometimes-difficult, always-sacred act of stepping back from the systems and assumptions that have been shaping us. In the book of Genesis, God uses a seventh day to stop and evaluate the creation that has emerged, declaring it good. We who are made in God's image also function best when we stop long enough to observe and evaluate. Observation and evaluation require a very different mode than creating or producing. As Sabbath reminds us, the practice of stepping away is crucial to nurturing a proper perspective on our role in the scheme of things.

This is one of the reasons why the Lilly Endowment Clergy Renewal Programs emphasize renewal leaves as experiences that pastors and congregations share. While pastors step away from the persistent obligations of daily congregational life, congregation members explore what renewal means for their community, including how they function with more space to exercise leadership and other pastoral gifts. Both constituencies encounter an upset, a disjunction with what has been their way of operating. But in healthy congregations, such disjunctions tend to reap benefits rather than anxiety.

It may not be ideal for pastor and congregation to return to the same way of operating as soon as a time of renewal ends. Some pastors arrive at renewal leaves worn out by their habitual ways of being pastor. Some congregations arrive at renewal leaves discouraged by familiar ways of being church. Some renewal leaves disrupt what Wayne Muller's *Sabbath: Finding Rest, Renewal, and Delight in Our Busy Lives* calls "the pattern of desperation that infects our thinking." These Sabbath-like disruptions, according to Muller, enable us "to see the healing that is already present in the problem."[8]

"The problem" could be role expectations that add up to an over-functioning pastor. "The problem" could be budgets that only fund a part-time clergy salary. "The problem," however, gets defined, if pastoral sabbaticals disrupt congregations in any significant way, then they offer clergy and laity alike a chance to reflect about what ministries need to happen and by whom.

In the case of planning a sabbatical, clergy and laity get to explore their current distributions of leadership and then perhaps live into new models, experimenting with potential models during the leave time. Those sabbatical months may seem strange or unnerving, but this need not be a negative. Preparing to negotiate a pastor's time away could mean discovering the presence of unexpected possibilities when we only anticipated absence. When communities practice sabbatical, we practice pausing to watch and listen for the unknown gifts of God that may be only just beginning to grow among us.

Process

A 2011 report by the Louisville Institute (LI)[9] upon the conclusion of its sabbatical grants for pastoral leaders program (2006-2011) offers impressive statistics: "80% of congregational representatives affirmed that the LI-funded sabbatical had strengthened the pastor's commitment to his or her parish" and "75% reported that the sabbatical had tangibly benefited the life of the church." That breadth of people benefitting—pastors as well as congregants—would alone have been impressive. But when the report calls pastors and congregations to "trust the process" of sabbaticals, we can take hope in more than just the sheer number of people touched. We can take hope in the potential for transforming our communities.

"Parish ministry can become a 'totalizing environment' that defines the whole life world of the pastor," explains the report, adding: "Wise pastors acknowledge their need to keep Sabbath as a regular rhythm and alternate tempo in their ministry. Sabbath keeping fosters pastoral imagination via negativa: saying 'no' to work, commerce, and daily routine in order to say 'yes' to contemplation, feasting, and friendship with Creator and other creatures." Pastoral sabbaticals have benefit beyond the leave time itself, in part because they have the implications of a spiritual practice.

Indeed, trusting the process of pastoral sabbatical to have transformative potential in our communities over time may involve engaging new practices even before the sabbatical begins. In a "How to Have a Good Sabbatical" section, the Louisville Institute report recommends: "Start now living the sabbatical disciplines you desire. If you plan to journal while away, begin today. Integrate into your way of life so these disciplines will become enduring habits after return."

Trusting the process may also involve looking beyond the close of a leave time. The Lilly Endowment Clergy Renewal Programs pay attention to this. Final grant report guidelines ask, "Will any aspects of this renewal program be continued after the grant period?" These reports ask congregations, specifically, "Are there any parts of the renewal experience that have been incorporated into the life of the congregation?" Of pastors the guidelines ask, "Are there any parts of the renewal experience that have been incorporated into the routine of your life?" We ask on the assumption that pastoral sabbatical may very well have given an entire congregation opportunities to attend to an "alternate tempo in their ministry," as the Louisville Institute report puts it, enacting rhythms with the potential to alter their business-as-usual pace.

Conclusion

At whatever point you are in discerning the wisdom of a renewal leave, allow yourself permission to dream beyond what such a leave is "supposed" to look like. Consider too how it might impact your congregation and what "success" could look like in your unique ministry context. Indeed, to the extent that a renewal leave plan is genuinely "of" the congregation rather than imposed upon it, it may be truly unique as regards both pastoral and congregational activities. But what can be expected is that the entire process of the practice—before, during, and after any particular leave—will provide rich opportunities to explore what renewal could mean to your congregation over time.

Notes

1. We come to the work of considering sabbatical as a pastoral practice on the basis of our work at Christian Theological Seminary in Indianapolis, where we have had the honor, for the last three years, of administering the Lilly Endowment National Clergy Renewal Program and Clergy Renewal Program for Indiana Congregations on behalf of Lilly Endowment, Inc.

A little background: both the seminary and the Endowment are based in Indianapolis. The Endowment has been offering grants to congregations to support their pastors taking a 3-4 month renewal leave (more on that terminology below) since 1999; however, in 2012, with the establishment of the Center for Pastoral Excellence at Christian Theological Seminary, the Center's staff began administering the programs on behalf of the Endowment. In these last three years, then, we have had the opportunity to interact with hundreds of congregations and pastors as they discern the timing and shape of what a renewal leave for the pastor might look like. We are blessed to be the recipients of hundreds of stories each year of how renewal leaves have reenergized the ministries of pastors and congregations. What follows are some theological and practical reflections learned along the way.

2. Beth Sirull. "Sabbaticals for Nonprofit Leaders Benefit the Executive, the Organization and the Communities It Serves," The Huffington Post, online, accessed 24. June 2015.

3. Walter Brueggemann, *Reverberations of Faith: A Theological Handbook of Old Testament Themes* (Louisville, KY: Westminster John Knox, 2002), 181.

4. Christian Theological Seminary, Lilly Endowment Renewal Blog, online, accessed, 20. June 2015.

5. Wayne Muller, *Sabbath: Finding Rest, Renewal, and Delight in Our Busy Lives* (New York: Bantam, 1999), 119.

6. A. Richard Bullock and Richard J. Bruesehoff, *Clergy Renewal: The Alban Guide to Sabbatical Planning* (Lanham, MD: Rowman & Littlefield, 2000), 28.

7. Laurie Haller, *Recess: Rediscovering Play and Purpose* (Canton, Michigan: Cass Community, 2015).

8. Muller,168.

9. The Louisville Institute, "The Louisville Institute Sabbatical Grants for Pastoral Leaders Program 1994–2011" *Resources for American Christianity*, online, accessed 5. May, 2016.

Chapter 18

Spiritual Direction as Clergy Self-Care

Rev. Teresa Blythe

We want our religious leaders to live healthy lives. A bright, energetic pastor who embodies joy and compassion is a true gift. One who knows when and how to draw appropriate boundaries, enjoys a robust life outside of work, and stays engaged with theological and spiritual questions is the ideal. Yet anyone who has spent much time around faith communities knows that pastors, priests, rabbis and religious educators frequently run into situations that drain life right out of them. Worse yet, the people they may want to talk to about their situation—parishioners—are likely the very people at the heart of what is contributing to the drain.

In light of such life draining experiences, spiritual direction is vital, especially for those clergy who refuse to be in denial about the changing face of the church and refuse to be a chaplain to a dying congregation. For the creative clergy, the habit of spiritual direction is a lifeline.

What is Spiritual Direction?

Spiritual direction is the practice of examining your life for the energy, presence and movement of the holy. "Our journeys are not meant to be utterly solitary," writes Marjorie J. Thompson. "Trying to be faithful to God can be a lonely and trying path."[1] A spiritual director listens with deep attention and lovingly explores with the one seeking direction (the directee) the meaning, lessons and gifts along that "trying path." Direction is not psychotherapy or pastoral counseling "nor is it to be confused with the mutuality of deep friendships, for it is unashamedly hierarchical," writes Margaret Guenther. "Not because the director is somewhat 'better' or 'holier' than the directee, but because, in this covenanted relationship the director has agreed to put himself aside so that his total attention can be focused on the person sitting in the other chair."[2] This practice of having one hour a month devoted to your life, your spiritual path and your relationship with God can seem like a luxury, but once experienced it becomes a self-care necessity for people working full-time in the care-of-souls business.

What makes a spiritual director most valuable to the religious professional is that the director is ethically bound to hold confidentiality and withhold judgment about the material brought to a session. Spiritual directors are trained to be a non-anxious presence with no agenda for you other than your spiritual growth—and how that happens is between you and God.

Training is an important part of the formation of a spiritual director. Directors are trained in contemplative listening, ethics, prayer practices and self-care. They are ethically bound to each have their own spiritual director and to participate in supervision, which is part of a director's continuing education and an essential practice for developing greater self-awareness as a director.

The Theology Behind Spiritual Direction

Theology matters in spiritual direction, but it is always practical theology—how a person lives out their faith—rather than systematic theology. Doctrine is not of great concern for the spiritual director since the focus of direction is more on a person's experience of God than of what he or she believes about God. Still, several theological assumptions are at work in spiritual direction, and it is helpful to be transparent about them.

1. God exists and desires a union of love with us. Whether the directee prefers the term "God" or some other term for the unseen

reality that is the source of all life, spiritual direction holds as foundational that this life force exists; the force is good and desires a two-way relationship of love with us. There are countless ways we understand this relationship.

2. God created us for relationship. God is not separate from creation but lives and breathes in all creatures, past, present, and future. Spiritual direction is the intentional, conscious invitation to experience this embodied presence.

3. God's desire for us is written in our hearts. "It is not too high or too far away—the Word is in your hearts for you to observe." (Deuteronomy 30: 10-20) Spiritual directors believe God is already at work in the hearts and minds of our directees, drawing them closer to God and leading them on the path that is right for them.

4. Relationship with God is developed through spiritual practice. When we are in love with a person, we stay connected to that person. The same is true with the divine. Living in a loving relationship with the source of life, we need to cultivate that relationship through regular spiritual practice which includes prayer, reflection, meditation, fasting, study and worship. Many other activities are spiritual practice for people—yoga, walking outdoors, gardening, dance, play and tending to pets. Spiritual directors encourage regular spiritual practice although we leave the choice of practice up to the directee.

5. God is bigger than any one religious or spiritual tradition. Directors come from their own religious or spiritual tradition and directees do as well. Dogma and doctrine are ways humans within institutions have sought to understand God, and as such they have their place. Spiritual direction works in a different realm--the realm of what we experience of God, even while understanding that a directee's beliefs about God influence that experience.

6. God is the true Director in spiritual direction. The spiritual director is not a guru giving out wisdom. At best, directors listen to the Spirit in the hope that whatever is said or done in each session helps the directee do the same.

7. God calls us into a world in need of God's healing presence. Spiritual direction encourages the balance between contemplation and action. God calls all persons to a good work in the world. Directors help directees discern what that work is for them and support them collegially as they take the action toward that call.

Why clergy need Spiritual Direction

The most important reason for clergy to engage in spiritual direction is to commit to a deeper relationship with God. The work that pastors do is difficult, emotional and deep and it requires time out for prayer, study and renewal. As Jesus might put it today, "what good is it if the spiritual leader helps a congregation thrive and grow but loses his or her own soul?" Spiritual direction helps us pay attention to what matters most in life.

Spiritual direction has three basic areas of interest: awareness of God; reflection on what that awareness means; and discernment--making choices in alignment with that understanding of God in one's life. It is so easy to lose awareness of God when you are busy "working for God." Awareness needs to be intentional if we are to learn and grow from it, which means we need to be still now and then. How many clergy are so busy that taking time for stillness seems impossible? Spiritual direction is a monthly reminder of the moments when God's presence was keenly felt and a time to relive it in a contemplative setting.

A spiritual director can be the one person a pastor can go to as an outlet for airing and processing the common frustrations of being the chosen and paid leader of that most distinctive of volunteer organizations—the religious congregation. In spiritual direction, you are given space to allow all emotions to be felt and listened to. Situations and conflicts can be "unpacked," and options discussed and prayed about. Some typical concerns clergy bring to spiritual direction include:

Difficulties with prayer and relationship with God
A loss of motivation and passion in work
Seeking more joy in life
Balancing work responsibilities with responsibilities to family
      or interests outside the congregation
Emotional highs and lows of being a spiritual leader
Desire to be accountable to better self-care practices
Secrets that are causing inner turmoil
Challenges with physical health and healing.

Beyond these, one of the most important services a spiritual director can offer a clergy person is assistance with discernment—the spiritual practice of making choices in alignment with one's faith and values for the purpose of deepening in relationship with God. Sifting and sorting through a situation, considering how the Spirit is moving in one's heart and then—at the appropriate time—making the choice and taking the action can be the material for months of direction sessions with a pastor who is experiencing distress and conflict on the job.

If you are a clergy reading this chapter right now you may be saying to yourself, "Hey, this description of spiritual direction is what I do for other people all the time." It is true. Clergy are, by default, spiritual guides for those they serve, which means they need never "go it alone." In addition to a spiritual director, clergy who do a lot of one-on-one work as a spiritual guide or pastoral counselor might consider having a supervisor as well.[3] Many clergy find that after being in spiritual direction awhile they develop a desire to attend a formation and training program and be formally trained as a spiritual director.[4]

Finding a Spiritual Director

Since this is such an important part of pastoral self-care, it is important for the pastor to find the right spiritual director. The most effective spiritual director for most clergy will be the "non-directive" type using what is sometimes called the evocative method. This is the empathic listener who doesn't give advice or steer the directee in any way. Evocative spiritual directors—the most common types found—allow ample freedom and space for the directee to do his or her own work. A wise spiritual director will encourage awareness of God, listen deeply, help the directee reflect on his or her life and situations that come up, allow emotions to be held and processed and keep confidentiality. He or she will also help the pastor gain a greater understanding of the systems and structures they are a part of. The non-directive director will encourage regular spiritual practice and keep a contemplative attitude throughout the session so that the directee can slow down and feel safe.

There are several ways to find a spiritual director. The professional organization Spiritual Directors International has a "Seek and Find Guide" on its website that will show you members of SDI by region.[5] Internet searches are also helpful since many directors now have websites that give a lot of information about their practice. Retreat centers usually keep a list of spiritual directors on hand. Once you get a list, it is recommended that you interview at least three directors by telephone before beginning sessions with one. Make sure they have the kind of training, experience and religious background you are looking for. In the interview, pay attention to your intuition and comfort level. You will know you have found the right director when you feel like you can safely reveal anything that needs to be revealed.

It may be wise for a pastor serving a congregation within a denomination to look for a spiritual director outside his or her denomination. It can be freeing to move outside one's zone of influence even if it means explaining polity and procedures of your denomination to your director. As people from a variety of backgrounds and religions now have training in spiritual direction, it is not uncommon to find Christian pastors receiving spiritual direction from Jewish or Buddhist directors (or vice versa).

Regardless of tradition, always look for a trained and experienced director. Most directors are paid for their time and depending on your geographical region, one session will cost anywhere from $40 - $100. Sliding scales are almost always offered if finances are a concern.

Making a Retreat

Many clergy have their first taste of spiritual direction on retreat--that special block of time away from the congregation for silence, rest, play and reflection. Many retreat centers have spiritual directors on hand to meet with retreatants on a daily or "as needed" basis. Or if you live near a retreat center, you can hire a local spiritual director to help you plan the retreat and meet with you on a pre-arranged basis. Retreats are as varied as the people who lead or plan them. There are guided retreats with lots of activities to choose from or you can plan your own solo retreat with unstructured time for a few days of rest. These times apart from our tightly-controlled daily lives invite us to slow down, reflect on what is real and necessary and help us get our bearings for what is to come.

The Disconnect

So why don't all clergy have spiritual directors? If it is so beneficial, should it not be a universal practice? Time constraints and financial concerns are sometimes barriers. Fear can stand in the way—fear that it is not truly confidential or a fear of being vulnerable. In some cases, pastors are not aware of the benefits of spiritual direction until a colleague shares how it has helped them. Sadly, spiritual directors aren't always very good at marketing.

Spiritual direction can often be disparaged as a fad, written off as just another of the many personal services people indulge in today. People have a fitness trainer, a life coach and a health coach, why not a spiritual director? But Tilden Edwards—one of the pioneers in the modern spiritual direction movement—does not think it is a fad. "It has endured in one form or another since the early days of the church, and its value is corroborated by every other deep spiritual tradition. Once experienced in an authentic form, I think its value will become apparent to most people."[6]

Conclusion

Spiritual direction is a unique experience that complements a host of other important relationships related to the vocation of ministry and most importantly grounds the centrality of pastoral practice in the work of a nurtured relationship with God. The therapist keeps confidentiality and listens, but may not delve deeply into spiritual experiences or assist with spiritual practices. Additionally, a close friend can listen and help the pastor process what is going on in the congregation, but the close friend may feel so invested in the friendship that he or she cannot be objective. Our friends find it hard to shed their opinions or judgments.

The right spiritual director will help the clergyperson find his or her own path through the valleys and mountaintops of ministry in this postmodern terrain, accompanying them but not choosing the path for them. And that can make the difference between surviving and thriving as a creative clergyperson in congregational leadership.

Notes

1. Marjorie Thompson, *Soul Feast* (Louisville: Westminster John Knox, 1995), 117.

2. Margaret Guenther, *Holy Listening* (Boston: Cowley, 1992), 3.

3. Supervision is the practice of reflecting on a case study or situation from your ministry work with a person or peer group designed to help you discover your inner motivations and feelings about that case. Spiritual directors have supervisors to help prevent them from developing unhealthy habits, to create and maintain healthy boundaries and to know when they need more inner work around a subject or theme that may come up in a session.

4. You can find formation and training programs listed on the Spiritual Directors International website, www.sdiworld.org.

5. Visit the "Seek and Find Guide" at www.sdiworld.org.

6. Tilden Edwards, *Spiritual Director Spiritual Companion* (Mahwah, NJ: Paulist, 1989), 22.

Chapter 19

Pastoring and Parenting: Experiments in Family Ritual

Rev. Courtney Stange-Tregear

All three of them lay in one big bed. Actually, it was two twin beds that had been pushed together in ramshackle fashion. Asleep, finally. With their sweet little faces at rest, and to the faint hum of quiet snoring, I exhaled. It might have been the first time I had actually exhaled all day, and I felt an overwhelming sense of shame and sadness.

"I'm just not good at this," I thought. I'm ruining them and their childhoods. Why go to the trouble, and cost, of going on vacation only to have me be the same short-tempered parent that I always am? Had I failed? As I backed out of the room and closed the door, I cried a little. This was our first time taking a real vacation as a family. I had packed up all three children and the car for a week at the beach. I had been looking forward to this week for months, yet just one day into vacation and I felt terrible.

While I had been looking forward to our family time at the beach, it somehow had not sunk in that my husband was not able to take a full week off from work. So I would be on my own with our three young kids at the beach, away from the comforts and routines of home, for the first four days. Reality struck as I had begun packing the car that morning. Resentment soon followed. I felt angry at my husband that he couldn't take more time off from work. I felt frustrated that the children were exhausted, for in their excitement they had not been able to fall asleep the night before and woke particularly early that morning. I felt embarrassed that I had been looking forward to this week as a time of rest and rejuvenation, but it was likely to feel more exhausting than the work-life "balance" I barely cobbled together in regular life.

As I walked to my room, knowing that the little one would be up and getting into my bed soon enough, I knew that I wanted to be better, to have more balance in my life. I didn't want my sense of failure, both feared and in reality, to dominate our first family vacation. Parenting is a vocation like any other, although with it there is a complication of balance with other parts of our lives, such as our jobs. I am a pastor and a parent, two vocations that consistently pour over into one another. How do we as clergy who have families set a proper balance? Are there habits that can sustain our family lives and ease our pastor-parent stresses? This family vacation was a symptom of a larger problem within the work of clergy and their families; it was a symptom of our constant worry that we will fail and a lack of proper balance. Something had to change.

Clergy and Imbalance

One of the greatest challenges that clergy face in our work is finding the appropriate boundaries for our lives, a challenge that is compounded when we have families. The lines between pastor and parent are blurry when we are at home. We might be in the middle of a conversation or a meal as a family when the phone interrupts with the news that someone has been sent to the emergency room or someone has died and our presence is needed. Or a phone call comes needing our attention with a matter of importance with the church and we have to excuse ourselves to address the concerns. In a corporate office at the end of the day, it is not often that the work environment makes its way into the home. With clergy families, these lines are blurred. When we are at home we can still be at work and when we are at the church office we still have to deal with sick kids, a vomiting dog, a school concern, or getting a meal on the table for everyone. The work of clergy interlinks and overlaps different worlds in our lives and this can cause stress, anxiety, and a strong sense of uncertainty unless we find a good way to set healthy boundaries.

What is more, if the work of a pastor is largely the work of spirituality and we spend a great portion of our time engaging others in their spiritual lives, how do we have the energy to do the same with our families? Do not our children and spouses deserve our same attention? But, as I recall my experience at the beach that day, my sense of imbalance, I realize that many clergy struggle with holding these same lines, this same need for balance and for healthy boundaries. I am not alone and my need to hold better balance from that day at the beach taught me that I need a spiritual practice, a habit, to ground me and my family. Sure, I could have developed a spiritual practice that would have been exclusive to me, but my life is not exclusive. My life is intertwined with four other lives in my home and I wanted to seek out and design a spiritual practice that would involve my entire family. My search took me back to my seminary days.

While in seminary I had taken a course on spiritual practices. As part of the course each student had to try several different spiritual practices and then commit to practicing one for the second half of the semester. I chose Sabbath keeping-and inflicted it upon my husband. We followed as much of the tradition as seemed practical, which meant not too much of it actually, but it did create a nice rhythm to our week. Though we enjoyed the practice to some varying degree, yet when the semester came to a close and I wrote up my report on the final project, we decided to stop keeping Sabbath. We had not taken on quite enough of the "spiritual" part of Sabbath for it to feel as rich and transformative as I had hoped for, and it didn't seem likely I was going to convince my agnostic husband to do more than we already were. As I recalled that Sabbath keeping experience on my search for balance, I remembered a significant amount of reading on mindfulness and meditation.

My initial reading in this area started as an interest in intercessory prayer and the concept of prayer healing. It was also fueled by a growing dissatisfaction with my prayer life. While prayer had played a large role in my becoming Christian in the first place, as I became more and more involved in church leadership, prayer had (sadly) become something I did for others. I was ashamed to admit that my personal prayer practice felt more obligatory than rewarding.

By chance, a friend gave me a book on the connection between prayer and bodily health called Healing Words, about different research and viewpoints on prayer healing.

I read another book on the topic and another, and through my research I discovered that there are measurable physical and health benefits of mindfulness meditation. Particularly formative was the work of Herbert Benson and his book *The Relaxation Response.*

Benson is a medical doctor, Harvard professor, and founder of the Henry-Benson Institute for Mind Body Medicine at Massachusetts General Hospital.[1] During his career Benson researched, developed, and tested a meditative practice called the Relaxation Response modeled after transcendental meditation. In the simplest terms, the Relaxation Response is a simple meditative practice of breathing deeply and intentionally, which has been shown to be very effective at stress reduction and healing the body of conditions such as hypertension, obesity, and mental illness.

I was drawn to the idea of a spiritual practice that would specifically benefit my physical self, one that wasn't something I did for church members and wasn't something I was, in any way, obligated to do. As someone who came to faith later in life and still wrestled with doubt, I was attracted to the idea of a practice that would be valuable to my person, for my health, even when I was in the midst of spiritual doubt. Because mindfulness meditation "works" even without any belief in God or the power of prayer, I saw the possibility that it could be valuable even in my most agnostic moments.

I longed to be the type of person who practiced mindfulness in any one of the various ways it can be practiced. I wanted to live as that person who went out walking each day and came back refreshed in body and spirit. Yet in the midst of an expanding family, this never seemed possible. I couldn't see how I would find time for any kind of meditation given the imbalance between my life as a pastor, a mother, and a wife. Meditation seemed like a good idea in theory, but it also just felt like one more thing to add to the chaos.

The more I looked at the puzzle of finding balance, the more I concluded, that I was simply not good enough at time management or else I would be able to schedule time away from all distractions for some practice that would serve as a regular injection of spiritual enlightenment. Perhaps if I were more devout, I would be able to see cleaning up toys as a reminder of the beauty of creation or bath time as an opportunity to remember their baptisms.

Alas I could do none of these practices. The hurdle felt too high, and I, too incapable. In the meantime, through the daily struggles of parenting and pastoring, I felt that I was becoming less spiritual, less compassionate, and less myself with each day. I needed a spiritual practice, a habit, that was strong enough to transform and ground the intertwining of my vocation as a pastor and my vocation as a mother and wife.

Discovering Family Devotion

When I closed the door that night at the beach, I knew something had to change. Through what I had already learned and experienced about spiritual practices and mindfulness, and with some persistent googling, I was able to create a personalized spiritual practice that was just a little bit of everything I was longing for. It was that night when the idea was born of our family devotional.

Of course a family devotional is something I had known about as an idea. I imagined it to be a bit like Sunday School at home. In my mind, this was for calm and quiet families in their idyllic loving homes; devoted families who share quality time, enriching their faith and praying together. But I needed something I could manage, something that didn't require me to possess a God-like patience. So I came up with something of my own, something that seemed possible in my hurried, unprepared, and impatient capacity. What we do at our house is, of course, open to a large range of adaptation, but here is what we do at our house and I simply offer it to the reader as an invitation to creatively figure out what kind of family ritual and prayers work for you.

Gathering

One of the greatest challenges of pulling together a family to specifically address matters of the Spirit is finding a time to gather. Our time after school, like most families, is busy and tense. The kids want to blow off steam after the stress of school. I feel pressure to make sure they get through their homework and eat dinner in the few short hours between school and sports. Often I have the added commitment of evening meetings back at the church. Even on the best days, afternoon is a stressful time of day and with plenty of other home distractions, pastoral care emergencies, and sports, I find it hard to pull this all together before rushing out the door again.

I knew that if this was going to be helpful or effective, I needed us to gather as soon as everyone was home from school. That way, no matter what else happened, I was guaranteeing ten minutes of quality family time together. And these ten minutes ultimately, became a great way for us to "reset," to ground and center us each afternoon, holding in balance various parts of our day. This time may not work for all families depending on schedules, but finding ten minutes of time to "reset" together can bring a life of imbalance into a healthier way of being. Whatever time of day makes that balance happen for you, adjust and make it work in your family. For us, the best time to gather came in the middle of our day between our early day activities and what would come of the rest of our evenings.

Setting the Scene

My children are used to being in church and can sit through worship reasonably well. But not having done anything like this in our home before, I knew it would be important to set the scene for them. I would need to make the time we spend in family devotion feel different and "set apart" from the other time we spend together as a family. Influenced by what I know about worship and retreat settings, as well as what I've observed in school and preschool classrooms, I developed a plan.

First, to encourage stillness, it would be important to root their bodies to a physical spot (just like circle time in preschool), so I bought inexpensive placemats from a home decorating store. Knowing that it's important to engage a multitude of senses, I found some old incense and an LED light. I carefully chose a space where they weren't used to playing; we are lucky to have a play room, so I decided to use the living room since they do not usually go into that room.

Because my kids tend toward the rambunctious side, I ask them to line up outside the room. This helps them to enter the room with a degree of seriousness they would not have otherwise. Once lined up and calm, they are invited into the room one at a time. Upon entering, they take a placemat and choose where they would like to sit. I allow them to sit anywhere they want with the rule that they must sit on the floor and cannot be touching one another. Then one of them is given the opportunity to light the incense while another is allowed to turn on the LED light.

Guided Meditation

Guided meditation definitely seems like an "adult" thing to do: how many children spend time following their breath for ten minutes? Yet this is the core of what we do together. This practice has been transforming mostly because it is unique compared to the chaos my family is used to throughout the rest of the day. I have written some of my own meditations, and read aloud some that have been written by others, but for the most part we listen to one of the many meditations that can be found online at www.shambala.com,[2] which are short and specifically geared towards children.

Believe it or not, once the children have gotten used to this practice, they will settle down with very little guidance.

Reading Scripture

The design of adding the scripture reading was mostly for my benefit. I spend a lot of time reading and interpreting scripture texts for the benefit of those I serve at church, but I have found rarely do I read it for my own or my family's edification. As a pastor and parent, I needed a better balance of sharing scripture with my congregation and with my family, so the addition of scripture as a tool in family devotions is multipurpose. Instead of randomly reading through the children's bible, I read the scripture that I am going to preach on that coming Sunday. I try to find the story first in their children's bible then step it up to reading it in the regular bible.

Reflecting and Sharing on the Word

I believe it to not be an unusual encounter for parents to experience their children providing a one-word answer to their questions after the school day. There must be a universal kid code:

"How was school today?" " Fine."

During this time of hearing scripture, however, I ask the family to respond and react to the reading. In these moments when I would expect my children to conform to the norm of one word answers, instead the conversation shifts. Since we have already centered ourselves with the mediation and listened to scripture, the question

I ask usually gets a more nuanced and thoughtful answer:

> What made you happy today?
> What made you sad today?
> What do you wish you had done better today?
> When was someone kind to you?
> When were you thoughtful towards someone else?
> Who needs our prayers today?
> What is the scripture/story saying to you?

Most days, but not always, I try to relate the question in some way to the scripture we read. Most of all I try to get them talking. To facilitate their responses, I require that they not respond to one another and that they each get a turn to answer the question. This particular element of the family devotion is also a window into their world for me as their mother. It allows me to know when they are happy or sad, and if I need to be aware of something in their life. Understanding this, I find this part of our time invaluable.

Closing Prayer

Once everyone has had a chance to answer the question, we have a closing prayer. When we first started doing this I was always the one to lead the prayer. I would say a simple prayer and that would be it. But after a few months, first my oldest child and then all three wanted an opportunity to say the prayer. It is touching and often rather profound to hear them pray, and this is perhaps the best part of the family devotion.

Treats: So the sweetness of Sabbath will linger on their lips

Years ago when we practiced Sabbath-keeping, we would end our Sabbath time with a sweet treat. My son would be allowed to pick out some sweet treat from the bakery or snack from the pantry. For a family that didn't eat a lot of sweets it was a memorable way to make the time special. I decided that eating a sweet treat was something that I wanted to carry over from our Sabbath keeping and into our family devotional.

After the closing prayer, we would put out the incense, turn off the LED light, stack up the placemats, and head to the kitchen where each child is given a small piece of chocolate or other treat. If nothing else, it works as a kind of bribery and makes them think devotion time is fun and exciting, rather than another harebrained scheme to which their mother is subjecting them.

I believe the sweetness of our time together is encouraged to linger by the sweetness of the closing treat.

Learning Curve and Application

On that first vacation at the beach, I knew that I needed a spiritual practice that offered me a strong sense of self care as a pastor and as one who loves her family. I needed a way to stay well. Many clergy can identify with this struggle for balance. We understand the need to set good boundaries, to stay healthy, and endeavor to share in practices of excellence for our vocation. We are asked to be knowledgeable about everything from the Bible to mission, from finances to administration, it can feel overwhelming to be exceptional in all the areas of our work. The feeling of being overwhelmed contributes to doubt, frustration, poor boundaries, and poor health for many of us, and these imbalances cause stress within our families. As a way of addressing these matters we need rituals and practices that can keep us grounded. In truth, there are very few resources out there for those of us seeking such things. Thus, the learning curve is wide and our creativity will no doubt cause us to fail, start over, and try again. How will we know if we have achieved the balance we seek? I know that the creative action I took with family rituals as a habit has worked for us because of how it has changed all of us, especially my children.

"Let me breathe!" My eight-year-old closed his eyes and breathed deliberately, sitting up straighter with breath going in and out of his lungs, hand on his stomach to feel the flow of air. After perhaps thirty seconds, he opened his eyes and said, with a surprising objectivity and clarity, what he was angry about. We were able to discuss his (valid) concern without any shouting, tears, consequences, or punishments. We hugged, and I felt full of love and compassion for this small person whose life I get to be a part of.

"Mama, help me breathe!" My three-year-old daughter, in the midst of a temper tantrum, with tears streaming down her face, climbed up into my lap so that I could help her breathe. I tuned into my own breath, feeling the air going in and out of my nostrils. I sit up straighter so that I can feel my chest expand with the air entering my lungs. I calmed my own body and my reaction to her tantrum. Soon she was breathing calmly as well. She stopped crying and was able to say what was upsetting her. I feel overwhelmed by gratitude for my child's wisdom.

These are two moments that stand out because they were dramatically different than they would have been before we started doing family devotions. While we started doing family devotions because I felt the need to feel more calm and centered, because I wanted a spiritual practice I could do in the midst of pastoring and parenting, the reality is that the family devotions have transformed our family life.

These experiments in family ritual are experiments: adapt to what will work for your family. In the end, this practice has been a blessing to my family and I hope it can be to yours.

Notes

1. Massachusetts General Hospital, "bhi," online, accessed, 5. May 2016.

2. Shambala, "Sitting Still Like a Frog." online, accessed, 5. May 2016.

Chapter 20

"Mind Fullness" and Mindfulness: The Practice of Clergy Mental Wellness

Kristina Lizardy-Hajbi

The patient must minister to [her]self.
— William Shakespeare, Macbeth

I was in elementary school the first time I had a panic attack. On the bus ride home from a school trip, I was suddenly gripped with an overwhelming sense of dread and panic. I couldn't breathe. I felt trapped. I wanted to get off of the bus immediately, and all I could do was envision running to the driver demanding immediately that he stop the bus. Sweat poured down my face, my heart raced, and I thought that I was dying. Having no idea what was happening to me, and afraid to tell someone, I kept this terrifying experience to myself. No one else knew what had happened to me—not my friends, teachers, or even my parents. This secret and silent struggle that I continued to experience regularly for many years after that day, dictated everything from my innermost thoughts to my daily actions. I felt alone in my own world much of the time, not knowing when these attacks would strike and with those around me never realizing that I held this deep, dark secret, this "flaw" in my design and character.

Throughout junior high and high school, I spent long lengths of time in the bathroom before car and bus trips, trying to "be ok enough" to get in the vehicle, regardless of whether our trip would be thirty minutes or three hours. Even as a student in seminary, I had to spend twenty minutes in the bathroom each time I entered the building just to be able to manage my anxiety for whatever task

I was facing—a class, a meeting, or work. Oftentimes, when I was invited to a party or other social gathering, I just could not bring myself to get out of the house and into the car, my mind and body gripped with fear.

Those were just some of the visible, outward manifestations of what were diagnosed many years later as panic disorder, anxiety disorder, and depressive mood disorder. Unfortunately, I didn't fully understand my experiences until I began seeing the seminary counselor in preparation for an award-funded study trip to Greece (I had no idea how I was going to manage my anxiety on a plane for ten hours!). There, in those sessions, I finally learned that my craziness had a name (or three) and that I was not alone.

The hardest part of any mental illness is the continuing realization that your mind is playing tricks on you, and then you have to spend the rest of your life keeping that internal trickster at bay. Most days, I accomplish this through medication, therapy, and a beautiful, messy, imperfect understanding and practice of mindfulness that counters the "mind fullness" I experience daily.

Mind Fullness as Light and Shadow

My own special brand of craziness revolves largely around the fact that my mind doesn't stop. Ever. If I let it go, it would simply run away with itself and control my entire body. Even in times of depression, the recordings in my mind continuously play; the thoughts are just different in nature. I suppose that is what every mental illness does, though some illnesses more extensively than others.

But this mind that plays tricks and runs away with itself is also a grand gestured gift from God. From the time I was three years old, it gave me the label of being "gifted." My teachers marveled at my intellectual abilities; and with my IQ being tested regularly in school, I ended up skipping a grade, graduating at barely seventeen years old. This mind of mine provided me with educational opportunities that I would never have had as an otherwise average Puerto Rican-Italian girl growing up in a poor, rural area and whose parents had never attended college. I traveled all over the state, country, and even internationally for spelling bees, speech competitions, and science fairs. It provided me with scholarships to attend college, seminary, and to eventually earn a Ph.D. In essence, "mind fullness," this capacity for holding unique or numerous thoughts and ideas within my mind, made me the person that I am.[1]

Parker Palmer, a highly gifted teacher and author who has written extensively about his own experiences with depression, says that we as people project both light and shadow.[2] I believe that every gift comes with its own shadow side, but some shadows are just a bit longer than others. Sarah Lund, in her poignant work *Blessed Are the Crazy*, shares her brother's brilliant intellectual gifts as a biochemistry professor; yet bipolar disorder forced him to leave his profession.[3] It is no coincidence that many of those who have made the greatest contributions to the world possessed an expansive capacity for mind fullness, that light-shadow juxtaposition of holding brilliant or immeasurable thoughts and ideas within the brain. I don't even pretend to compare myself to the host of exceptional creatives who have traversed this planet yet struggled because of the deep shadow sides of their mind fullness: Vincent van Gogh, Max Weber, Sylvia Plath, Scott Joplin, Georgia O'Keefe, Kurt Cobain, Virginia Woolf, Tennessee Williams, Leonard Bernstein, Leo Tolstoy, Franz Liszt, and the list goes on and on.

My own mind has been quite dulled—I've been on medication for so long that it has deeply impacted the crispness of my brain's neural connections. I miss the way that my brain used to generate and process ideas with lightning speed and agility. In this manner, mental wellness is always a trade-off. Author and columnist Diana Spechler writes about her need to take antidepressant medications in order to regulate her mental illness, yet this medication also caused writer's block and thwarted her creative process: "My favorite escapes from depression are meds and writing. But I can't do both at once."[4] Spechler recounts that with each decrease in dosage, writing came more easily.

Many individuals have attempted to explain the nuances of this light-shadow phenomenon when it comes to mind fullness. My favorite description comes from Peter Zapffe's 1933 essay "The Last Messiah." Zapffe refers to depression as an over-evolution of the mind and writes that people with anxiety or depression may be more awake, or more connected to profounder realities, than others.[5] While others are able to more readily utilize defense mechanisms against these profounder realities such as isolation, anchoring, distraction, and sublimation, individuals with depression and anxiety may not be able to incorporate these protections into thought patterns as comprehensively.

While framing mind fullness in these terms of light and shadow is extremely helpful, more is needed to actually curtail biochemical imbalances. Even with medication and therapy, monitoring and regulating mind fullness requires something more. My mind needs simply to be instead of moving constantly. It needs to pause regularly; and when it doesn't receive routine down time, my entire body suffers. My family suffers. My colleagues suffer. My community suffers. Most of all, my relationship with the Holy suffers—worry, doubt, and endless internal chatter hinders my ability to listen to the nudging of the Spirit. Depressive thoughts block God's invitation to deep rest and glimpses of the oneness in spirit that my being seeks.

Clergy Mind Fullness

One in five adults in the United States experiences mental illness in a given year.[6] These numbers do not decrease when examining the prevalence of mind fullness among clergy. Though clergy mental wellness has not been studied consistently, studies have indeed confirmed that clergy experience mental health challenges at similar and, in most cases, increased rates when compared with the general public.[7]

In reality, the nature of our work as clergy lends itself to greater stressors affecting mental wellbeing. While some of us have experienced lifelong struggles around mind fullness (which carries its own stigmas fueled by the silence within our faith traditions), others have come to be acquainted with this phenomenon more recently as a result of this demanding and emotionally fraught calling. It is no secret that clergy burnout is common and pervasive; and the systems in which we carry out our daily activities make clergy more susceptible to anxiety, depression, and other mental and emotional challenges. Relating with people and the intricacies of their individual and collective lives takes its toll, no matter how extroverted the clergyperson. We hold others' experiences—their joys, pains, triumphs, and failures—in our hearts and in our minds. Day in and day out, we engage with others' variations of mind fullness, their own particular brands of crazy that require additional amounts of energy, focus, and emotional differentiation on our part. These factors alone are enough to rattle the sanest of individuals.

Another phenomenon has reared its ugly head in recent years which magnifies these factors. With the rise of our now fast-paced, constantly plugged-in world, more people are drawn into the clutches of the over-filled, over-active mind. Clergy, regardless of where they find themselves on the diagnostic mental wellness spectrum, are prone to suffer from this more common type of mind fullness as a result of the outside world having 24/7 electronic access to us and, in turn, us having 24/7 access to the outside world. The new normal of our culture communicates that we are "always on" or "always in" and can respond via text, instant message, or email outside of stated work hours. As clergy, this is especially problematic; and even the most boundary-adhering clergy can get bogged down with all of the mental and emotional space that this level of connectivity occupies.

In our connecting to others through social media and the internet, Jon Kabat-Zinn, a prominent scientist and expert on mindfulness, argues that we are in a state of "continual partial attention" which will eventually render us unable to give our full attention to any one task or thought.[8] With our focus so often fixated on online connections and the reporting of our experiences through social media, there is little time to experience fully the present moment. There is no space to be "in" and "on" for ourselves.

Mind fullness also connotes that the thoughts, experiences, and emotions of each day remain in the circular thought processes of one's mind well beyond their necessary timeframe. The lack of clear separation between work and home due to our constant connectivity creates the ideal environment for increased mind running. Psychologists sometimes call this over-focusing, and increased connectivity provides greater opportunities for over-focusing on situations. For example, engaging in a difficult series of email communications in the evening while at home focuses our thoughts and attentions on work-related issues and occupies mental space that should be utilized for rest and time with self and family. Browsing social media in the evenings or on Sabbath days can cause clergy to over-focus on ministry-related issues. Additionally, clergy may choose to participate in online conversations or threads that re-focus our much-needed mental and emotional "down time" back to the outside world. In the end, not only do our daily in-person interactions possess the potential to incite mind fullness; but now our smartphone interactions exacerbate these tendencies during the exact times and spaces that originally were set aside for something else.

Considering Mindfulness

With all the varying degrees of mind fullness that clergy can experience, the practice of mindfulness is now more critical to our thriving and creativity than at any other point in postmodern history. Personally, I have a love-hate relationship with the term "mindfulness."[9] The way that this word has been over-commercialized and rebranded as a spiritual elixir to all that ails the human condition is a far cry from its deeply significant religious origins. At any bookstore or library, one can find in the self-help section innumerable books on mastering mindfulness in every aspect of life—parenting, work, giving birth, eating, stress, and, yes, overall mental wellness.

Despite this over-exposure, the concept is simple, yet incredibly profound. My favorite definition comes from Thich Nhat Hanh, in which mindfulness is simply "keeping one's consciousness alive to the present reality."[10] He articulates that this practice "can call back in a flash our dispersed mind and restore it to wholeness."[11] Plainly stated, mindfulness is the practice of paying attention.

Kabat-Zinn sees mindfulness as an "openhearted, moment-to-moment, nonjudgmental awareness."[12] In our daily lives, we live in a state of partial awareness and never give our full attention to the tasks we are undertaking in the present moment. When looking at a particularly colorful sunset, the mind thinks, "Wow, this is a great sunset. I need to take a picture and share it with my sister." Or, "I wonder how the staff meeting will go tomorrow ... will the administrative assistant have another open conflict with the Christian Education director?" Rarely do we focus on the present moment before our minds wander to the other, the next, and the last.

How many times do we engage in household chores and focus solely on those tasks? When brushing our teeth while getting ready for the day or preparing for sleep, what would it look and feel like to focus only on that act? To feel wholly the bristles of the toothbrush against each tooth, to hear and experience the swish of water in our mouths, and to discover peace and gratitude in that present moment for water, for teeth, for life? It may sound absurd; but mindfulness, when practiced, can lead to a state in which the mind stops running and starts being. Kabat-Zinn provides a strong case for this:

"Attention, not neurotic self-preoccupation and hypochondriasis, reestablishes and strengthens connection or connectedness. Connection leads to greater regulation, which leads to a state of dynamic order, which is the signature of ease, of wellbeing, of health, maintained and nourished by intention."[13] Mindfulness has the potential to give the mind a break; and particularly for those of us who struggle with biochemical mental wellness, this is invaluable.

I was introduced to the general practice of mindfulness meditation (though it wasn't called mindfulness at the time) while attending a Catholic middle school. Each year, Father Bob would hold a mandatory two-day retreat at the adjacent convent for each grade level. Trying to get fifteen eighth graders to meditate for this period of time was no small task; and as much as my peers tested Father Bob's (and my) patience, I found myself relishing this practice. It wasn't until many years later that I was able to make the connection between mindfulness meditation and its impact on my mental wellbeing. In seminary, I was introduced to the Buddhist concept of mindfulness and was able to relate it to contemplative Christian practices that I had utilized for years. While not identical in conception, both traditions possess some aspects of mindful meditation that made it easier for me to grasp more fully the particular nuances of mindfulness.[14]

Because mindfulness has become more mainstream in recent years, its benefits have been studied by psychologists and others in the medical profession.[15] Mindfulness-based cognitive therapy (MBCT) is now a widely-known, widely-practiced phenomenon.[16] For individuals with anxiety and depression, studies have confirmed that MBCT teaches decentering skills, or "the ability to step back and observe in a less self-identified way one's own thinking as it is occurring, seeing one's thoughts simply as thoughts, as events in the field of awareness, rather than as necessary accurate reflections of reality or of oneself, whatever their content might be."[17] Even individuals who are relatively new to the practice of mindfulness meditation have been shown to exhibit similar biochemical changes in the brain to monks who have been practicing for years; and these changes reflect a "refining of one's capacity for paying attention and for residing in greater empathic awareness . . . it also suggests that meditation training can modulate the circuitry responsible for emotional processing in the brain."[18]

More practically, mindfulness can provide clergy with an increased ability to take both distance from and perspective on the emotional and mental slog of day-to-day ministry. When we as ministers are able to separate our thoughts and emotions (as well as our actions) from our identity as God's beloved, it provides a centeredness from which creativity can flourish. Our awareness of ourselves and our interactions heighten the ability to be present in the moment to the people and situations that call for our attention. For those of us who tend to be mind-wanderers and who get caught up in thought cycles that are exacerbated by biochemical imbalances in the brain, cultivation of this practice is transformational. Kabat-Zinn calls mindfulness "a radical act of love" wherein sitting down and sitting up becomes "a way to take a stand in your life as it is right now, however it is."[19] It is a radically sane act for the insane.

Practicing Mindfulness

Practicing mindfulness is simultaneously difficult and easy. I'll be honest: I'm not very good at it. However, I will say that it becomes easier the more regularly I practice it (by easier, I mean more intuitive and automatic to my daily being and doing). Many books have been written on the how-to of mindfulness; and for the most part, any book that one selects will provide helpful tips and practices to get one started.[20]

Here are some key elements of mindfulness that I have found to be essential to my own wellbeing and that are generally foundational to this practice:

Breath awareness

Our breath is the "bridge from the body to the mind" and keeps us grounded in the present moment. [21] It reminds us that we are alive! I find that deep breaths while saying to myself, "I am breathing in" and "I am breathing out" as mantras, even for a few minutes, brings me to myself again and calls my mind to loving attention. Sometimes, when I'm particularly stressed by my thoughts, I simply need to count from one to five as I inhale and from five to one as I exhale. Doing this five times lowers my blood pressure, releases chemicals that refocus and relax my body and mind, and refocuses my attention. All mindfulness practice involves attentiveness to one's breath. It is what grounds this creative act of self-care, providing a foundation for the other aspects of this practice.

Body awareness

Mindfulness can be cultivated in any body position, though I find it most beneficial to sit on the floor cross-legged or in a chair with my back and shoulders at a ninety degree angle to the ground. This calls me to attention, whereas lying on the floor or bed calls me to close my eyes and doze off. In any case, choose positions that are comfortable and pain-free yet allow you to be attentive to the practice. Once in that position, I conduct a mental body scan. I gain an awareness of how my body is connecting with the surface on which I am sitting (or standing). I then move up and down, doing a mental awareness check of my body—how my legs, hands, torso, neck, eyes, are feeling, releasing any tension along the way.

When I am engaged in mindful practices involving activity such as walking, washing the dishes, or listening to another speak, I try to remain fully present physically. When walking, I am feeling my legs take each step, different parts of my foot touching the ground, my rapid breathing, the raindrops or sunlight touching on my face. Sometimes, I say with each step, "I am walking" or "I am grateful."[22] With washing the dishes, I encounter the warm water rushing over my hands as I use a circular motion to wipe the dish. I'm grateful for water in all its lovely qualities—its ability to cool, nourish, and cleanse the green, ceramic dish that holds my food. When engaged in conversation, I mentally commit to cultivating an awareness of my body in the present moment and its relationship to the other person—I may be sitting across from someone having a meal, tasting each spoonful in my mouth and following it as I swallow each bite. I may be seated in a comfortable chair with my feet dangling above the floor (I'm short so this happens fairly often) and playing with the rings on my fingers. I may be standing and facing someone, my weight resting on my right leg and my breathing shallow from the emotionally-laded nature of the person's words. Wherever I find myself bodily, I gently call my awareness to the space in order to be here, now.

Mood awareness

Moods are powerful elixirs of emotions, thoughts, and chemicals that contribute to the type of energy we radiate at any given moment. It is important to cultivate an awareness of our moods, as they are a critical piece of who we are. For those of us who struggle with mental wellness, it is not a coincidence that our conditions have often been labeled as "mood disorders" since ailments like anxiety and depression are understood most concretely with this vocabulary. I have found that a simple acknowledgement of my current mood—without placing any judgment on the mood or on myself for experiencing it—goes a long way toward putting some distance between me and my energy. In that regard, attention to mood becomes an extension of grace for me and for others; and I can more clearly begin to view contexts and relationships with some perspective and possibility. Moods are what they are—nothing more, nothing less—and defining them as such (rather than automatically trusting them as "necessary accurate reflections of reality or of oneself") unleashes a certain freedom and peace.

Thought awareness

This is perhaps the most difficult part of any form of meditation, but it lies at the crux of our practice. Our thoughts rule us, and mindfulness offers the gift of focusing those thoughts on the task at hand, whether breathing, walking, doing house chores, providing support and care, preaching, writing, driving, singing, or helping your child with homework. It makes what has become unconscious— the ongoing internal conversation of thoughts, worries, and to-do lists—much more conscious, giving us a sense of objectivity and control over our thoughts and feelings.

In the course of focusing on the present moment, it is inevitable that my mind will wander. All I simply need to do is notice the chatter, hold it with compassion, and return to the present focus. Thinking is what our mind does, so it is important to remember that thoughts and emotions are neither good nor bad and that I should not feel annoyance, shame, sadness, or anger if certain thoughts arise during meditation (but if I do experience any of those emotions, I simply call myself back to my breath and the mantra I'm using at that moment to reinstate focus).

Many individuals also try mindfulness meditation with the hopes of getting rid of negatively-associated emotions or habits. I have found that this doesn't work. At the heart of mindfulness is non-doing, non-striving; it is about "connecting with what is here and holding it in kind and compassionate awareness."[23] This is especially important for those of us who want to use mindfulness to lessen or eliminate anxiety and depression. I am a goal-oriented person whose inner workings tend toward an achievement-based framework; and for this reason, mindfulness is especially challenging to my modus operandi. Awareness is an internal journey with no beginning and no end, though it does alter perspectives of self, others, and the world; but in the letting go of trying to change through mindfulness, mindfulness itself can produce change. The paradox is striking.

Though MBCT and the cultivation of mindfulness is a regular, intentional part of my life, my anxious thoughts and emotions are seen for what they are; and as a result, I am able to better understand and monitor them through heightened awareness. My mind still runs away with itself from time to time, but it no longer rules my life. I have not had a panic attack in years; and when I have felt an attack approaching, I have been able to focus on my breath and acknowledge the thoughts and fears that were causing increased anxiety. Sometimes I say to myself, "This is fear" or "This is what fear is like." Naming the emotions interrupts the unconscious reaction that I am having within any particular situation and gives me a sense of understanding and power that I was not able to have that day on the school bus many years ago. As someone who once possessed incredible amounts of anxiety about flying in airplanes, I now find myself traveling once or twice a month for ministry. I actually relish flying these days because it provides me with space for practicing mindfulness and enjoying the present moment!

Creativity: Where Mindfulness and Mind Fullness Meet

We know that the work of ministry fuels mind fullness. Mindfulness, on the other hand, creates awareness, clarity, and space. Whether we as clergy serve within the context of a church, hospital, military setting, regional or national denominational office, non-profit organization, or anyplace in between, mindfulness practice releases the mind and body from being held captive by the day-to-day stressors of our vocation. In this freedom, this opening up of mental and emotional space, lies the potential for creativity and multiple alternatives.

Additionally, as ministers we are often called to bear witness to the realities of the present moment, whether that be sitting with the family of a recently deceased loved one or standing on the steps of the county courthouse to call for an end to an unjust law. We hold and then reflect the feelings, thoughts, and emotions of our contexts back to our communities and point people toward God in the moment. Bearing witness in this way may not seem like much, but it is the ultimate creative act of mindfulness. "The more bearing witness while dwelling in openhearted awareness becomes a way of life for all of us," according to Kabat-Zinn, "the more the world will shift, because the world itself is none other than us."[24] Openhearted awareness is the catalyst for new possibilities in a world fraught with suffering. It is the beginning of change.

For that reason, mindfulness as a creative act is of utmost relevance for today's church. Perhaps the most radical action that a community of faith can take in discerning their future is to commit to practicing mindfulness. It is certainly a necessary act for the pastor who leads any congregation. Because of the changing nature of mainline Protestantism as we know it within the United States, many churches are facing decline and difficult decisions about buildings, finances, and programs. Conflicts abound in churches, whether they are influenced by these outside factors or not; and these conflicts are often distractions from the mission of the church, the church in the here and now.

Therefore, the most faithful deed in this moment, in this time and place, is to practice mindfulness. What if the church stopped worrying and making decisions based on an uncertain future and focused on ministry in the present? What if the church were to commit to practicing mindfulness in all of its being and doing for a period of one year? This might include weekly mindful walks through the neighborhood, incorporating more mindful practices and expressions within worship, or setting aside a time for mindfulness meditation in committee meetings. A compelling sermon series might ask the question, "How can we be faithful in this moment?" Or, "How can we be more aware, more attentive to what's happening within ourselves, our congregation, and our community?" What if one of these questions became the question of discernment for a community of faith for an entire year? How would that transform us? In the end, it comes down to this: "We need to dare to be sane, to take on our craziness unabashedly and hold it with compassion, to face it, name it, and in doing so, be bigger than it, no longer caught by it, and therefore, intimately in touch with our wholeness, not only sane, but saner than sane. Especially when what passes for sane these days on the world stage is often madness itself."[25]

Most of us, whether or not we struggle with mental wellness, need to work at being sane. The "blessing" of having a biochemical imbalance is that it forces me to do the work. In that sense, mindfulness is not really a choice for me. I pray that it may become a habit for all of us, sane and insane alike.

Notes

1. I prefer to use the term "mind fullness" instead of "mental illness" or "mental health," though I will use all three terms somewhat interchangeably in this piece. Mind fullness reframes my condition in a way that helps me to treat it—and myself—more gently and lovingly. Mind fullness depathologizes and redirects the spectrum toward an orientation of balance; whereas, mental illness and mental health tend to be framed along a relative binary of clinical sickness and non-sickness. Fullness simultaneously connotes a sense of satiety while still calling attention to regulating thoughts and biochemical processes in order to avoid imbalance and overload. This reframing may not be helpful for others who traverse the mind fullness spectrum, but I've found it to be a liberating phrase that also acknowledges the gifts (the light) that comes with this shadow. Other terms utilized within the chapter to emphasize this perspective include "wellness" and "wholeness." I use all terms throughout this chapter in order to frame the issue in a way that is accessible to the widest audience possible.

2. Parker Palmer, *Let Your Life Speak: Listening for the Voice of Vocation* (San Francisco: Jossey-Bass, 2000).

3. Sarah Lund, *Blessed Are the Crazy: Breaking the Silence about Mental Illness, Family, and Church* (St. Louis: Chalice, 2014).

4. Diana Spechler, "Reducing My Dose, Unblocking My Muse," *The New York Times*, online, accessed, 26. May 2015.

5. Peter W. Zapffe, "The Last Messiah," trans. Gisle R. Tangenes, *Janus* (1933), online, accessed 4. May 2016.

6. "Mental Health by the Numbers," National Alliance on Mental Illness, online, accessed 7. July 2015

7. A few denomination-specific studies have explored clergy mental health in recent years, as follows. Research on Church of Nazarene pastors in New Mexico found that 17% of the clergy suffered from depression, and similar studies of Roman Catholic clergy demonstrated depression and anxiety rates of 18% to 20% (Rae Jean Prosechold-Bell, et al., "Using Effort-Reward Imbalance Theory to Understand High Rates of Depression and Anxiety among Clergy," *Journal of Primary Prevention* 34, no. 6 (2013), 439–453). A survey by the Evangelical Lutheran Church in America reported that 13% of its clergy take prescription antidepressants (Paul Vitello, "Taking a Break from the Lord's Work," *The New York Times*, [1. Aug. 2010], online, accessed 4. May 2016. The United Methodist

Church General Board of Pension and Health Benefits found that 26% of all clergy had at least some functional difficulty resulting from depressive symptoms and that 5% of all clergy suffered from diagnosed depression, a significantly greater percentage than demographically comparable adults ("Annual Clergy Health Survey," [2013], online, accessed 4, May 2016. Additionally, the Clergy Health Initiative at Duke Divinity School, a ten-year program intended to improve United Methodist clergy health and wellbeing in North Carolina, reported clergy depression rates of 9.6% in 2012 and both anxiety and depression rates of 7%. Moreover, 15% of clergy reported receiving treatment for depression, anxiety, or stress in the past year (Duke Divinity School, "Clergy Health Initiative: What We're Learning," [2015], online, accessed 4. May 2016.

8. Jon Kabat-Zinn, *Coming to our Senses: Healing Ourselves and the World through Mindfulness* (New York: Hyperion, 2005), 157.

9 Virginia Heffernan explains in a *New York Times* article ("The Muddied Meaning of 'Mindfulness,'" [14. April 2015], that while the concept of *sati* is based upon Buddhism, the English translation possesses its roots in the colonial legacy of the British Empire. In the late nineteenth century, the British magistrate of Sri Lanka sought to grasp more fully this concept while adjudicating Buddhist clerical conflicts; consequently, he labeled it "mindfulness," which was actually a synonym for "attention" from 1530 (as in "mind your manners").

10. Thich Nhat Hanh, *The Miracle of Mindfulness: An Introduction to the Practice of Meditation* trans. Mobi Ho. (Boston: Beacon, 1987), 11.

11. Ibid., 14.

12. Kabat-Zinn (2005), 24.

13. Ibid., 121.

14. It is important to note that there are some distinct differences between the contemplative Christian tradition and mindfulness practice. For further reading, see Rita M. Gross and Terry C. Muck, eds., *Christians Talk about Buddhist Meditation: Buddhists Talk about Christian Prayer* (New York: Bloomsbury, 2003).

15. See Daniel Goleman, ed., *Healing Emotions: Conversations with the Dalai Lama on Mindfulness, Emotions, and Health* (Boston: Shambhala, 1997).

16. A poignant autobiographical account of the positive impact of MBCT is Julie Myerson, "How Mindfulness Based Cognitive Therapy Changed My Life," *The Guardian*, [11. January 2014], online, accessed 4. May 2016.

17. Kabat-Zinn (2005), 432.

18. Ibid., 374.

19. Ibid., 84.

20. Some of the books that I have found most helpful have been included in other footnotes within this chapter. Additional resources include the following: Christopher Titmuss, *Mindfulness for Everyday Living* (New York: Barron's, 2003); Jon Kabat-Zinn, *Mindfulness for Beginners: Reclaiming the Present Moment—and Your Life* (Boulder: Sounds True, 2012), which comes with an accompanying CD of guided meditations; Jon Kabat-Zinn, *Wherever You Go, There You Are: Mindfulness Meditation in Everyday Life* (New York: Hyperion, 1994); Karen Armstrong, *Twelve Steps to a Compassionate Life* (New York: Alfred A. Knopf, 2010), which includes a short chapter on mindfulness; and Martha Davis, Elizabeth Robbins Eshelman, and Matthew McKay, *The Relaxation and Stress Reduction Workbook*, 6th ed. (Oakland: New Harbinger, 2008), 35–36, 58–63.

21. Naht Hanh, 23.

22. A brief, yet compelling book on mindful walking is Thich Naht Hanh, *How to Walk* (Berkley: Parallax, 2015).

23. Jeffery Brantley, *Calming Your Anxious Mind: How Mindfulness and Compassion Can Free You from Anxiety, Fear, and Panic* (Oakland: New Harbinger, 2003), 162.

24. Kabat-Zinn (2005), 519.

25. Ibid., 457.

Chapter 21

Disrupting Sabbath

Rev. Rachel G. Hackenberg

The sabbath is not meant for you.

Did you think you could rest?
Did you believe that now
now
you could lay it down
pause in peace
celebrate
finish
before life itself
is finished, or that
you could be done
before
I
am done?
Come now.
Come now.
I am not done.
Do not sit down
there on the grass
beside the road
in delusions of
heaven's final chorus
heralding your efforts
while
I myself

have not completed
the song I am orchestrating
here
and
now
for all creation
and all people
to sing in harmony.
Do not rest in the grass.
Neither should you
fall down
discouraged
in the dust
exhausted
and weary of hoping.
I
am
not
done.
Repeat it again
and make this your praise:
I
am
not
done.
Stand up,
find your feet again.[1]

In the course of my work in judicatory ministry, I try to make
this statement at every opportunity to those aspiring to ordained
ministry: "The sabbath is not meant for you."[2] I intend it as a reality
check and as a challenge. While it's wise to enter ordained ministry
with a clear awareness of the burnout pitfalls and poor health trends

among clergy, and with established habits of self and spiritual care, in reality no amount of best practices can negate the fact that ministry is difficult and exhausting. It requires hard work, long hours, interpersonal conflict, heartbreaking choices, grace under pressure. It causes wear and tear on the soul from which sabbath cannot protect us. My challenge to aspiring ministers regarding sabbath also aims to disrupt underlying assumptions about the ownership of ministry. Because ordination sets apart one's life for the sake of the Church and for the sake of Christ, one's ministry is therefore communal in both purpose and endeavor—including in practices of sabbath and self-care.

"The sabbath is not meant for you" insists upon a distinction between self-care and sabbath, for we clergy have fallen into the habit of treating these words as synonymous: sabbath has become a theological code word for self-care, and while both are important, they are not the same. Sabbath is an activity (yes, an activity) commended to us by God, much like loving our neighbor and breaking bread in remembrance of Christ and washing one another's feet. Self-care is an activity directed toward the self, and while not necessarily narcissistic, nevertheless its aim and motivation are self-focused rather than God-focused.

For this reason, self-care is inherently flawed and fails as a synonym for sabbath. Perhaps I betray my own life experiences too much if I confess that "self-care" falls short for me as both a goal and a motivating mantra, not due to pride in self-sacrifice or to scorn of selfishness, but because the self in my experience has been an undermined and devalued entity. Growing up, I learned to pray for God's grace but to rely on hard work, a "God Bless The Child" theology of sorts. As an adult in an abusive marriage and subsequent manipulative relationship, my self was denigrated, name-called, and deemed untrustworthy. Today as a single mother, my self necessarily focuses its energies on my children. For better and for worse, "self-care" holds no motivation for me. While our personal stories of self vary widely, I share my own experiences to emphasize the point: self-care is inevitably encumbered and limited by our views of the self, by our vanities and our frailties alike. Self-care at its best is therapeutic work, which is essential for faithful ministry, but it is not by definition "sabbath."

The practice of sabbath, according to scripture, serves two purposes—neither of which is the self. First, from Exodus 20, the purpose of sabbath is to remember God's creativity and rest: "Remember the sabbath day, and keep it holy. For in six days the LORD made heaven and earth, the sea, and all that is in them, but rested the seventh day; therefore the LORD blessed the sabbath day and consecrated it."[3] Second, from Deuteronomy 5, the purpose of Sabbath is to provide a fair respite for others, especially those whose work we oversee or cause:

> Observe the sabbath day and keep it holy, as the LORD your God commanded you. You shall not work ... so that your male and female slave may rest as well as you. Remember that you were a slave in the land of Egypt, and the LORD your God brought you out from there with a mighty hand and an outstretched arm; therefore the LORD your God commanded you to keep the sabbath day.[4]

Exodus 20 posits that sabbath honors God's rhythms of work and rest. Deuteronomy 5 hallows space for those most weary and put-upon to rest. The first reminds us that we are not God and that we cannot—indeed, we need not—work unceasingly. The second requires our awareness of the demands and injustices of systems (economic, social, ecclesial, etc.). To be more succinct: the two reasons of sabbath are because God and because Other. Sabbath is not meant for you.

If sabbath is not for us individually, how might we clergy practice it? What might creative sabbath habits look like? Reexamining our sabbath assumptions and developing creative practices can be accomplished by further exploring the two scriptural purposes of sabbath.

Sabbath Because God

For everything there is not enough time;
not enough time to work to rest
to savor to surrender
to remember to dream.
Not enough time, not enough!
But the One Who Holds All Time whispers:
"What are you trying to do
beyond what I have given you
to do? What else do you hope to gain
beyond life, breath, love?
You fuss over yesterday and
bite your nails about tomorrow
but I Have Been
from the beginning
and I Will Be
to the end.
Time does not belong to you;
you are only chasing dust with your
frantic busyness. But listen:
Meet me at the beginning.
Let me walk with you to the end.
Make peace already with working and resting,
savoring and surrendering,
remembering and dreaming.
It is enough.
I am forever enough."[5]

Sabbath because God. Because God, the practice of sabbath mirrors God's interplay of working and resting, of savoring creation and surrendering to limits, of remembering promises and dreaming of new stories. Because God, sabbath is not the either/or myth of balance that the world insists can be achieved if only we purchase the right products, if only we achieve the ideal lifestyle. Instead, sabbath is the harmonization of a holy tune that understands God's glory in all things. Resting sings alongside working, not just for one day out of seven but within every day. Surrendering deepens savoring's chord to ground in mystery our incarnational experiences. And dreaming dares remembering to learn a new song that riffs on old favorites.

Because God, sabbath is living and life-giving, adapting to bless what is needed. I am concerned when I hear clergy vent, "A parishioner had the nerve to call me on my day off to ask me to make a hospital visit, even though I announce my sabbath day every week in worship!" as though we are Pharisees who forbid the healing of a hand on the Sabbath.[6] Such sabbath orthodoxy is a not-unfounded but nevertheless reactionary response to those clergy who served before us saying, "I must always go—I cannot rest," to which today's clergy have drawn a line in the sand saying, "I must rest—I cannot always go." But the negotiation between ourselves and others, between work and rest, between (let's be honest) ourselves and God is not a zero sum game if we truly believe that the aim of our sabbath practices and of our ministry is God. If God is our aim and if God is enough, then sabbath is a call to trust in the fullness of God and to live continually into the fullness of who God creates us to be—in both work and play, in the creative as well as the rote, within ourselves and within our relationships.

Sabbath Because Other

We are asking:
Where will I find the money?
Where will I find a moment's rest?
Where will I find a job, a spouse, a home?

We are asking:
How will I get my way amidst partisanship?
How will I secure prosperity for "me and mine"?
How will my voice be heard over fame and money and chaos?

God is asking:
What did I do wrong
that idols of wealth and contentment
are worshiped more than the One of life and community?

God is asking:
Who are these who are
crying out in prayer and singing in praise
yet pursuing their own benefits and pleasures day by day?

We confess:
That we miss those times
when we trusted you, when we loved without fear,
when we were content to commit our lives to your work.

We pray:
For awe to replace pride,
for love of one another to root out fear,
for holy purpose to define our daily laboring.

We rejoice:
That you are our treasure,
our daily peace and provocation;
in your shadow, our souls are surprised and satisfied.

We offer:
Our lives to be a blessing
to your glory and to one another's living,
in the name of Jesus who sets an abundant table for all.[7]

Sabbath because Other. Because Other, the practice of sabbath strives after the relief of the world in imitation of God who, across time, has preferenced the cause of the poor and the oppressed. Because Other, sabbath uncenters the self in humble recognition that our personal work and our individual rest are not possible without others. Our 21st century work relies not only on the existence of those communities who call us into ministry but also on the persons who maintain the technology we use to email, call, text, and tag; on the workers of transportation infrastructures so that we can drive, fly, walk, and bus to be present in ministry; on farmers and hired hands, grocers and bakers, factory workers and customer service representatives, so that the paten and chalice might hold the Body of Christ. Our 21st century rest needs others as much as our work: whether we spend our rest paying bills for others' work, treating ourselves to a mani-pedi by someone else's hands, sleeping on the labors of mattress builders and linen weavers, or hiking on rubber soles stitched tightly to leather for our feet's protection.

Because Other, sabbath is a practice of humble confession that we are not the islands we dream of being. We are interdependent and interconnected, but not equally so: our connections are not democratic or power-neutral. They are systems in which we live and have our being, habits both social and institutional that maintain power and bequeath privilege. Resting apart from the system is impossible; actively joining the work against the injustices of the system by increasing our commitment to Other is the second aim of sabbath.

Because Other, sabbath is living and life-giving, adapting in order to understand what is needed. It is the call to make sacrifices for the sake of others' well-being. It is the honoring of God's heart of justice and of God's seasons of mercy. Because Other, sabbath is not practiced alone. Not only do we join the efforts of social justice, learning as we participate, but we also teach others to value habits of sabbath that bring healing and renewal. If, for example, our congregations demand that their staff be always "on" and always present at every single event; if our predecessors in pastoral positions could be called at any hour of any day for non-crisis pastoral care; then we clergy have an opportunity and obligation to teach our congregations how to hallow sabbath just as we would teach any other tenet of faith: through preaching, through education, through time and love, with grace. Demanding our days off in the name of "Sabbath" without giving care to education is poor pastoral leadership that wraps the employee-employer relationship with misappropriated theological language.

Sabbath as Harmonization

A recent blogpost (among many articles and blogposts on the topic of pastors practicing sabbath) illuminates the modern entanglement of self-care and sabbath. Titled "7 Ways I Protect My Sabbath," the post by Ron Edmonson makes this claim: "Protecting my Sabbath has proven to be crucial in protecting my ministry." Edmonson's seven ways include "Make it a priority" and "Prepare for it."[8] The goal of sabbath according to this blogpost is revealed unapologetically to be the self: it is "my" sabbath and "my" ministry and "my" plans for myself. At stake in protecting the self-fulfilling sabbath, we are told, is pastoral burnout, a state of physical-mental-spiritual exhaustion that we clergy vainly believe can be avoided by the mythological miracle of balance. But burnout is an inevitable consequence of the work of handling Holy Fire, as I've argued elsewhere.[9] The challenge is not to avoid burnout; the challenge is to recognize burnout as it happens so that we might not do harm as a result of it and so that we might seek out renewal and growth before, during and after burnout.

The inevitability of clergy burnout returns us to the necessity of therapeutic self-care—whether found on the couch of a qualified professional, with one's feet soaking in a tub at the salon, on a long walk away from people and technology, or over a caffeinated venti drink at a coffee shop (as I am often inclined to do). To practice self-care faithfully is to cultivate self-awareness and personal healing. We cannot engage in ministry in creative ways if we do not know who we are and Whose we are, if we do not know the stumbling blocks within our own selves. This is important; nevertheless we must not practice self-care and deceive ourselves that we have simultaneously practiced sabbath. To honor the sabbath is not to pay attention to the self for the sake of the self. To honor the sabbath is to pay attention to the self as situated in the world for the sake of the Other to the glory of God. Sabbath because Other. Sabbath because God.

Thus the activity of sabbath—to return to an earlier metaphor—is an exercise in tuning and retuning our harmonizations with God and with the Other throughout our working and resting, savoring and surrendering, remembering and dreaming. The practice of sabbath listens for dissonance and consonance between our rhythms and God's rhythms, between our needs and the Other's relief. If our tunes for work have no space for the ethereal descants of delighting in God, for example, then our work will quickly fall flat. If our lullabies of rest are drowned out by errands and social media and yes, even the busyness of self-care, then the lullabies will be lost and we will forget to sing them alongside the Other. The music of sabbath is constant, not alternately "on" or "off" as though ministry has a mute button, as though the self can be renewed on one day out of every seven while God and the Other are relegated to the other six. To practice sabbath creatively, we must continually practice the song; we must habitually attend to and listen for the Other and God in order to fine-tune our harmonic contributions to the music.

To honor sabbath, harmonize working and resting. In all activities, practice sabbath by sharing joy daily with the Other and giving praise daily to God. Take your time in conversations and visits; travel slowly between visits and appointments; tilt your head back and marvel at the sky. Commit to uninterrupted love and time with a family member, with a congregant, with God. Calculate a new math in which work is not greater than rest and rest is not greater than work, in which the Other is neither greater nor less than the self, in which nothing is of higher value than God, in which the pursuit of your call (work) and the joy of your call (rest) are equal. If the math feels unequal, if the tune sounds discordant, pause to map out the energies and emotions of your day—hospital visits and worship prep, committee meetings and community coffee hours, a local clergy gathering and a long walk, times with God in fellowship and times with God in solitude and times with God's absence. Where are the moments of catching your breath to renew your delight in God and the Other? How does your work diminish your delight, and how does your rest distract from it?

Engage an activity that is wholly separate from both work and rest, an activity that reminds you of the fullness to which God calls your being beyond the identity of "minister." My sense of self as a soccer mom, for example, gives me the regular opportunity to delight in my children and in the natural world from the vantage point of a sideline. During games and practices, I am very much "on" as a mother and I am still "on" as a minister, but I am also restful and joyful in the simple experience of being a soccer fan who tries not to be too vocal in her opinions about the referees' management of a game. What are your God-given gifts and passions that connect you to life beyond the daily rhythms of ministry? Who else are you in God's image and in relationship to the world?

To honor sabbath, harmonize savoring and surrendering. Practice an appreciation of these truths: you are not God, and you are not the Other. Because you are not God, savor the mystery of what God is doing and surrender to the knowledge that much of life is out of your control. Pray fervently for discernment over both. Take something that you think is yours and delegate it appropriately. Because you are not the Other, savor and seek out the opportunity to hear Others' stories—in person and online, in both fiction and non—especially the stories of those outside of your ministry context and personal experience. Surrender your self-care to another: accept a stranger's kindness or submit your flesh to the work of a massage therapist.

Savor and surrender the confession that your ministry is not yours. Practice this critical sabbath confession by supporting a colleague's ministry or extending a lunch invitation to the new pastor in town. Write a note of appreciation to your judicatory minister. Read the newsletter of another denomination. Contemplate which metaphorical instrument your congregation plays in the symphony that is God's work in the world, acknowledging that no single faith community can play them all. Which part of the symphony is your church's part to play, and which parts are not? Which instrument's voice makes your heart soar and melt at the same time?

To honor sabbath, harmonize remembering and dreaming. Delight in stories, both past and possible. A former congregant of mine loved to tell the story of how he received a vision from Jesus in a dream of how best to wire lighting for the golden cross in the sanctuary so that Christ's light would radiate from that cross into the world. Almost every time I visited him, he retold this story. And in truth, the story was stunning and humbling every time, because with each retelling of his story, I relearned the mystery and power of God speaking into a person's life. Listen closely to the Other's stories. Write down your own stories, both past and possible. Search occasionally for another job; imagine what could be in order to clarify the story that is.

Delight—O delight!—in scriptural stories, both canonized and continuing. Practice telling the Bible's stories with a modern lens. The 2 Samuel story of Absalom's death, for example, recently coincided on the lectionary schedule with the unending hashtagged names of the #BlackLivesMatter movement, providing a stirring and disturbing parallel of stories about young beloved men dying violent and unnecessary deaths. Take these stories into your preaching, and teach your congregation how to listen for their own stories in scripture. Be unceasing in seeking out the continuing themes of God's story: Where has God been? Where is God moving? How is God inspiring and upending?

"The sabbath is not meant for you." The present and emerging Church needs creative clergy who are unafraid of working hard and rolling up their sleeves for pastoral care, for congregational (re)visioning, for community activism. It needs clergy who expect burnout but who—having learned the lessons of previous clergy generations—are wise to the ways of self-care. It needs clergy who unceasingly foster awareness within themselves and within their communities of the world's fatigue and of God's abundant imagination. It needs clergy who regularly pause to reorient their ministries and their perspectives toward the Other and toward God. It needs clergy who practice sabbath in such a way as to contribute to the renewal of the Other and the praise of God, believing that neither sabbath nor ministry belong to themselves. Creative clergy intentionally interweave working and resting, savoring and surrendering, remembering and dreaming as an ongoing daily practice of sabbath, rejecting both the old orthodoxy of sacrificing sabbath and the new orthodoxy of idolizing sabbath, in order instead to delight in God and Other.

Notes

1. Rachel G. Hackenberg, "Unsatisfied" (28. June 2013), online, accessed 4. May 2016.

2. For this essay, it's my choice to use "sabbath" rather than "Sabbath" in order to focus on the spiritual practice(s) rather than the weekly day of s/Sabbath. In addition, the simple uncapitalization of sabbath may offer a visual disruption of our presumptions about s/Sabbath.

3. Exodus 20:8, 11 (NRSV).

4. Deuteronomy 5:12, 14–15 (NRSV).

5. Rachel Hackenberg "Ecclesiastes 3" (10. May 2014), online, accessed 4. May 2016.

6. Matthew 12: 9–13 (NRSV).

7. Adapted from Rachel Hackenberg, "Labor Day" (1. September 2013), online, accessed 4. May 2016.

8. Ron Edmonson "7 Ways I Protect My Sabbath," (4. Aug. 2015), online, accessed 4. May 2016.

9. Rachel Hackenberg, "Is Clergy Burnout Really a Crisis?" (23. Jan. 2012), online, accessed 4. May 2016.

Chapter 22

A Clergy Rising from the Ashes

Rev. Chad R. Abbott

I was never one to thrive on the science fair. However, I fully understand the thrill of putting together a project that must use experimentation to test a working theory. As people gather around science fair tables, students are given the opportunity to make their argument, to test their theory in public and then leave it up to the people to decide whether or not the theory has merit. The power of using experimentation as a model is that it does not begin with a guarantee that it will work. Experimenting is a model unto itself and the only guarantee that comes with it is that there is "possibility" and "potentiality" inherent in the very act itself. I believe this bodes well for the Church. If we are honest with ourselves, the decline of the Church in the last four to five decades indicates that the models of ministry that we have engaged in over these many years have failed to sustain the Church as a central and respectable place in the dialogue of the public squares in our culture. Continuing in these same models and expecting to get different results will only end in doors of churches closing all across the country. But, possibility? But, potentiality? If these are the things that experiments in ministry will produce, then what do we have to lose?

I remember getting a call from the Rev. Mike Mather (a fellow author in this book) when I was on his staff that he wanted our entire Broadway Church staff to meet in the community room. We gathered waiting, unsure of what he had up his sleeve this time. As the staff gathered he told us that he wanted to take a break from meeting as a staff for a while to do some experiments. Each staff person was given the same task of going to visit two people from our parish in their work environments. We were to set this up with these persons ahead of time and we were to go and do two main things. First, we were to observe their work, see how their customers or co-workers interact with them. If they were in a leadership role, examine what they brought to that role—to observe everyday kinds of details about the work environment and what gifts that person was bringing to their work. Then, second, we were to sit down with that person and talk about their hopes and dreams for their work, talk with them about how they got into their line of work, and talk about what made them passionate, what made them get out of bed each morning and give energy to their work. What was their story?

This was a huge task. It did not matter if you were a custodian, an administrative assistant, or one of the clergy, we all were asked to do this experiment. We were given several weeks to schedule these encounters with people in their work. The idea behind this particular experiment was that Mike desired to find a creative way to convince the people who attended church that their particular ministry was not within the walls of the church, but rather in their classrooms, boardrooms, local parks, and construction sites. Yes, they gather for worship in our sanctuary each week to renew their spirit, but the true transformative work is what happens with the passions and gifts that people have for the work they do day in and day out. So, my task was to spend time with a man who owned a chain of Subway restaurants, a woman who worked at the Indianapolis Museum of Art, and also a woman who was an elementary school teacher working with special education kids. After all the staff met with their assigned persons, we would then meet again as a staff to tell stories, to give testimony to where God is at work in the lives of those we spent time with, and to ask ourselves as a staff how we could be involved in supporting what God is doing in the lives of people in our parish every single day.

It was an experiment in how we do ministry in the church and served as a reminder that we must get outside of the all too familiar ways of doing work in churches. Like Mahatma Gandhi, we must find ways to do experiments in truth. One of the most famous blogs in recent memory is Leo Babauta's "Zen Habits" blog, where he forms habits over twenty one days of time as an experiment to see if it will be lasting and sustaining. He experiments in everything from food and exercise, to meditation and times of silence. Both Gandhi and Leo Babauta can teach pastors a great deal about how to discover habits that will be sustaining for our work. Their methodology of experimentation is the new frontier of pastoral work and will offer us ministries that can bring "possibility" and "potentiality" for the transformation of the world. Experimentation means a willingness to fail and the Church must be willing to fail, for it is in failing that we discover anew the path God has for us.

In this book, hopefully the reader has encountered a host of clergy and scholars who are willing to fail, willing to experiment, in order to discover our way forward as the Church. Will each of these habits work for every church? Of course not. But, the creativity involved in the collective wisdom of these pages offers me hope that the Church has a future. If nothing else, the reader will have received inspiration to consider holy experiments of his or her own.

In the end, we must not give in to apathy as clergy or as the Church. A great frontier is ahead of us and it will require the rise of the creatives. We need creative clergy willing to break free of the chains that bind so many of our churches. We need creative lay leaders that can see their everyday work in the world as ministry and can bring their creativity to the embracing of God's realm in their work and in the work of the Church. We need creative denominations that do not shy away from experimenting with new church starts and addressing racism or building multi-denominational collaborative models that will be sustainable. Out of the ashes of five decades of congregational decline must rise a creative phoenix of clergy willing to be vulnerable in their work and humble in their failings. It is a new day, friends. Join us, the creative clergy, in building a creative church willing enough to die that we may be resurrected. Rise, O Church, rise.

Afterword

Open Wide Shut: Sensing Theologically in the Midst of Chaos

Dr. Gregory C. Ellison II

For years I have worn the labels of professor, pastor, and activist like an ill-fitting suit. More often than not, in classrooms, I found myself preaching. I stepped out of pulpits onto sanctuary floors to call parishioners to action. In community centers and on street corners, I swapped words with unlettered professors and wise sages. In all of this shape shifting, I found my heart opening wide to the hybridity of creative ministry. But the institutions that formed me valued the convenience of vocational labels that wedged me in and shut me down. Like the authors in this book, I sought freedom within the bounds of scripture, doctrine, and traditions. I yearned for ways to see differently, hear more acutely, and work for change in an increasingly chaotic world that challenged me to transcend categorization.[1]

Just as the three monikers hung off me with unkempt fashion, so, too, did my theology. After years of study, rote memorization, and what I perceived as mundane ministerial activity, I began to see the world with dull graceless eyes. I heard age-old hymns in monotone. In reading theological texts, I rarely felt the unction of internal change or the catalytic force to change the world around me. My theological outlook flattened, my creative zeal for ministry collapsed, and my vocational fervor for writing, teaching, and justice efforts withered in the mirror before my eyes. In the midst of chaos, change was imperative.

On April 2, 2009, my inner world shifted on its axis, when a slimy squirming baby girl literally fell into my hand. I recall the seconds before her birth like a grainy black and white film. Besides the cars that sped by my pregnant wife and me as she labored on the side of the road, all other sounds were muted. On that rainy midnight, I knelt on the highway's shoulder by the passenger seat. The dim light from the visor mirror illumined my wife's face in grayscale. With an uneasy calm, I beckoned, "Push . . ." Those seconds felt like decades, but in divine timing, creativity burst forth in Technicolor and Anaya's high-pitched cry was a tuning fork to my soul that had since grown tone-deaf. Seeing in color and hearing with vibrancy compelled me to sense the world anew.

Life shifted. No longer were theories just words on a page. Both life and theology had texture. The creative practices of writing poetry, learning from nature, reading novels, and hearty conversation with strangers over a good meal had epistemic value. By this, I mean, the creative practices of living informed how I thought about God and creation just as much as reading and writing. Likewise, in bold new ways, theological texts grew more formative in daily practices of interacting with others and engaging the world around me. Practice informed theory. Theory formed new practices. For the first time, I was sensing theology.

Theology titillated all of my senses. It smelled like freshly cut grass and flew on butterfly's wings. Theology tasted like minestrone soup shared with residents at the senior center and sounded like the jangling coins in the street pharmacist's pockets. Like tall steeple church bells those jangling coins alerted me to the holiness of fearless dialogue, as this drug dealer and I stood on the corner discussing identity politics, mass incarceration, and the presence of an interrupting hope. Participating in the birth of my baby daughter borne within me a new way of engaging theology. On a daily basis, I stumbled upon altars that transported me into sacramental moments of discovery, even in the midst of chaos.[2]

Sensing theology is about seeing more clearly and hearing more acutely to notice the mysteries of God in an increasingly chaotic world. Trained alongside this book's editor as a pastoral theologian, I believe that the primary role of the caregiver is to see that which the ordinary person overlooks and hear that which is unspoken. This philosophy not only re-aligned my studies to stand alongside persons on the margins who felt muted and invisible, it also recalibrated my internal clock. I felt challenged to alter my pace so that I might sense the mysteries of God's creation all around me. These three epiphanies pushed me forward on the journey of sensing theology and casting off the labels that stunted my creativity.

Slow Down and Contemplate! The customary response to crisis or chaos is to fight or flee, both of which are often done at quickened pace. Meet this paper deadline, write that sermon, change a diaper, cook dinner, visit the sick, eat with the homeless, counsel the teenager in juvenile detention . . . these demands accelerate our lives. But, what does the pace of our life inadvertently communicate to others about living in faith? During my years of seminary, a dear pastoral care professor would sit on the chapel steps during finals and read a book. Though he also held a demanding schedule, his visible presence signaled his availability to speak with and counsel students in the midst of chaos. This image remains as a visible reminder of how altering pace may creatively build God's kingdom. If only for a moment, let your speedometer drop, so you can see more clearly how and where God is at work in the world around you.

Contemplate on the fly. As cultivators of the spirit, we have been called to engage life's deepest mysteries; to contemplate. A common misnomer is that contemplation is about silence and serenity, when in fact contemplation is defined as an act of considering with attention. In this sense, reading attentively until you hear the author's voice, revising a sermon until it is excellent, or having a good conversation with someone from a different background can be contemplative acts that draws you closer to the Divine. Even in crisis, revelation is possible when we can contemplate in the midst of chaos and not contemplate on the chaos itself.[3]

Creativity and Hope in Chaos thrive in a Community of Reliable Others. As a caregiver who senses theology, I have come to believe that the human spirit, at its core, is resilient and hopeful, but still longs for a community of reliable others. "Creativity and hope are borne out of collaborative interchange. For example, an individual who feels deprived of meaning may be inspirited to hope after reading an account in the Sunday newspaper of a villager in a war-torn township who overcame incomparable difficulties to survive. I offer this example because the community of reliable others that generates hope [and creativity] may not always be physically present. Instead, this community may be any combination of textual, scriptural, historical, or even virtual supports."[4] Isolation flattens the imagination and forestalls the fruitful growth of hope. Seek support in a community of reliable others to fortify hope and embolden creative ministry.

I'm only three years into tailoring my ill-fitting suit. Now I don the vocational coat of "artist." While not perfect, this moniker fits much more snugly than the boxy hand-me-down that tagged me as professor, pastor, and activist. Likewise, I walk more freely in pants that sense theology, than the theology from my seminary training that cut little slack for lived experience. As I fashion a new existence as an artist who senses the movement of God, I pay homage to the master seamstress' from the past and in the future who tailored my approach and altar-end my path.

In the spirit of the creative practitioners who have opened themselves to divine possibility, I conclude this afterword with a brief poem I wrote my first semester in seminary. At my scantly lit dormitory desk, on the evening of September 25, 2000, I sensed theology moving within me and artistry pulsing in my soul as I wrote "Open Wide Shut."

I have purposely woven myself into a cocoon of sorts.

I rest tirelessly…
Perched high above the troubles of yester year
The burning rays of modern day racism and crisp winds of classism
pounding upon the soft exterior of my thinly coated shell. [Tremors of Unrest]

Yet, I endure…
Blanketed with the prayers of my ancestors, and enveloped by the encouraging words of saintly supporters. [Vibrant Warmth]

Slumbering in this nest,
I focus, to familiarize myself with voices…
Voices of rebellion, change, creativity
that at one point crouched in similar cocoons of mental and spiritual transformation [Ecstatic Enlightenment]

Preparation…
for the day of metamorphosis.
I am challenged by the rhythmic beats of unborn hearts [Intimate Inculcation]

For we are responsible for the birth of a new nation.

My prayer is that you have been compelled from the words in this book to open your heart and your mind to a sensory theology that transcends time, stimulates creativity, and brings meaning in the midst of chaos.

Notes

1. These words are inspired by four women: Anaya, Antoinette, Barbara, and Bonnie. They continually teach me to see more clearly, hear more acutely, and find God in theoretical abstraction and the seemingly mundane.

2. For a closer look at the presence of the divine in seemingly mundane activity, I encourage a thorough read of Barbara Brown Taylor's *An Altar in the World: A Geography of Faith* (New York: HarperOne, 2010).

3. For more on contemplation and chaos see Bonnie J. Miller McLemore, "Contemplation in the Midst of Chaos: Contesting the Maceration of the Theological Teacher" in *The Scope of Our Art: The Vocation of the Theological Teacher*, eds. Gregory Jones and Stephanie Paulsel (Grand Rapids, Michigan: Eerdmans, 2001), 53.

4. For more on the community of reliable others, see Gregory C. Ellison II, *Cut Dead but Still Alive: Caring for African American Young Men* (Nashville: Abingdon, 2013), 82.